Lecture Notes in Computer Science 4357

Commenced Publication in 1973
Founding and Former Series Editors:
Gerhard Goos, Juris Hartmanis, and Jan van Leeuwen

Levente Buttyán   Virgil Gligor
Dirk Westhoff (Eds.)

Security and Privacy in Ad-Hoc and Sensor Networks

Third European Workshop, ESAS 2006
Hamburg, Germany, September 20-21, 2006
Revised Selected Papers

 Springer

Volume Editors

Levente Buttyán
Budapest University of Technology and Economics
BME-HIT, PO Box 91, 1521 Budapest, Hungary
E-mail: buttyan@crysys.hu

Virgil Gligor
University of Maryland
Electrical and Computer Engineering Department
College Park, Maryland 20741, USA
E-mail: gligor@umd.edu

Dirk Westhoff
NEC Europe Ltd., Network Laboratories
Kurfürsten-Anlage 36, 69115 Heidelberg, Germany
E-mail: dirk.westhoff@netlab.nec.de

Library of Congress Control Number: Applied for

CR Subject Classification (1998): E.3, C.2, F.2, H.4, D.4.6, K.6.5

LNCS Sublibrary: SL 5 – Computer Communication Networks
and Telecommunications

ISSN   0302-9743
ISBN-10   3-540-69172-3 Springer Berlin Heidelberg New York
ISBN-13   978-3-540-69172-3 Springer Berlin Heidelberg New York

Springer is a part of Springer Science+Business Media

springer.com

© Springer-Verlag Berlin Heidelberg 2006
Printed in Germany

Typesetting: Camera-ready by author, data conversion by Scientific Publishing Services, Chennai, India
Printed on acid-free paper   SPIN: 11964254   06/3142   5 4 3 2 1 0

Preface

These proceedings contain the papers of the 3rd European Workshop on Security and Privacy in Ad Hoc and Sensor Networks (ESAS 2006), which was held in Hamburg, Germany, September 20–21, 2006, in conjunction with the 11th European Symposium on Research in Computer Security (ESORICS 2006).

This year, a total of 44 full papers were submitted to ESAS. Each submitted paper was reviewed by at least three expert referees. After a short period of discussion and deliberation, the Program Committee selected 14 papers for presentation and subsequent publication in the workshop proceedings. This corresponds to an acceptance rate of 32% – a respectable rate by any measure.

In addition to the presented papers, this year's workshop also featured two keynote speeches and seven project presentations. In the first keynote, Jean-Pierre Hubaux (EPFL) gave an overview of "Security and Cooperation in Wireless Networks". The second keynote was given by Pim Tuyls (Philips) on the interesting topic of "Grey-Box Cryptography: Physical Unclonable Functions". The project presentations covered the following European Projects: S3MS, SeVeCom, BIONETS, CASCADAS, MOBIUS, EYES and UbiSecSens. Unfortunately, the extended abstracts of these presentations could not be included in the proceedings.

As the Chairs of ESAS 2006, we are very happy with the outcome of the workshop that clearly demonstrates the continued importance, popularity, and timeliness of the topic: Security and Privacy in Ad Hoc and Sensor Networks.

Many people contributed to the success of ESAS 2006. First of all, we are thankful to the authors of the submitted papers for their confidence in this venue. We are also grateful to the members of the Program Committee for reviewing the submitted papers and for putting together the workshop program. The following external experts helped the work of the Program Committee in the reviewing process: Asmaa Adnane, Frederik Armknecht, Jared Cordasco, Stefano Crosta, Laszlo Csik, Ari Juels, Jerome Lebegue, Jin Wook Lee, Marcin Poturalski, Maxim Raya, and Liu Yang; we appreciate their contribution very much.

We are also thankful to the participants of the workshop in particular, to the keynote speakers, the session chairs, and to those who presented their papers or their projects. Many thanks go to the organizers of ESORICS for accommodating ESAS and taking care of the logistics. We are thankful to Claude Castelluccia and Susanne Wetzel for serving as Publicity Chairs, and to Gergely Acs for maintaining the Web site of ESAS 2006 (www.crysys.hu/ESAS2006). Finally, we are grateful to NEC Europe for sponsoring the workshop and to Springer for publishing the proceedings.

Levente Buttyan (Program Co-chair)
Virgil Gligor (Program Co-chair)
Dirk Westhoff (General Chair)

Organization

General Chair

Dirk Westhoff, NEC Europe Network Lab, Germany

Program Chairs

Levente Buttyn, BME, CrySyS Lab, Hungary
Virgil Gligor, University of Maryland, USA

Publicity Chairs

Claude Castelluccia, INRIA, France
Susanne Wetzel, Stevens Institute of Technology, USA

Program Committee

Imad Aad, DoCoMo Lab Europe, Germany
N. Asokan, Nokia, Finland
Sonja Buchegger, University of California, Berkeley, USA
Srdjan Capkun, Technical University of Denmark, Denmark
Claude Castelluccia, INRIA, France
Xuhua Ding, Singapore Management University, Singapore
Roberto Di Pietro, Università "di Roma La Sapienza", Italy
Hannes Hartenstein, University of Karlsruhe, Germany
Yih-Chun Hu, University of Illinois UC, USA
Markus Jakobsson, Indiana University, Bloomington, USA
Frank Kargl, University of Ulm, Germany
Yongdae Kim, University of Minnesota, Minneapolis, USA
Breno de Medeiros, Florida State University, USA
Ludovic Me, Supelec, France
Pietro Michiardi, Eurecom, France
Gabriel Montenegro, Microsoft, USA
Cristina Nita-Rotaru, Purdue University, USA
Guevara Noubir, Northeastern University, USA
Kaisa Nyberg, Helsinki University of Technology, Finland
Panagiotis Papadimitratos, EPFL, Switzerland
Adrian Perrig, Carnegie Mellon University, USA
Radha Poovendran, University of Washington, USA
Frank Stajano, Cambridge University, UK

Andre Weimerskirch, escrypt GmbH - Embedded Security, Germany
Dirk Westhoff, NEC Europe Network Lab, Germany
Susanne Wetzel, Stevens Institute of Technology, USA
Jeong Hyun Yi, Samsung Advanced Institute of Technology, Korea
Imad Aad, DoCoMo Lab Europe, Germany

Table of Contents

Security and Cooperation in Wireless Networks

Jean-Pierre Hubaux

Laboratory of Computer Communications and Applications (LCA)
EPFL -Lausanne, Batiment BC,
Switzerland
jean-pierre.hubaux@epfl.ch

According to most technology pundits, progress in wireless and sensor networks will lead us into a world of ubiquitous computing, in which myriads of tiny, untethered sensors and actuators will communicate with each other. Information technology will thus deliver its most encompassing and pervasive accomplishment to mankind, promptly taking care of the needs and wishes of everyone.

Or maybe not. The described evolution is driven primarily by market forces and vastly ignores the users' intentions. Yet the recent history of the Internet has shown that these intentions can have devastating effects; for example, spam, viruses, "phishing" and denial of service attacks have unfortunately become commonplace. The misbehavior of a relatively small number of users is leading to a substantial inconvenience to the whole community. Similar or even worse misdeeds are and will be perpetrated in wireless networks.

Anyone would agree that forecasting the attacks against a network before its deployment is a very difficult task, and that the countermeasures are not purely technical, as the human dimension needs to be taken into account. Yet the current practice consisting in patching the problem a posteriori, once it has been detected, is of course not acceptable; after all, we should be able by now to draw the lessons from many years of Internet security experience.

An additional problem is that the speed to the market is in contradiction with the design of a well-thought (and possibly standardized) secure architecture; the solution to this recurrent problem probably resides in the evolution of the designers' attitude, and therefore requires appropriate education on this issue.

To summarize, our purpose is to prevent ubiquitous computing from becoming a pervasive nightmare.

This talk addresses the fundamental questions related to this problem, in particular:

How are users and devices identified? How can a security association be established between two wireless peers? How can packets be securely and cooperatively routed in a multi-hop network? How can the fair share of bandwidth between nodes located in the same radio domain be guaranteed? How do wireless operators behave, if they have to share a given chunk of the spectrum? How can naturally selfish players be encouraged to behave cooperatively? And, above all, how is privacy protected?

L. Buttyan, V. Gligor, and D. Westhoff (Eds.): ESAS 2006, LNCS 4357, pp. 1–2, 2006.
© Springer-Verlag Berlin Heidelberg 2006

All these issues are addressed in a graduate textbook co-authored with Levente Buttyan, to appear in 2007.

The book treats each of these questions from a theoretical point of view and illustrates them by means of concrete examples such as mesh, ad hoc, vehicular, sensor, and RFID networks. More information about the book can be found at http://secowinet.epfl.ch/. The current version V1.0 (430 pages) can be downloaded from there.

Grey-Box Cryptography: Physical Unclonable Functions

Pim Tuyls

Philips Research Laboratories,
Prof. Holstlaan 6, 5656 AA Eindhoven, The Netherlands

Cryptography is a fundamental component of any information security infrastructure. It allows two parties, a sender and a receiver, to exchange messages in a secure and authentic way. For this goal the parties use a publicly known algorithm that depends on a secret key. The main assumption in cryptography is that the honest parties have some secure hardware containing the secret key. This is the so-called *black-box* model. Within this model, cryptography has developed many useful secure algorithms and protocols. The security level of these algorithms is well understood. It can for instance be guaranteed that mathematical attacks are very difficult. This difficulty is even made precise in terms of a security parameter. When the black-box assumption does not hold however, the security guarantees provided by cryptography do not hold anymore.

Because of the reasons mentioned above, in real life many attackers perform physical attacks on the devices carrying out the cryptographic operations. Based on the fact that information and computation are physical systems and processes, it follows that the physical state of the device might be a weak link. Since the state of a device is determined amongst other things by the secret that is used, information on the secret can in principle be obtained by somebody having physical access to the device. These theoretical facts are confirmed in real life by the success of many so-called physical attacks: Simple Power Analysis (SPA), Differential Power Analysis (DPA), Electromagnetic Analysis (EMA), Etching, Probing, Focused Ion beam attacks, etc. It follows also from current practices, that the construction of devices that can perform operations depending on a secret without leaking any information to physical attackers, will be very difficult if not impossible. Therefore, it is necessary to develop security components that provide a high level of security even when the attacker has access to some part of the internal state of the device. This is what we call *Grey-Box Cryptography*.

In order to deal with this critical situation, several groups have started to investigate the problem of security under the presence of physical attacks [2]. Recently some theoretical progress has been made and the notion of *algorithmic tamper proofness* was developed. Within this theory three components were identified to provide security under physical attacks: i) Read-Proof Hardware i.e. hardware that can not be read by an enemy ii) Tamper-Proof Hardware i.e. hardware in which the data can not be changed by an attacker iii) Hardware with a self-destruction capability.

L. Buttyan, V. Gligor, and D. Westhoff (Eds.): ESAS 2006, LNCS 4357, pp. 3–5, 2006.

In this paper we focus on the hardware implementation of Read-Proof Hardware. Although this notion is clear from a theoretical point of view, it has a wide variety of practical aspects. In a practical situation Read-Proof hardware has to be resistant against an attacker using invasive attacks [1], fault attacks and side-channel attacks. Here, we investigate resistance against invasive attacks.

In order to protect cryptographic keys against read-out by physical attacks, we propose the following principles: i) Do not store the (long-term) key into a memory like ROM, EEPROM,... ii) Generate the key only when needed and iii) Delete the key after its security functionality has been performed. In order to implement these three principles, we use a *cryptographic* and a *physical* component. The physical component consists of a PUF implemented on an IC. The cryptographic component is then a Fuzzy Extractor (Helper Data Algorithm [1,3]) which allows to convert a noisy PUF measurement into a secret key.

In particular, we propose a so-called Coating PUF [4] for this purpose. A Coating PUF consists of a coating, containing randomly distributed particles covering the IC. Just underneath the coating, in the top metal layer of the IC, an array of sensors is laid down. By application of a voltage to the sensors the capacitance values of the local capacitors are read-out. Since the coating has randomly varying dielectric properties, the capacitance values contain quite some randomness. It was shown that with this set-up 6.6 secure bits can be maximally extracted per sensor. The Fuzzy Extractor is then used to remove the noise from the measured values and to extract the randomness i.e. for the generation of a secure key.

A demo with the actual hardware has been developed. It consists of an IC with a measurement circuit on board and thirty sensors that can measure the various capacitance values. Additionally a Fuzzy Extractor has been implemented to extract the key bits from the measured capacitances. In this implementation, we extract three bits per sensor from the capacitance values. Since, these capacitance values are continuous values, the Fuzzy Extractor implements an additional step: quantisation. Next, an error correction code is applied to remove the noise and extract the keys. This leads to a key of 60 secure bits, i.e. two secure bits per sensor.

We have used this demo set-up to investigate the strength of the Coating PUF against Focused Ion Beam (FIB) attacks. With a FIB we have made several holes in the coating. These holes had various sizes and depths. From the experiments it follows that such attacks can damage the key substantially, i.e. after such an attack the key is substantially randomized from an attackers point of view. Moreover it turns out that the sensors can detect that holes have been made into the coating and hence that an attack on the IC was performed. This information can be used to take appropriate measures e.g. shut down the IC. We refer to [4] for more details.

---

[1] An invasive attack is informally defined as an attack where the attacker physically breaks into the device by modifying its structure.

References

1. Y. Dodis, M. Reyzin, and A. Smith. Fuzzy extractors: How to generate strong keys from biometrics and other noisy data. In C. Cachin and J. Camenisch, editors, *Proceedings of Eurocrypt 2004*, volume 3027 of *Lecture Notes in Computer Science*, pages 523–540. Springer-Verlag, 2004.
2. R. Gennaro, A. Lysyanskaya, T. Malkin, S. Micali, and T. Rabin. Algorithmic tamper-proof security: Theoretical foundations for security against hardware tampering. In *Theory of Cryptography, First Theory of Cryptography Conference, TCC 2004, Cambridge, MA, USA*, number 2951 in Lecture Notes in Computer Science, pages 258–277. Springer-Verlag, 2004.
3. J.P. Linnartz and P. Tuyls. New shielding functions to enhance privacy and prevent misuse of biometric templates. In J. Kittler and M. Nixon, editors, *Proc. of the 3rd Conference on Audio and Video Based Person Authentication*, volume 2688 of *Lecture Notes in Computer Science*, pages 238–250. Springer-Verlag, 2003.
4. B. Skoric J. van Geloven R. Verhaegh P. Tuyls, G.J. Schrijen and R. Wolters. Read-proof hardware from protective coatings. In *Proceedings of the Workshop on Cryptographic Hardware and Embedded Systems (CHES)*, 2006.

Low-Cost Elliptic Curve Cryptography for Wireless Sensor Networks

Lejla Batina, Nele Mentens, Kazuo Sakiyama,
Bart Preneel, and Ingrid Verbauwhede

Katholieke Universiteit Leuven, ESAT/COSIC,
Kasteelpark Arenberg 10, B-3001 Leuven, Belgium
{lbatina,nmentens,ksakiyam}@esat.kuleuven.be

Abstract. This work describes a low-cost Public-Key Cryptography (PKC) based solution for security services such as key-distribution and authentication as required for wireless sensor networks. We propose a custom hardware assisted approach to implement Elliptic Curve Cryptography (ECC) in order to obtain stronger cryptography as well as to minimize the power. Our compact and low-power ECC processor contains a Modular Arithmetic Logic Unit (MALU) for ECC field arithmetic. The best solution features 6718 gates for the MALU and control unit (data memory not included) in 0.13 μm CMOS technology over the field $\mathbb{F}_{2^{131}}$, which provides a reasonable level of security for the time being. In this case the consumed power is less than 30 μW when operating frequency is 500 kHz.

Keywords: sensor networks, pervasive computing, Elliptic Curve Cryptography, authentication, key-distribution, hardware implementation.

1 Introduction

The field of embedded security is in constant evolvement and new applications are constantly emerging. Extreme examples are sensor nodes and RFID tags as they put new requirements on implementations of Public-Key protocols with a very low budget for the number of gates, power, bandwidth *etc.* Especially the security in wireless sensor networks is of crucial importance as a large number of nodes is exposed in sometimes hostile environments and if only one node is captured by the attacker, the impact to the complete network can be devastating. Therefore, various cryptographic services are required for these applications and common use of symmetric-key algorithms such as AES and MACs are not just imposing problems such as key protection and management but can be at the same time even more expensive. Although for example, authentication can be obtained by means of symmetric-key cryptography, it is evident that PKC substantially simplifies security protocols. In addition, the use of PKC reduces power due to less protocol overhead [2].

To the best of our knowledge very few papers discuss the possibility for PKC in these applications although the benefits of PKC are evident especially for

L. Buttyan, V. Gligor, and D. Westhoff (Eds.): ESAS 2006, LNCS 4357, pp. 6–17, 2006.

key distribution between the nodes and various authentication protocols. For example, the authentication of the base station is easily performed assuming the public key of the base station can be stored in each node [3]. If only resistance against passive attacks is needed, the algorithm of Schnorr [9] can be used for this purpose as it is known that this scheme is secure against passive attacks under the discrete logarithm assumption. The main cost of this algorithm for the case of ECC is just one point multiplication.

In this paper we investigate the possibility for PK services for pervasive computing. We show that ECC processors can be designed in such a way to qualify for lightweight applications suitable for wireless sensor networks. Here, the term lightweight assumes low die size and low power consumption. Therefore, we propose a hardware processor supporting ECC that features very low footprint and low-power. We investigate ECC over binary fields $\mathbb{F}_{2^p}$ where p is a prime as proposed in standards [4].

The paper is organized as follows. Section 2 lists some related work. In Sect. 3 we give some background information on Elliptic Curve Cryptography and supporting arithmetic. In Sect. 4 we elaborate on a suitable selection of parameters and algorithms and we outline our architecture and describe our hardware implementation. Our results are discussed in Sect. 5. Section 6 concludes the paper.

2   Related Work

Two emerging examples of PKC applications dealing with extremely constrained environments are sensor networks and radio frequency identification tags (RFIDs). They put new requirements on implementations of PK algorithms with very tight constraints in number of gates, power, bandwidth *etc.* Therefore, as related previous work we mention implementations of Public-Key cryptosystems for these applications.

Wireless distributed sensor networks are expected to be used in a broad range of applications, varying from military to meteorological applications [3]. As the current generation is powered by batteries, ultra-low power circuitry is a must for these applications. On the other hand, there is a clear need for PKC in this context, especially for services such as key-exchange protocols that are typically provided by means of PKC.

RFID tags are passive devices consisting of a microchip connected with an antenna. Typically, they have no battery, but they obtain power from the electromagnetic field produced by the RFID reader. Today they are mainly used for identification of products but recent applications include also counterfeiting [10]. The application areas for RFIDs vary from supply chain management, inventory management, preventing banknotes counterfeiting to vehicles tracking, security of newborn babies *etc.* In short, RFID tags are meant to be a ubiquitous replacement for bar codes with some added functionality.

The work of Gaubatz *et al.* [3] discusses the necessity and the feasibility of PKC protocols in sensor networks. In [3], the authors investigated implementations of two algorithms for this purpose *i.e.* Rabin's scheme and NTRUEncrypt. The conclusion is that NTRUEncrypt features a suitable low-power and small footprint solution with a total complexity of 3000 gates and power consumption of less than 20 μW at 500 kHz. On the other hand, they showed that Rabin's scheme is not a feasible solution. In [2] the authors have compared the previous two algorithm implementations with an ECC solution for wireless sensor networks. The architecture of the ECC processor occupied an area of 18 720 gates and consumed less than 400 μW of power at 500 kHz. The field used was a prime field of order $\approx 2^{100}$.

Some more efforts for PKC processors for RFID tags include the results of Wolkerstorfer [11] and Kumar and Paar [5]. Wolkerstorfer [11] showed that ECC based PKC is feasible on RFID-tags by implementing the ECDSA on a small IC. The chip has an area complexity of around 23 000 gates and it features a latency of 6.67 ms for one point multiplication at 68.5 MHz. However, it can be used for both types of fields *e.g.* $\mathbb{F}_{2^{191}}$ and $\mathbb{F}_{p^{192}}$. The results of Kumar and Paar [5] include an area complexity of almost 12 kgates and a latency of 18 ms for one point multiplication over $\mathbb{F}_{2^{131}}$ at 13.56 MHz. The operating frequency is in both cases too high for those applications and therefore the results cannot be properly evaluated. Namely, with such a high frequency the power consumed becomes too large, which has the most crucial impact on the feasibility of the implementations. We compare the previous implementations with our results in Section 5 in more detail.

3   Elliptic Curve Cryptography

ECC relies on a group structure induced on an elliptic curve. A set of points on an elliptic curve together with the point at infinity, denoted ∞, and with point addition as binary operation has the structure of an abelian group. Here we consider finite fields of characteristic two. A non-supersingular elliptic curve E over $\mathbb{F}_{2^n}$ is defined as the set of solutions $(x, y) \in \mathbb{F}_{2^n} \times \mathbb{F}_{2^n}$ to the equation: $y^2 + xy = x^3 + ax^2 + b$ where $a, b \in \mathbb{F}_{2^n}, b \neq 0$, together with ∞.

The main operation in any ECC-based primitive such as key-exchange or encryption is the scalar multiplication which can be viewed as the top level operation. The point scalar multiplication is achieved by repeated point addition and doubling. All algorithms for modular exponentiation can also be applied for point multiplication.

At the next (lower) level are the point group operations *i.e.* addition and doubling. The point addition in affine coordinates is performed according to the following formulae. Let $P_1 = (x_1, y_1)$ and $P_2 = (x_2, y_2)$ be two points on an elliptic curve E. Assume $P_1, P_2 \neq \infty$ and $P_1 \neq -P_2$. The sum $P_3 = (x_3, y_3) = P_1 + P_2$ is computed as follows [1]:
If $P_1 \neq P_2$,

$$\begin{aligned}
\lambda &= (y_2 + y_1) \cdot (x_2 + x_1)^{-1} \\
x_3 &= \lambda^2 + \lambda + x_1 + x_2 + a \\
y_3 &= \lambda(x_1 + x_3) + x_3 + y_1.
\end{aligned}$$

If $P_1 = P_2$,

$$\lambda = y_1/x_1 + x_1$$
$$x_3 = \lambda^2 + \lambda + a$$
$$y_3 = (x_1 + x_3)\lambda + x_3 + y_1 .$$

There are many types of coordinates in which an elliptic curve may be represented. In the equations above affine coordinates are used, but so-called projective coordinates have some implementation advantages. The main conclusion is that point addition can be done in projective coordinates using only field multiplications, with no inversions required. More precisely, only one inversion needs to be performed at the end of a point multiplication operation.

The lowest level consists of finite field operations such as addition, subtraction, multiplication and inversion required to perform the group operations. More details on ECC and its mathematical background can be found in [1].

4 Elliptic Curve Processor (ECP) for Pervasive Computing

4.1 Algorithms Selection and Parameters

For the point multiplication we chose the method of Montgomery (Algorithm 1) [8] that maintains the relationship $P_2 - P_1$ as invariant. It uses a representation where computations are performed on the x-coordinate only in affine coordinates (or on the X and Z coordinates in projective representation). That fact allows us to save registers which is one of the main criteria for obtaining a compact solution.

Algorithm 1. Algorithm for point multiplication

Require: an integer $k > 0$ and a point P
Ensure: $x(kP)$
  $k \leftarrow k_{l-1}, ..., k_1, k_0$
  $P_1 \leftarrow P, \quad P_2 \leftarrow 2P.$
  for i from $l - 2$ downto 0 **do**
    If $k_i = 1$ then
    $x(P_1) \leftarrow x(P_1 + P_2), x(P_2) \leftarrow x(2P_2)$
    Else
    $x(P_2) \leftarrow x(P_2 + P_1), x(P_1) \leftarrow x(2P_1)$
  end for
  Return $x(P_1)$

We chose as starting point for our optimizations the formulas of Lopez and Dahab [7]. The original formulas in [7] require 2 or 3 intermediate registers if the point operations are performed sequentially or in parallel respectively. In the case of sequential processing it is enough to use two intermediate variables but in our case we eliminate one more intermediate register, which added a few more steps to the original algorithms. The results of our optimizations are shown in Algorithm 2.

Algorithm 2 requires only one intermediate variable T, which results in 5 registers in total. The required registers are for the storage of the following variables: X_1, X_2, Z_1, Z_2 and T. Also, the algorithm shows the operations and registers required if the key-bit $k_i = 0$. Another case is completely symmetric and it can be performed accordingly. More precisely, if the addition operation is viewed as a function $f(X_2, Z_2, X_1, Z_1) = (X_2, Z_2)$ for $k_i = 0$ due to the symmetry for the case $k_i = 1$ we get $f(X_1, Z_1, X_2, Z_2) = (X_1, Z_1)$ and the correct result is always stored in the first two input variables. This is possible due to the property of scalar multiplication based on Algorithm 1.

Algorithm 2. EC point operations that minimize the number of registers

Require: X_i, Z_i, for $i = 1, 2$, $x_4 = x(P_2 - P_1)$
Ensure: $X(P_1 + P_2) = X_2$, $Z(P_1 + P_2) = Z_2$
1: $X_2 \leftarrow X_2 \cdot Z_1$
2: $Z_2 \leftarrow X_1 \cdot Z_2$
3: $T \leftarrow X_2 \cdot Z_2$
4: $Z_2 \leftarrow Z_2 + X_2$
5: $Z_2 \leftarrow Z_2{}^2$
6: $X_2 \leftarrow x_4 \cdot Z_1$
7: $X_2 \leftarrow X_2 + T$

Require: $b \in \mathbb{F}_{2^n}$, X_1, Z_1
Ensure: $X(2P_1) = X_1$, $Z(2P_1) = Z_1$,
1: $X_1 \leftarrow X_1^2$
2: $Z_1 \leftarrow Z_1^2$
3: $T \leftarrow Z_1^2$
4: $Z_1 \leftarrow X_1 \cdot Z_1$
5: $T \leftarrow T^2$
6: $T \leftarrow b \cdot T$
7: $X_1 \leftarrow X_1^2$
8: $X_1 \leftarrow X_1 + T$

4.2   Binary Fields Arithmetic

From the formulae for point operations as given in Algorithm 2 it is evident that we need to implement only multiplications and additions. Squaring is considered as a special case of multiplication in order to minimize the area and inversion is avoided by use of projective coordinates. We assume that conversion to affine coordinates can be computed at the base station's side. Note also that, if necessary, the one inversion that is required can be calculated by use of multiplications. In this way the area remains almost intact and some small control logic has to be added.

4.3   Global Architecture

Our Elliptic Curve Processor (ECP) is shown in Fig. 1. The operational blocks are as follows: a Control Unit (CU), an Arithmetic Unit (ALU), and Memory (RAM and ROM). In ROM the ECC parameters and the constants x_4 and b are stored. On the other hand, RAM contains all input and output variables and it therefore communicates with both, the ROM and the ALU.

The Control Unit controls the scalar multiplication and the point operations. In addition, the controller commands the ALU which performs field multiplication, addition and squaring. When the START signal is set, the bits of $k = \sum_{i=0}^{n_k-1} k_i 2^i$, $k_i = \{0,1\}$, $n_k = \lceil \log_2 k \rceil$, are evaluated from MSB to LSB resulting in the assignment of new values for P_1 and P_2, dependent on the key-bit k_i. When all bits have been evaluated, an internal counter gives an END signal. The result of the last P1 calculation is written to the output register and the VALID output is set. The CU consists of a number of simple state machines and a counter and its area cost is small. The processor memory consists of the equivalent to five n-bit $(n = p)$ registers.

As our ALU deals with modular arithmetic in a binary field we refer to it from now on as the Modular Arithmetic Logic Unit (MALU) for which give more details in the following section.

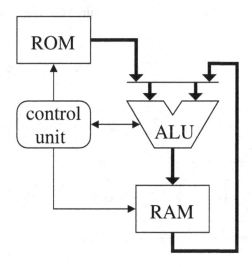

Fig. 1. ECP architecture

4.4 Modular Arithmetic Logic Unit (MALU)

In this section the architecture for the MALU is briefly explained. The datapath of the MALU is an MSB-first bit-serial $\mathbb{F}_{2^n}$ multiplier with digit size d as illustrated in Figure 2. This arithmetic unit computes $A(x)B(x) \mod P(x)$ where $A(x) = \sum a_i x^i$, $B(x) = \sum b_i x^i$ and $P(x) = \sum p_i x^i$. The proposed MALU computes $A(x)B(x) \mod P(x)$ by following the steps: The MALU$_n$ sums up three types of inputs which are $a_i B(x), m_i P(x)$ and $T(x)$, and then outputs the intermediate result, $T_{next}(x)$ by computing $T_{next}(x) = (T(x) + a_i B(x) + m_i P(x))x$ where $m_i = t_n$. By providing T_{next} as the next input T and repeating the same computation for n times, one can obtain the multiplication result.

Modular addition, $A(x) + C(x) \mod P(x)$ can be also supported on the same hardware logic by setting $C(x)$ to the register for $T(x)$ instead of resetting register $T(x)$ when initializing the MALU. This operation requires additional multiplexors and XORs. However the cost of this solution is much cheaper compared to the case of having a separate modular adder. This type of hardware sharing is very important for such low-cost applications.

The proposed datapath is scalable in the digit size d which can be determined arbitrary by exploring the best combination of performance and cost.

In Fig. 2 the architecture of our MALU is shown for finite fields operations in $\mathbb{F}_{2^{163}}$. To perform a finite field multiplication, the cmd value should be set to 1 and the operands should be loaded into registers A and B. The value stored in A is evaluated digit per digit from MSB to LSB. We denote the digit size by d. The result of the multiplication will be provided in register T after $\lceil \frac{163}{d} \rceil$ clock cycles. A finite field addition is performed by giving cmd the value 0, resetting register A and loading the operands into registers B and T. The value that is loaded into T is denoted by C. After one clock cycle, the result of the addition is provided in register T. The cmd value makes sure that only the last cell is used for this addition.

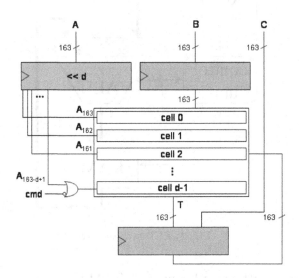

Fig. 2. Architecture of the MALU

The cells inside the MALU all have the same structure, which is depicted in Fig. 3. A cell consists of a full-length array of AND-gates, a full-length array of XOR-gates and a smaller array of XOR-gates. The position of the XOR-gates in the latter array depends on the irreducible polynomial. In this case, the polynomial $P(x) = x^{163} + x^7 + x^6 + x^3 + 1$ is used. The cmd value determines whether the reduction needs to be done or not. In case of a finite field multiplication, the reduction is needed. For finite field addition, the reduction will not be performed.

The output value T_{out} is either given (in a shifted way) to the next cell or to the output register T in Fig. 2. The input value T_{in} is either coming from the previous cell or from the output register T.

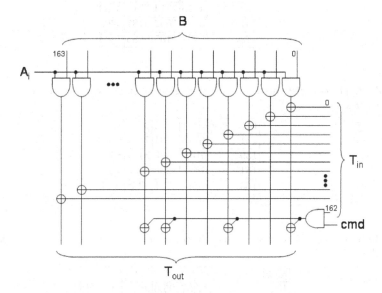

Fig. 3. Logic inside one cell of the MALU

The strong part of this architecture is that it uses the same cell(s) for finite field multiplication and addition without a big overhead in multiplexors. This is achieved by using T as an output register as well as an input register. The flip-flops in T are provided with a load input, which results in a smaller area overhead compared to a solution that would use a full-length array of multiplexors.

5   Results and Discussion

Now we give the results for area complexity and the latency in the case of ECC point multiplication. The designs were synthesized by Synopsys Design Vision using a 0.13 μm CMOS library. We used binary fields from bit-size 131 to 163 as recommended by NIST. ECC with key sizes of around 160 bits is usually compared with RSA for 1024 bits although those are only rough estimates. Namely, according to the work of Lenstra and Verheul 163 bit long key sizes for ECC correspond to RSA keys that are much longer than 1024 bits [6]. More precisely, one could achieve that level of security with around 130 bits long ECC keys. Therefore, we can assume that ECC over $\mathbb{F}_{2^{131}}$ provides a good level of security for these applications.

The results of the area complexity for various architectures with respect to the choice of fields and the size of d for the MALU are given in Table 1. The

Table 1. The area complexity of MALU in gates of the ECC processor for various fields and digit sizes

Field size	$d=1$	$d=2$	$d=3$	$d=4$
131	4446	4917	5376	5837
139	4716	5214	5712	6189
151	5117	5652	6187	6700
163	5525	6105	6685	7243

Table 2. The complete area complexity in gates of the ECC processor for various fields and digit sizes

Field size	$d=1$	$d=2$	$d=3$	$d=4$
131	6718	7191	7645	8104
139	7077	7635	8132	8607
151	7673	8205	8738	9252
163	8214	8791	9368	9926

Table 3. The complete area complexity in μm^2 of the ECC processor for various fields and digit sizes

Field size	$d=1$	$d=2$	$d=3$	$d=4$
131	34936.7	37395.6	39754.4	42139
139	36802.9	39702.5	42287.6	44755.2
151	39901.2	42666	45439.5	48109.2
163	42714.4	45714.2	48715.8	51617.1

results for the complete architecture in gates and in μm^2 are given in Table 2 and Table 3 respectively.

The graphical representations of our results for area are shown in Fig. 4 and Fig. 5. We can observe that the upper bound for the area of the MALU is slightly more than 7 kgates. On the other hand the complete area, so MALU and the CU together is less than 10 kgates.

The graphical representations of our results for area in μm^2 and for the total power consumed are shown in Fig. 6 and Fig. 7. The power estimates were made assuming the operating frequency of 500 kHz. With this frequency the power stays between 20 and 30 μW which is assumed to be acceptable for sensor networks applications.

Next we give the numbers for the performance. For the point multiplication we used Algorithm 1 and for point operations Algorithm 2. We calculate the total number of cycles for each field operation by use of the following formulae for field operations. The total number of cycles for one field multiplication is $\lceil \frac{n}{d} \rceil + 3$ where n and d are the bit size of an arbitrary element from the field in which we are working and the bit size respectively. On the other hand, one field addition takes 4 cycles. The number of cycles required for one point multiplication in the

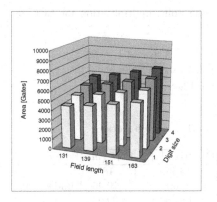

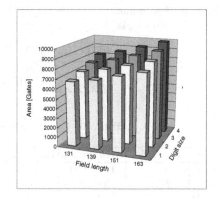

Fig. 4. Results for area complexity of the ECC-dedicated MALU for various fields and digit sizes

Fig. 5. Results for complete area complexity of ECC processor for various fields and digit sizes

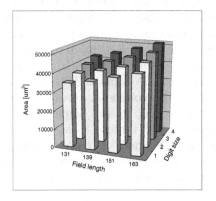

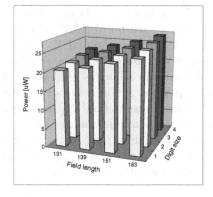

Fig. 6. Results for area complexity in μm^2 of the ECC-processor for various fields and digit sizes

Fig. 7. Results for the power consumed by the ECC processor for various fields and digit sizes

case of field $\mathbb{F}_{2^p}$, where p is a prime is: $(n_k - 1)[13(\lceil \frac{(n_k-1)}{d} \rceil + 3) + 12]$. Here, n_k denotes the number of bits of the scalar k *e.g.* the secret key.

The results for the total number of cycles of one point multiplication for fields $\mathbb{F}_{2^{131}}$ and $\mathbb{F}_{2^{163}}$ are given in Table 4. To calculate the time for one point multiplication we need an operating frequency. However, the frequency that can be used is strictly influenced by the total power. We assumed an operating frequency of 500 kHz as suggested in [3] in order to estimate the actual timing. We get 115 ms for the best case of ECC over $\mathbb{F}_{2^{131}}$ ($d = 4$) and 190 ms for the best case of ECC over $\mathbb{F}_{2^{163}}$ ($d = 4$). Our results are compared with other related work in Table 5.

Table 4. The number of cycles required for one point multiplication for ECC over fields $\mathbb{F}_{2^{131}}$ and $\mathbb{F}_{2^{163}}$

Field size	$d=1$	$d=2$	$d=3$	$d=4$
131	210 600	109 200	74 880	57 720
163	353 710	182071	124 858	95 159

Table 5. Comparison with other related work

Ref.	Fin. field	Area [gates]	Techn. [μm]	Op. freq. [kHz]	Perf. [ms]	Power [μW]
[5]	$\mathbb{F}_{2^{131}}$	11 969.93	0.35	13 560	18	-
[2]	$\mathbb{F}_{p_{100}}$	18 720	0.13	500	410.45	under 400
[11]	$\mathbb{F}_{2^{191}}$, $\mathbb{F}_{p_{192}}$	23 000	0.35	68 500	9.89	n.a.
our	$\mathbb{F}_{2^{131}}$	8104*	0.13	500	115	under 30

We underline again that our result for the area complexity does not include RAM. The amount of storage that is required for our implementation is to store $5n$ bits, where n is the number of bits of elements in a field. Assuming factor 6 for each bit of RAM, which is quite conservative, the total area of our processor would be around 12 kgates. This result is close to the result of [5], but only with respect to area. Assuming the same frequency for their processor would result in a latency of almost half a second, which is probably to slow for real applications. The work of Wolkerstorfer is also considering area in mm^2 and power consumption[1] for various technologies. As another comparison our architecture consumes an area smaller than 0.05 mm^2, without RAM.

We can conclude that our architecture presents the smallest known ECC processor for low-cost applications. The performance and power estimates are also implying a feasible solution for various applications of pervasive computing.

6   Conclusions

This work gives a low-power and low footprint processor for ECC suitable for sensor networks. We give detailed results for area and performance estimates for ECC over $\mathbb{F}_{2^p}$ where p is a prime of bit-length varying from 131 to 163. We also include the power numbers obtained by the simulation.

Acknowledgements

Lejla Batina, Nele Mentens and Kazuo Sakiyama are funded by FWO projects (G.0450.04, G.0141.03) and FP6 project SESOC. This research has been also partially supported by the EU IST FP6 project ECRYPT and by IBBT, and K.U. Leuven (OT).

---

[1] An estimated power is 500 $\mu W/MHz$.

References

1. I. Blake, G. Seroussi, and N. P. Smart. *Elliptic Curves in Cryptography*. London Mathematical Society Lecture Note Series. Cambridge University Press, 1999.
2. G. Gaubatz, J.-P. Kaps, E. Öztürk, and B. Sunar. State of the Art in Ultra-Low Power Public Key Cryptography for Wireless Sensor Networks. In *2nd IEEE International Workshop on Pervasive Computing and Communication Security (PerSec 2005)*, Kauai Island, Hawaii, March 2005.
3. G. Gaubatz, J.-P. Kaps, and B. Sunar. Public Key Cryptography in Sensor Networks - Revisited. In *1st European Workshop on Security in Ad-Hoc and Sensor Networks (ESAS 2004)*, Heidelberg, Germany, August 2004.
4. IEEE P1363. Standard specifications for public key cryptography, 1999.
5. S. Kumar and C. Paar. Are standards compliant elliptic curve cryptosystems feasible on RFID? In *Proceedings of Workshop on RFID Security*, Graz, Austria, July 2006.
6. A. Lenstra and E. Verheul. Selecting cryptographic key sizes. In H. Imai and Y. Zheng, editors, *Proceedings of Third International Workshop on Practice and Theory in Public Key Cryptography (PKC 2000)*, number 1751 in Lecture Notes in Computer Science, pages 446–465. Springer-Verlag, 2000.
7. J. López and R. Dahab. Fast multiplication on elliptic curves over $GF(2^m)$. In Ç. K. Koç and C. Paar, editors, *Proceedings of 1st International Workshop on Cryptographic Hardware and Embedded Systems (CHES)*, volume 1717 of *Lecture Notes in Computer Science*, pages 316–327. Springer-Verlag, 1999.
8. P. Montgomery. Speeding the Pollard and Elliptic Curve Methods of Factorization. *Mathematics of Computation*, Vol. 48:243–264, 1987.
9. C.-P. Schnorr. Efficient Identification and Signatures for Smart Cards. In Gilles Brassard, editor, *Advances in Cryptology — CRYPTO '89*, volume LNCS 435, pages 239–252. Springer, 1989.
10. P. Tuyls and L. Batina. RFID-tags for Anti-Counterfeiting. In D. Pointcheval, editor, *Topics in Cryptology - CT-RSA 2006*, Lecture Notes in Computer Science, San Jose, USA, February 13-17 2006. Springer Verlag.
11. J. Wolkerstorfer. Scaling ECC Hardware to a Minimum. In ECRYPT workshop - Cryptographic Advances in Secure Hardware - CRASH 2005, September 6-7 2005. invited talk.

Re-visited: Denial of Service Resilient Access Control for Wireless Sensor Networks

Frederik Armknecht[1], Joao Girao[1], Marc Stoecklin[2], and Dirk Westhoff[1,*]

[1] NEC Europe Ltd.
{frederik.armknecht,joao.girao,dirk.westhoff}@netlab.nec.de
[2] Swiss Federal Institute of Technology - Lausanne
marc.stoecklin@epfl.ch

Abstract. The appliance of wireless sensor networks to a broad variety of applications doubtlessly requires end-user acceptance. End-users from various computer network unrelated disciplines like for example from the agriculture sector, geography, health care, or biology will only use wireless sensor networks to support their daily work if the overall benefit beats the overhead when getting in touch with this new paradigm. This does first and foremost mean that, once the WSN is deployed, it is easy to collect data also for a technical unexperienced audience. However, the trust in the system's confidentiality and its reliability should not be underestimated. Since for end-users from various disciplines the monitored data are of highest value they will only apply WSN technology to their professional activities if a proper and safe access control mechanism to the WSN is ensured. For FIPS 140-02 level 2 or level 3 conform sensor devices we provide an access control protocol for end-users of civilian WSN applications that i) ensures access to the monitored data only for authorised parties, ii) supports user-friendly data queries and iii) is DoS resilient to save the sensor nodes' battery capacity.

1 Introduction

Recently considerable contributions have been made in the area of wireless sensor networks (WSN) to effectively request and receive environmental data from a WSN. We observe two principle directions to apply a WSN: The first type of WSNs, which we term *synchronous* WSNs are WSNs where the monitored data is fluctual and is most likely to be used for some real-time control monitoring. Data are transmitted in a push or in a pull mode. In contrast, we define an *asynchronous* WSN as one that provides information to an authorised reader only seldomly. Here the data provision to the end-user is exclusively in pull mode.

---

* The work presented in this paper was supported by the European Commission within the STReP UbiSec&Sens of the EU Framework Program 6 for Research and Development (IST-2004-2.4.3). The views and conclusions contained herein are those of the authors and should not be interpreted as necessarily representing the official policies or endorsements, either expressed or implied, of the UbiSec&Sens project (http://www.ist-ubisecsens.org) or the European Commission.

L. Buttyan, V. Gligor, and D. Westhoff (Eds.): ESAS 2006, LNCS 4357, pp. 18–31, 2006.

The network continiously monitors and stores environmental data as a function over the time and/or over the monitored region. Consequently, after a period of monitoring and storing, the WSN contains a very fine granular environmental fingerprint. Such information can be requested via some external reader device by the end-user, e.g. a winemaker, a geologist, or other professionals.

For synchronous WSNs Madden et al. in [10] and Hellerstein et al. in [7] provide an SQL-based query model for tiny in-network aggregation in WSNs addressing specific monitoring durations of the network. Queries address monitoring periods in the present and in the future. However, although in [7] the concept of storage points allows to buffer a streaming view of recent data, the fully-fledged architecture to store monitored data of an event of the past within the WSN is not addressed in their work.

With respect to asynchronous WSNs the problem of how to use the limited persistent storage capacity of an asynchronous WSN to store sampled data effectively has been discussed by Tilak, Abu-Ghazaleh and Heinzelmann in [13]. The authors provide a cluster-based collaborative storage approach and compare it to a local buffering technique. Collaborative storage is a promising approach for storage management because it enables the use of spatial data aggregation and redundancy control among neighboring sensors to compress the stored data and to optimize the storage use.

Although it is unrealistic to expect that all the aforementioned approaches survive the competition to market, such a diversity of storage architectures and information gathering concepts for WSNs on the one side, and the ultimative need for a simple, user-friendly and consistent query interface on the other side, manifests that a flexible data access framework will be a coactive part of future service-oriented WSNs. Moreover, since for end-users from various disciplines the collected data are of highest value they will only apply WSN technology to their professional activities if a proper and safe data management is ensured. This includes the encrypted storage and transport of data which have been monitored over the time but also mechanisms to access the collected data in an authenticated way. For the first we proposed solutions in [15] for synchronous WSNs and in [6] for asynchronous WSNs. It is the contribution of this work to provide a secure and efficient access control mechanism to allow only an authenticated reader to request data from the WSN. We assume a distributed and encrypted storage- and transmission architecture for reliable long-term storage of data in the WSN as well as a translation framework to map user-friendly database queries into controlled flooding messages. For the latter we introduce a generic query translation model which we subsequently apply to show that the proposed access control protocol for WSNs is applicable to any WSN database architecture. An early version of this work has been presented at [16].

When considering access control, one must define the assets one is protecting and the environment. In this particular model, we protect access to the network and, in doing so, we provide an authorization mechanism which only allows a valid reader to perform one query per interaction with a supervising entity, the sink. In parallel we provide a mechanism which fits the query model described in Section 3 and provide the link between the user world and the WSN world and bind it to the access control information which can be validated at both sink and sensors.

2 Network Model and Device Characteristics

The WSN considered in this work is static and densely distributed. It is presented by a graph $\mathcal{G} = (\mathcal{N}, \mathcal{L})$ with $|\mathcal{N}|$ nodes and $|\mathcal{L}|$ links. Each node represents a wireless sensor node, e.g., a MicaZ mote, and each link represents a bidirectional communication channel over a shared medium, e.g., the RF channel specified by IEEE 802.15.4 WPAN. There is one single stated node S, the sink node. The sensor nodes that compose a WSN are typically small in size, wireless, and have very limited communication, computation, storage and power capabilities. For example, the Berkeley Sensor Motes use an 8-bit 4MHz microcontroller with 4KB of memory and a radio tranceiver with a maximum 10 kbps data rate. One consequence of limited computing and storage capacities is that modular arithmetic with large numbers is difficult and, therefore, asymmetric cryptography should only be used very carefully. In particular, standard Diffie-Hellman key exchange protocols and even low exponent RSA techniques are prohibitively expensive for sensors. Based on the above, extremely low-cost mechanisms are needed. Furthermore, it has been pointed out that, in WSNs, sending a bit is roughly 10^2 times more expensive than executing a processor instruction [8].

The NIST standard FIPS 140-02 [4] defines four levels of physical security for cryptographic devices. In this work we assume the sensor nodes being level 2 or level 3 devices, namely devices that implement tamper evidence mechanisms or devices that in addition to tamper evidence mechanisms also implement tamper response mechanisms like top-metal sensor meshes or light-sensors. An adversary, who destroys a sensor line or shortens it to ground or power, causes the device to self-destruct. Partly protected devices prevent clever outsiders to read out sensitive information from the sensor nodes. However, knowledgable insiders or funded organisations which spend several 100,000 EURs for an attack can clearly read out the data. We expect FIPS 140-02 level 2 and even level 3 enabled devices to be reasonable in future in terms of costs also for the usage for some types of WSN.

3 Query Translation Model

The goal of this paper is to present a denial of service resilient access control for WSN applications that support "user-friendly" data queries. However, we will see that the "user-friendliness" imposes conditions on the communication between reader and sensor nodes that have to be considered in an access control protocol.

For a "user-friendly" distributed database, it is mandatory that any query $q \in \mathcal{Q}$ from the end-user's *query space* can be mapped to a "network-friendly" controlled *flooding message* $\varpi \in \mathcal{M}$, i.e., the existence of a function $f : \mathcal{Q} \to \mathcal{M}$. However, in practice f should provide a semantical appropriate interpretation of q. This means that ϖ should reflect the user's query as good as possible on the WSN's side. We will call such a function *adequate*.[1] But here the following problem arises. On the one hand, ϖ relies on the topology of the WSN. Therefore we cannot expect that an "end-user friendly" query from the user space can *adequately* be translated into a query from the WSN query message flooding space unless additional information are available. On the other hand, the user should be bothered only to a minimum with the technical details of the WSN. The queries should contain as much information as possible but not more than necessary.

Let the domain $\mathcal{T}$ represents the topology information of the WSN. Obviously, it is only available after the roll-out of the network. Some information on $\mathcal{T}$ are certainly necessary to formulate a "network-friendly" flooding message. On the other hand, major parts of $\mathcal{T}$ should be hidden from the end-user as otherwise "user-friendliness" would not be fulfilled. We therefore divide $\mathcal{T}$ in $(\mathcal{T}_U, \mathcal{T}_N)$ whereas $\mathcal{T}_U$ represents only those information about the WSN's which are relevant for the end-user to generate context-sensitive user queries. Contrary, $\mathcal{T}_N$ contains topology information which are mandatory to formulate WSN architecture specific flooding messages and which should be hidden from the end-user.

Consequently, to get an adequate function, we consider functions $f^* : \mathcal{Q} \times \mathcal{T} \to \mathcal{M}$ instead of $f : \mathcal{Q} \to \mathcal{M}$. Given such a mapping f^*, we can doubtlessly infer that such a translation exists and we can build a framework that can translate (q, t_U) with t_U from $\mathcal{T}_U$ into an ϖ for a specific WSN architecture. Examples for WSN architectures are tinyDB, TAG or tinyPEDS.

Remarks

- With respect to the entropy of a message in principle it holds $|q| = |\varpi|$. Although due to the involvement of $\mathcal{T}$ in f^* one could expect $|\varpi| > |q|$. We argue that the gain of information comes with the implicit knowledge about the network's topology and it does not need to be transmitted in the message itself.
- the domain $\mathcal{M}$ relates to the WSN's architecture. Known WSN architectures are e.g. *tinyDB*, *TAG*, *tinyPEDS*, etc. Any $\varpi \in \mathcal{M}$ considers the architectural semantic and thus we point out that for different WSN architectures the domain $\mathcal{M}$ is a separate one.
- the domain $\mathcal{T}$ relates to the WSN topology. In principle $t = (t_U, t_N) \in \mathcal{T}$ is dynamic. For simplicity we assume t to be static. It describes the topology of the WSN directly after the roll-out.
- The existence of an adequate mapping f^* can best be proven over the detour of comparing $r_U \in \mathcal{R}_U$ with $r_N \in \mathcal{R}_N$ with $f_U : \mathcal{Q} \to \mathcal{R}_U$ and $f_N : \mathcal{M} \to$

---

[1] An example for a non-adequate function f would be one that maps any query q to the same flooding message ϖ. This is principally possible but wouldn't make any sense in practice.

$\mathcal{R}_N$: $r_U \overset{?}{\approx} r_N$ (approximation to the expected value). $\mathcal{R}_U$ and $\mathcal{R}_N$ represent the query response space from the user's perspective respectively from the network side.

– The topology $\mathcal{T}_N$ can automatically be generated by the WSN initially after the roll-out of the WSN. However, the mapping to $\mathcal{T}_U$ needs to be done by an administrator. Concretely the mapping is to assign a symbolic region to each node or group of nodes.

– The time should also be mapped to a WSN friendly value. Human readable expressions like days or hours have to be expressed in number of epochs for the WSN query. The sink knows the duration of an epoch and when t_0 occurred, hence the translation for time is a trivial task.

4   Query Translation to TinyPEDS

For a better understanding of the introduced query translation model, we exemplarily illustrate the translation from (q, t_U) to $\varpi \in \mathcal{M}$ and $\mathcal{M}$ representing the *tinyPEDS* semantic. We elaborated a user-friendly SQL-like language very similar to *tinyDB* [18]. Our *tinyPEDS* query syntax is as follows:

```
SELECT agg<expr> | <expr>, ...
[FROM sensors | <expr>]
[WHERE <pred>]
[TIME [BETWEEN <expr> AND <expr> | LAST <expr>]]
[GROUP BY <expr>]
[HAVING <pred>]
```

One can notice that the FROM term is optional. When not set, the default value is 'FROM sensors'. This language aims to provide the most functionality to the user, though it is limited compared to the full SQL language set. There are for example no nested queries. Furthermore, our language should be easily extendable to synchronous WSNs queries. By having a similar syntax to the most used synchronous WSN database, which is *tinyDB*, we ensure larger acceptance among end-users. The essential differences between *tinyDB* and *tinyPEDS* are discussed in the Annex A.

As an example of user-friendly (SQL-like) query $(q, t_u) \in \mathcal{Q} \times \mathcal{T}_U$:

```
SELECT AVG(light), room FROM sensors
WHERE room = 'kitchen' OR room = 'library'
TIME BETWEEN '12:00' AND '13:00'
GROUP BY room
```

The format of a "WSN friendly" *tinyPEDS* flooding message is $\langle region,$ $duration, aggregation, TTL, QT\rangle$. Our model supports hierarchical topologies and here *region* is any subregion of the WSN. In *tinyPEDS*, typically *region* can be noted as $region = \langle level_1 \triangleright level_2 \ldots \triangleright level_l\rangle$ with $level_i \in \mathcal{P}(ALL)$ and $ALL := \{\mathcal{Q}_{(i,1)}, \ldots, \mathcal{Q}_{(i,4)}\}$ for $1 \leq i \leq l$. As a consequence, the smallest unit of an area to which a symbolical location can be mapped is one of the lowest hierarchical subregion of the WSN. Duration is any subinterval over the WSN's current lifetime, aggregation describes the mode of in-network processing, which can be the addition or comparisions operations. The parameter TTL is the time-to-live and QT describes the query type which can be either "continuous (C)" or "disaster (D)". The problem of mapping the SQL-like query to the WSN query is further discussed in Section 5. A controlled flooding message $\varpi = \langle region, [t_x, t_y], aggregation, ttl_{max}, C \rangle$ is handled by receiving sensors $s \in \mathcal{N}$ as denoted in Algorithm 1. In *tinyPEDS*, data monitored is stored at the aggregator node itself, and at one of its neighbouring aggregator. Notice that the query model for distributed database entries of the WSN is different prior and after a disaster strike. After a disaster, where a large number of nodes have died in a limited area, the query is flooded to the complementary region of where the data was originally monitored, as described in Algorithm 2. Thus a disaster query would hopefully harvest the monitored data of the dead nodes in their backup nodes, it is only issued when a continuous query has failed. With the data harvested from the continuous and disaster query responses, one can reconstruct the data completely.

For the concrete setting of $\varpi = \langle \mathcal{Q}_{(1,1)} \triangleright \mathcal{Q}_{(2,2)} \triangleright \mathcal{Q}_{(3,1)} \cup \mathcal{Q}_{(2,4)} \triangleright \mathcal{Q}_{(3,1)}, [t_x, t_y], +, 20, C \rangle$ and the WSN characteristics listed in table 1, ϖ translates into the controlled flooding pattern depicted in the figure 1 of our the GloMoSim simulation. $\mathcal{Q}_{(x,y)}$ denotes a subregion (quarter) of $\mathcal{N}$, whereas x $(1 \leq x \leq l)$ stands for the quarter's hierarchy level and y $(1 \leq y \leq \omega)$ identifies the ω quarters in a cycled order of the corresponding hierarchy level l.

Algorithm 1. *Continuous Database Query /* for any receiving sensor node* $s \in \mathcal{N}$ **/*

---

    if $s \in \mathcal{Q}_{(x,y)}$ **AND** $\mathcal{Q}_{(x,y)} \subseteq pathTo(region)$ **then**
        if $ttl_{current} > 1$ **then**
            $ttl_{current} = ttl_{current} - 1$
            $s \rightarrow * : \langle region, [t_x, t_y], aggregation, ttl_{current}, C \rangle$
            if $aggregation = true$ **AND** $storage_{[t,t+1]} \cap region \neq \emptyset$ **AND** $t_x \leq t \leq t_y$ **then**
                $s \rightarrow R : \langle storage_{[t,t+1]} \rangle$
            end if
        end if
    else
        $ttl_{current} = 0$
    end if

---

5   Problem Statement

We are now in the position to formulate the problem statement of this work: Given a $\mathcal{T} = (\mathcal{T}_U, \mathcal{T}_N)$ for a $\mathcal{M}$ that ensures that an adequate $f^* : \mathcal{Q} \times (\mathcal{T}_U, \mathcal{T}_N) \rightarrow \mathcal{M}$ exists, how to make the originator of any $q \in \mathcal{Q}$ verifiable for the receiver of $\varpi \in \mathcal{M}$ over the detour of f^* (and not f)?

Algorithm 2. *Disaster query*

---

if $s \in \mathcal{N} \backslash \mathcal{Q}_z$ **then**
  if $ttl_{current} > 1$ **then**
    $ttl_{current} = ttl_{current} - 1$
    $s \rightarrow * : \langle region, [t_x, t_y], aggregation, ttl_{current}, D \rangle$
    if $aggregation = true$ **AND** $storage_{[t,t+1]} \cap region \neq \emptyset$ **AND** $t_x \leq t \leq t_y$ **then**
      $s \rightarrow R : \langle storage_{[t,t+1]} \rangle$
    end if
  end if
else
  $ttl_{current} = 0$
end if

Table 1. GloMoSim simulation parameters

WSN size, quadrant size	400x400, 50
num. nodes	240-407
node's transmission range	50
hierarchy levels (l)	3
num. quarters per level (ω)	4
radio layer	CSMA
propagation pathloss	two-way

Table 2. Concrete topology setting for $\mathcal{T} = (\mathcal{T}_U, \mathcal{T}_N)$

$\mathcal{T}_U$	$\cdots$	library	kitchen	$\cdots$
$\mathcal{T}_N$	$\cdots$	$\mathcal{Q}_{(2,2)} \triangleright \mathcal{Q}_{(3,1)}$	$\mathcal{Q}_{(2,4)} \triangleright \mathcal{Q}_{(3,1)}$	$\cdots$

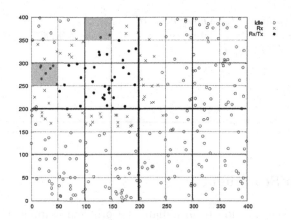

Fig. 1. Controlled flooding of the continuous database query $\langle \mathcal{Q}_{(1,1)} \triangleright \mathcal{Q}_{(2,2)} \triangleright \mathcal{Q}_{(3,1)} \cup \mathcal{Q}_{(2,4)} \triangleright \mathcal{Q}_{(3,1)}, [t_x, t_y], +, 20, C \rangle$ in a WSN with $l = 3$ and $\omega = 4$

The precondition of our problem statement addresses the fact that for a semantical appropriate interpretation of q one has to provide additional information t_N to translate q in a corresponding ϖ. However, to still ensure a user-friendly query process we must hide t_N from the end-user, namely t_N must be incorporated into the query process *after* the user has formulated his query. This implies that f^* can only be applied after q has been formulated by the user. This observation has different impact for the previously introduced different WSN types:

a) *asynchronous WSN*: In this setting the functionalities of the reader and the sink node are co-located. The end-user formulates a query (q, t_U). However, t_N is available at the sink node respectively the reader and it is due to the query translation framework to translate (q, t_U) to ϖ:

$$
\begin{array}{cc}
reader/sink & sensor \\
(q, t_U) & \\
\downarrow & \\
f^*(q, t_U, t_N) = \varpi \rightarrow & \varpi
\end{array}
$$

b) *synchronous WSN*: In this setting the reader device and the sink node are two separate units. A multitude of reader devices can access the WSN from anywhere in the core network via the sink node. In such a setting it is unrealistic to assume that $\mathcal{T}_N$ is known to each reader device. Instead $\mathcal{T}_N$ should solely be located at the sink node. Therefore, we assume the following setting:

$$
\begin{array}{ccc}
reader & sink & sensor \\
(q, t_U) \rightarrow f^*(q, t_U, t_N) = \varpi \rightarrow & & \varpi
\end{array}
$$

Our problem statement addresses the security problem that arises due to the fact that t_N is subsequently incorporated into a query (q, t_U) *after* the end-user entry. How to ensure query message originator verification between the end-user and the verifying sensor nodes on (q, t_U) although sensor nodes finally receive ϖ? Note that this is of highest relevance for *synchronous WSNs* in which the reader device and the sink node are separate units.

6   Truncated Hash Chains

We introduce the notion of dedicated security primitives and define a hash-chain, which is also known as Lamport's hash-chain [9], as $x_{i+1} = h(x_i)$ with x_0 being the anchor and h being an un-keyed one-way hash function which maps bit-strings to t bits. One-wayness means that given x, the image $y = h(x)$ can be easily computed, but the other way around, that is given y finding a pre-image, is difficult. We denote $x_i = h^i(x_0) = h(...(h(x_0))...)$. We define $x_{i+1}^{[1,t-k]}$ to be a $(t-k)$-truncated hash value from a t-bit secure hash function: $x_{i+1}^{[1,t-k]} \hookleftarrow h(x_i)$. W.l.o.g. $[1, t-k]$ indicates that $x_{i+1}^{[1,t-k]}$ consists out of the first $t-k$ bits of $h(x_i)$.

7 Access Control for Synchronous WSNs

We propose an access control protocol for (synchronous) WSNs which

1. supports the mapping from user-friendly queries to a WSN architecture appropriate flooding message,
2. hides the WSN's master secret from the set of reader devices,
3. supports newcomers to the set of reader devices, and
4. securely links the access protocol part from the WSN with the protocol part from the infrastructure.

Topic 1) ensures that in particular a message flow as described in Section 5b) is supported. Topic 2) ensures that readers cannot directly send queries to the WSN, namely skip the sink node. In addition, the set of the reader devices may be huge and the knowledge of each client about the master secret would be unacceptable.

Table 3. WSN access control protocol for the i-th query of the reader device

Transmitting:	Processing:
1. $R \to S : (q, t_U) \| H_{x_{n-i}}(q, t_U)$	$S : x_{n-i} = h^{n-i}(x_0)$
	$H_{x_{n-i}}(q, t_U) \stackrel{?}{=} H_{x_{n-i}}(q, t_U)$
	$x_{n-i-1} = h^{n-i-1}(x_0)$
	$f^*(q, t_U, t_N) = \varpi$
	$z_0 = x_0 \oplus y_{m-j}$
2. $S \to R : \varpi, z_0, H_{x_{n-i-1}}(x_{n-i}, \varpi)$	$R : x_{n-i-1} = h^{n-i-1}(x_0)$
	$H_{x_{n-i-1}}(x_{n-i}, \varpi) \stackrel{?}{=} H_{x_{n-i-1}}(x_{n-i}, \varpi)$
	$y_{m-j} = z_0 \oplus x_0$
3. $R \to S : \varpi, H_{x_{n-i-1}}(x_{n-i}, y_{m-j}, \varpi)$	
$\quad H_{y_{m-j}}(\varpi)$	
4. $S \to s : \varpi, H_{y_{m-j}}^{[1,t-k]}(\varpi)$	$s : y_{m-j} = h^{m-j}(y_0)$
	$H_{y_{m-j}}^{[1,t-k]}(\varpi) \stackrel{?}{=} H_{y_{m-j}}^{[1,t-k]}(\varpi)$

Compared to the scarce radio link connecting the sink node and the sensor nodes we assume the bandwidth requirements between the reader device and the sink node to be rather relaxed. We further assume the sink node to be tamper-resistant and to provide enough storage space to administrate a list of all end-users (readers) who are allowed to access the WSN. For such a setting one solution for a user-friendly and DoS resilient access control protocol to the WSN may be based on

- a challenge-response based on a keyed one-way function,
- two hash chains, and
- a truncated (keyed) hash function.

The challenge response protocol runs between the reader device (R) and the sink node (S) whereas we solely apply a truncated hash function on the scarce radio link between S and a sensor (s). This ensures a weak but still reasonable secure query message authentication at the sensor nodes to prevent DoS attacks from "any" unauthorised reader which simply circumvents the sink node S. Without such a mechanism it would be possible to cheat and to directly address a query request to the WSN. We apply two hash chains. Hash chain number one which is generated based on a secret anchor x_0 is known by the sink node and one particular reader device. The sink node stores for each particular reader a different pair (x_0, n) whereas each reader stores the secret (x_0, n). The value n represents the number of iterations of the applied hash function, namely x_n is the hash value $x_n = h^n(x_0)$. The hash value x_n is public and reveals no secret. Hash chain number two is generated based on the secret anchor y_0. The tuple (y_0, m) is known by the sink node and each sensor node in the WSN. This tuple is stored by the manufacturer within the sensor nodes preliminary to the roll-out of the WSN. Again $y_m = h^m(y_0)$ is public not revealing any secret. Both hash chains are applied in a simple yet efficient way to control access to an asynchronous WSN. The basic idea is to apply intermediate hash values $x_i = h^i(x_0)$ with $1 \leq i \leq n$ and $y_j = h^j(y_0)$ with $1 \leq j \leq m$ to keyed hash functions $H_{x_i}(\varpi)$ respectively $H_{y_j}(\varpi)$, namely message authentication codes (MAC). The $(n - i)$-th hash value which can be derived from x_0 is used by the particular reader for its i-th query addressing the WSN. The $(m - j)$-th value which can be derived from y_0 represents the j-th request of any reader device. However, due to the extreme bandwidth limitation on the radio (IEEE 802.15.4 WPAN) and due to the fact that the number of transmitted bits directly translates into a reduced lifetime of the WSN we propose to use $(t - k)$-truncated keyed hash values $H^{[1,t-k]}_{y_{m-j}}(\varpi) \leftarrow H_{y_{m-j}}(\varpi)$. The full protocol is described in table 3.

Remarks

- the secret (x_0, n) is known by the sink node and a specific reader device. The secret (y_0, m) in particularly is not known by the reader devices. It is exlusively stored at the sensor nodes and at the sink node. To still enable a reader device to compute $H_{y_{m-j}}(\varpi)$ and to know y_{m-j}, in Step 1 the sink node performs the $\oplus$ function (bitwise addition modulo 2) on x_0 and the actual WSN secret y_{m-j}. In Step 2) the reader device bitwise adds x_0 to z_0 to compute the actual WSN key which is valid for the actual flooding message ϖ.
- if everything works well, it is not really necessary to provide R the knowledge of y_{m-j}. But as the experience shows, it is rather unrealistic to assume that the sink S can always communicate with each sensor s. For example, in huge WSN, intermediate nodes are necessary to transport a message from S to s. If this connection is broken, R can use the knowledge of y_{m-j} to get directly in contact with s. As s updates the value of y_{m-j} to y_{m-j-1} for the next flooding message, y_{m-j} provides only a kind of temporary permission to get information from s, what limits the damage R could cause.

- any $s \in \mathcal{N}$ where $H_{y_{m-j}}^{[1,t-k]}(\varpi) \overset{?}{=} H_{y_{m-j}}^{[1,t-k]}(\varpi)$ is true, locally broadcasts the message $\varpi, H_{y_{m-j}}^{[1,t-k]}(\varpi)$, otherwise it drops the query.
- the problem of message loss over the wireless can be handled at any $s \in \mathcal{N}$ by also validating if $H_{y_{m-j}}^{[1,t-k]}(\varpi) \overset{?}{=} H_{y_{m-j-2}}^{[1,t-k]}(\varpi)$ in case the check $H_{y_{m-j}}^{[1,t-k]}(\varpi) \overset{?}{=} H_{y_{m-j-1}}^{[1,t-k]}(\varpi)$ failed. Iff the second check succeeds s forwards the query and sets $j = j - 1$.
- only $t - k$ additional bits over the scarce wireless are needed. An adversary who eavesdrop the value $H_{y_{m-j}}^{[1,t-k]}(\varpi)$ might misuse this knowledge to replace ϖ by his own flooding message. However, as the value y_{m-j} is secret, the problem is to find a value $\varpi' \neq \varpi$ such that $H_{y_{m-j}}^{[1,t-k]}(\varpi) = H_{y_{m-j}}^{[1,t-k]}(\varpi')$ for an unknown value y_{m-j}. This is also know as a *target collision*. We expect a hash function suitable for a hash chain to be *target collision resistance*. Note that it is widely believed that for $t = 80$ finding a target collision is as hard as factoring an RSA modulus of 1024-bits. On the Berkeley motes e.g. RC5 based hash chains and MACs are quite competitive in terms of speed (2.22-4.18ms), code size (1738 Bytes) and data size (136 Bytes).

8   Proposed Approch for Data Concealment in WSNs

Access control for WSNs is only valuable if data concealment over the wireless is provided. Approaches like TinySec with RC5 respectively Skipjack or IEEE 802.15.4 WPAN's AES-CTR provide link layer security in a hop-by-hop manner. However, since query response traffic is characterised by in-network processing and data aggregation of reverse multicast traffic each aggregating node must decrypt all receiving data, aggregate the data and subsequently encrypt the aggregated value again. This is suboptimal due to i) a lack of security at the aggregating nodes and ii) due to the energy waste for multiple decryption and encryption operations. Therefore in [15] we propose for the aggregation functions *sum, average, movement detection* and *variance* to apply a *symmetric/asymmetric additively privacy homomorphism (PH$_S$)* to conceal reverse multicast traffic end-to-end. A *PH$_s$* is an encryption transformation which has the property

$$a + b = D_k(E_k(a) + E_k(b)) \tag{1}$$

where a and b belong to the plaintext domain and E and D are encryption respectively decryption transformations on the key k. Using such an *PH$_s$* in WSNs means that an aggregator node can perform above aggregation functions on incoming ciphertexts. With conventional encryption schemes it would need to decrypt incoming ciphers before performing the aggregation function.

9   Related Work

The first work in progress report investigating the problem of authenticated querying in sensor networks appeared in 2005 from Benenson [2]. Beneson introduced the problem of node querying and analysed the design space for authenticated queries in WSNs. Although Beneson describes techniques for authenticated querying she does not provide a concrete solution to the problem of authenticated queries. Recently a concrete solution to this problem followed in [3]. It it based on the idea of using 1-bit MACs per sensor node. A sensor node receiving a query can infer with probability 1/2 if the query stems from an authenticated reader device.

Zhou and Ravishankar [19] have proposed the use of dynamical Merkle trees and one-way hash chains in order that the sensors are able to authenticate mobile sinks. The mobile sinks must get for each activity the necessary credential from the base station, so that they can then locally query the sensors. The sensors can then verify the authenticity of mobile sinks by just storing the prior knowledge of the root of the Merkle tree. Contrary to the work at hand, these approaches are focused on the WSN and not on the fixed network.

More generally, a set of authentication approaches for restricted devices have been proposed. We restrict ourselves by refering to the resurrecting duckling approach from Stajano and Anderson [12], the Guy Fawkes protocol [1], the TESLA approach from Perrig et al.[11], and the Zero Common-Knowledge (ZCK) protocol [14].

10   Conclusion

We introduced the problem of end-user friendly WSN queries and DoS resilient access control to WSNs. We propose to use an access control protocol which is based on a challenge-response protocol and truncated hash values over the scarce wireless to overcome the introduced problems. The access control mechanism provides two way mutual authentication between the reader device and the sink node as well as a lightweight query authentication at the sensor nodes. The latter is mandatory to prevent un-authorised users from flooding query messages to the WSN by circumventing the sink node. The proposed data storage architecture on the WSN side is tinyPEDS which ensures an encrypted distributed data storage.

Acknowledgment

We would like to thank Axel Poschmann and Andre Weimerskirch for their input to Section 2. We would also like to thank Alban Hessler who gave input to the camera ready version of this paper.

References

1. R. Anderson, F. Bergadano, B. Crispo, J.-H. Lee, C. Manifavas, R. Needham, "A New Family of Authentication Protocols", ACM Operating Ssystems Review, 1998.
2. Z. Benenson "Authenticated Queries in Sensor Networks", Second European Workshop on Security and Privacy in Ad Hoc and Sensor Networks, ESAS'05, LNCS 3813, pp. 54-67, Visegrad, Hungary, 2005.

3. Z. Benenson, L. Pimenidis, F.C. Freiling, S. Lucks "Authenticated Query Flooding in Sensor Networks", 4th IEEE Conference on Pervasive Computing and Communications Workshops, pp. 644-647, Pisa, Italy, 2006.
4. FIPS PUB 140-2, "Security Requirements for Cryptographic Modules", Federal Information Processing Standards Publication, National Institute of Standards and Technology.
5. W. Heinzelmann "Application-Specific Protocol Architectures for Wireless Networks", PhD thesis, MIT, 2000.
6. J. Girao, D. Westhoff, E. Mykletun, T. Araki, "TinyPEDS: Persistent Encrypted Data Storage in Asynchronous Wireless Sensor Networks" to appear as regular paper in Elsevier Ad Hoc Journal.
7. J. M. Hellerstein, W. Hong, S.Madden, K. Stanek, "Beyond Average: Towards Sophisticated Sensing with Queries", In *Workshop on IPSN'03*, Palo Alto, CA, USA, April 2003.
8. H. Karl, A. Willig, "Protocols and Architectures for Wireless Sensor Networks", Wiley, 2005.
9. L. Lamport, "Password authentication with insecure communication", Commun. ACM 24(11), pp. 770–772, ACM Press, New York, NY, USA, 1981.
10. S. Madden, M. J. Franklin, J. Hellerstein, W. Hong, "TAG: a Tiny AGgregation Service for Ad-Hoc Sensor Networks" In 5th Symposium on OSDI, 2002.
11. A. Perrig, R. Canetti, J.D. Tygar, D. Song, "The TESLA broadcast authentication protocol", RSA CryptoBytes, 5(Summer), 2002.
12. F. Stajano, R. Anderson, "The resurrecting duckling: Security issues for ad hoc wireless networks", 7th International Workshop, volume 1796 of Lecture Notes in Computer Science, pp. 172-194. Springer-Verlag, Berlin Germany, 2000.
13. S. Tilak, N. B. Abu-Ghazaleh, W. Heinzelmann, "Collaborative Storage Management in Sensor Networks", Journal of Ad Hoc & Ubi. Comp.
14. A. Weimerskirch, D. Westhoff, "Zero-Common Knowldge Authentication for Pervasive Networks", 10th Selected Areas in Cryptography, SAC'03, Springer-Verlag LNCS 3006, pp. 73-87, Ottawa, Ontario, CA, August 2003.
15. D. Westhoff, J. Girao, M. Acharya, "Concealed Data Aggregation for Reverse Multicast Traffic in Wireless Sensor Networks: Encryption, Key Pre-distribution and Routing", in *IEEE Transactions on Mobile Comuting*, Vol. 10, October 2006.
16. D. Westhoff, "End-user friendly and DoS Resilient Access Control for WSNs", 13th International Conference on Telecommunication, ICT, Portugal, May 2006.
17. J. Girao, D. Westhoff, M. Schneider, "CDA: Concealed Data Aggregation for Reverse Multicast Traffic in Wireless Sensor Networks", In *IEEE International Conference on Communications (ICC'05)*, Seoul, Korea, May 2005.
18. Samuel R. Madden, Michael J. Franklin, Joseph M. Hellerstein, Wei Hong, "TinyDB: an acquisitional query processing system for sensor networks", ACM Trans. Database Syst., Vol. 30 No 1, 2005
19. Li Zhou, Chinya V. Ravishankar, "Dynamic Merkle Trees for Verifying Privileges in Sensor Networks", In *IEEE International Conference on Communications (ICC'06)*, Istanbul, Turkey, June 2006

A   Comparing TinyPEDS with TinyDB

We argued in Section 4 that the *tinyPEDS* front-end language is very similar to the one of *tinyDB*, because we do not want the user to learn a new query syntax for each WSN database. However, one has to keep in mind that the underlying databases and mechanisms are fundamentally different. Due to space restrictions we only sum up the main differences. They are listed in table 4:

Table 4. Databases features

	tinyPEDS	*tinyDB*
WSN type	Asynchronous	Synchronous
Storage policy	In-network	At sink Some storage points possible
Dissemination model	Controlled flooding	Multicast (tree routing)
System security	Encrypted storage End-to-end confidentiality	None

The data model has the same shape for both WSN databases. We can see the WSN as one table, i.e. *sensors*, which has a colum for each type of data, e.g. temperature; and a row for:

- each node and interval of time in tinyDB
- each lowest subregion and epoch in tinyPEDS

One major difference is that *tinyDB* uses acquisitional queries, meaning that records of the table are only materialized as needed to satisfy a query and subsequently stored for a short period of time or delivered out of the network. Consequently queries in *tinyDB* only concern present or future values. In opposite to *tinyPEDS*, where queries harvest data of the past thanks to the in-network persistent storage.

Tiny 3-TLS: A Trust Delegation Protocol for Wireless Sensor Networks

Sepideh Fouladgar, Bastien Mainaud, Khaled Masmoudi, and Hossam Afifi

Institut National des Télécommunications, 9 rue Charles Fourier,
91011 Evry Cedex, France
{sepideh.fouladgar,bastien.mainaud,khaled.masmoudi,
hossam.afifi}@int-evry.fr

Abstract. Adapting security protocols to wireless sensor networks architectures is a challenging research field because of their specific constraints. Actually, sensors are computationally weak devices, unable to perform heavy cryptographic operations like classical asymmetric algorithms (RSA, Diffie-Hellman). In this paper, we introduce Tiny 3-TLS, an extension and adaptation of TLS handshake sub-protocol that allows establishing secure communications between sensing nodes and remote monitoring terminals. Our protocol aims at guaranteeing the integrity and confidentiality of communications between sensors and distant terminals, after having established mutual authentication between the two parties. In order to achieve these security goals without putting too much burden on sensing devices, Tiny 3-TLS rely on an intermediate node, the sink node. Depending on the trustworthiness of this sink node and on the applications, we propose two versions of our proposition. Besides, we provide a formal validation of the protocol's security goals achievement and an evaluation of its computation and delay performances.

1 Introduction

Wireless sensor networks (WSN) have been generating much interest in the last few years. The need for efficient security is more and more appealed since the most of sensor applications require wireless communications for flexible deployment purposes. Besides, the accuracy and the integrity of the conveyed data may be of very high importance. For instance, WSN may be deployed in e-health applications, including medical monitoring and remedies administration, which are critical as the patients' lives are at stake. Most WSN architectures rely on a central node that collects and processes the data. It is generally an entity located outside the WSN, and is linked to it through an interconnecting architecture (usually the Internet), either an ad hoc or an infrastructure-based network. The interconnection between WSN and Internet is made by means of a gateway acting as a radio base station: the sink. This gateway modifies the message from the WSN in order to be compliant to Internet, usually IP-based, protocols. The complete operation of this gateway is not detailed in this document.The need for security is a request of WSN community. On the one hand,

L. Buttyan, V. Gligor, and D. Westhoff (Eds.): ESAS 2006, LNCS 4357, pp. 32–42, 2006.

the major constraint is the weak resources of such nodes in terms of memory, processing capacity and power consumption. That's why it is not possible to use classical cryptographic algorithms and security protocols in networking architectures that include WSNs. On the other hand, TLS (Transport Layer Security protocol) [6] has become the de facto secure application-level tunneling protocol; in order to adapt it in the context of wireless sensor networks, we propose a solution which enables establishing TLS tunnels between a node of the WSN, and a monitoring remote device. The negotiation may rely on the sink node to perform as much cryptographic operations as possible. The remainder of this paper will unfold as follows: the next section will focus on the existing tunneling technologies and the security mechanisms for WSN. Next, we describe our solution to support traditional sensor networks security mechanisms, followed by an evaluation of the computation time of our protocol over Avrora platform [1] and a formal validation of the protocol from a security point of view using an automatic protocol analyzer. Finally we conclude and provide some possible extensions to our work.

2   Related Work

TLS, is an application-independant set of protocols that enables encryption, authentication and integrity for data exchanged between a client and a server. TLS consists of many subprotocols, among which Handshake protocol. This latter allows a client and a server to negotiate a cyphersuite, authenticate each other and obtain a shared master key, usually using public key algorithms. Once the shared master key established, the two parties derive symmetric keys and use symmetric algorithms for fast encryption and authentication of application data. Thus, TLS Handshake protocol uses public key technology to support symmetric key management. Although many prior security proposals for sensor networks considered that sensor constraints were incompatible with public key cryptography, many more recent work showed that public key technology can also be deployed in the realm of sensor networks. Watro et al.[3] conceived a security scheme, Tiny PK, based on public key technology, for providing authentication and key exchange between an external party and a sensor network. The fact is that TinyPK is based on a precautionous implementation of RSA cryptosystem albeit Elliptic Curve Cryptography (ECC) appears as an alternative to RSA for resource constrained devices. Indeed, ECC can offer equivalent security for fairly smaller keys. Moreover, TinyPK uses checksums to insure message integrity during its key management protocol, whereas checksums have shown to be poor and easily misled integrity mechanisms. An end-to-end security architecture for low power devices (Sizzle), which lies on ECC, has been implemented by Gupta et al.[4]. It allows embedding a secure web server in low power devices for monitoring and control purposes. Sizzle architecture is composed of a control station located somewhere in the internet, the sensors being controlled and a gateway that serves as a bridge between these two elements. The gateway connects to the internet using an ethernet-like high-speed link and connects to the sensors via a lower-speed wireless link such as 802.15.4 [13]. In Sizzle, the gateway does not perform any cryptographic operation as all data stays encrypted when crossing the gateway. It just transmits the messages between the control station and the sensors. As a consequence, all the burden of cryptographic operations is on the sensors. Moreover the gateway does not authenticate itself neither to the control station nor to the sensors; and these, are not authenticated either. Therefore, man in the middle attacks are easily achievable.

3   Tiny 3-TLS

3.1   Trust Model and Security Goals

The goal of our solution is to provide an end-to-end secure communication between a remote device and a wireless sensor network . Tiny 3-TLS achieves the following security functionalities:

- *injective agreement on a shared session key between a remote terminal and the WSN, possibly through the help of the gateway,*
- *mutual authentication between the gateway and the remote node*

These goals are validated using an automatic protocol analyser, as described in section 5.

Even though classical TLS Handshake achieves these goals, it is not adapted as is to our context. We use concepts from IEEE 802.1X standard [15] trust model to build trust between the WSN, the gateway and the remote node (see figure 1). In this scheme, the WSN acts as the authenticator (the resource), the remote node as the supplicant and the gateway as the authentication server.

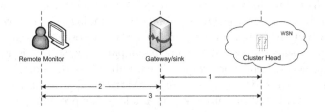

Fig. 1. Trust establishment sequence

Figure 1 shows the pre-establishment of trust between the security gateway and the group of sensors in (1). Once trust is established between the gateway and the remote node (2), it is transitiveley achieved between the remote node and the WSN (3).

3.2   Problem Statement

Partially Trusted Versus Fully Trusted Gateway:
Tiny 3-TLS adapts TLS handshake sub-protocol in order to have secure communications between a remote client terminal and a sensor network. To balance

sensors' low computational capabilities, the Tiny 3-TLS architecture is based on a third party [5], the security gateway (GW) that assists the sensors for cryptographic computations.

Henceforth, we consider two cases:

— In the first case, the security gateway is partially trusted by the sensors and will only help the two parties to authenticate each other. Loosely speaking, by partially trusted, we mean that the gateway introduces the group of sensors to the distant terminal and reciprocally this latter to the sensors, but will not interfere further in the sensors/terminal relationship. In fact, this mutual authentication will help establishing a shared secret, unknown to the gateway, between the two parties, allowing the data exchanged between the terminal and the sensors to remain encrypted when crossing the gateway. Thus, at the end of Tiny 3-TLS handshake, we will have a secure end to end tunnel between the two entities.

— In the other case, the security gateway is fully trusted. That is to say, the gateway will not only help the authentication between the two parties but will also possess the shared secret between both entities.

Use Cases:

Among project MAGNET-Beyond [14] scenarios, one could consider *MAG-NET.Care*. In this scenario, a patient is connected to the external world through his Body Area Network (BAN), which includes a set of sensors reporting health data like the current temperature and blood pressure to a coordinator/receiver, acting as a cluster head, which in turn sends reports to a remote monitoring device. The coordinator is connected to the external world by means of a gateway. Whenever the remote monitor polls the BAN for data, the gateway acts as a reverse proxy, authenticates the monitoring device and then grants access.

One possible application of the partially trusted gateway scenario could be that of an attending medical practitioner who wants to monitor his patient's

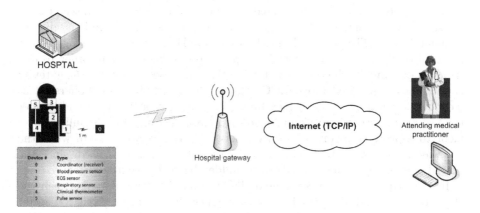

Fig. 2. A partially trusted gateway use case

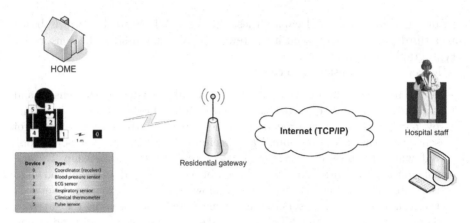

Fig. 3. A fully trusted gateway use case

health condition while he is at the hospital. He can connect his laptop to the hospital gateway (Security Gateway) and query the sensors connected to the patient. Then the gateway authenticates the laptop to the patients sensors. However, if the gateway is not fully trusted, it won't see the information exchanged between the physician laptop and the sensors, for evident privacy reasons. This use case is shown in figure 2.

On the other hand, if the patient is at home and, the physicians at the hospital want to retrieve some health data (see figure 3), the monitoring device authenticates to the patient's residential gateway. The reverse proxy in this case is part of the personal network of the patient and therefore should be fully trusted.

Protocol Assumptions and Statements:

Tiny 3-TLS handshake involves three parties among which a sensor network. When the gateway is partially trusted, in order to establish a shared secret master key which is unknown to the gateway between the sensors and the distant terminal, Tiny 3-TLS uses ECDH (Elliptic Curve Diffie-Hellman) key agreement protocol [7, 8]. In fact, asymmetric cryptography is necessary in order to distribute safely among the targeted entities, the shared secret, even if the gateway is watching. As precised above, ECC (Elliptic Curve Cryptography) offers asymmetric cryptography with considerably lower computational burden and smaller key sizes than traditional asymmetric cryptosystems and thus, is fully convenient to a protocol involving a sensor network. On the other hand, when the gateway is totally trusted, the classical TLS key agreement is used, since the shared master key no more needs to be hidden from the security gateway.

In this paper, we have considered that the handshake is done between the client terminal and a cluster head sensor. Once the master key (shared secret between the two entities) is derived, the cluster head sensor will broadcast the keys in a secure manner to other sensors. This broadcast is out of the scope of this paper.

We assume that the security gateway and the sensor network share a symmetric key K that is used to encrypt any message between both entities. We will use in the table 1 syntax to describe Tiny 3-TLS.

Table 1. Figure 1 and 2 syntax

$BigAlice, GW, TinyBob$	Principals
K	Symmetric Key shared between the gateway and TinyBob
PK_x	Public key of principal x
ID_x	Identifier of principal x
$Cert_x$	Certificate of principal x
$H(.)$	Hash function
$ECDH_x$	Elliptic curve Diffie-Hellman public values of principal x
PK_x^{-1}	Private key of principal x
$\{M\}\_K$	M encrypted with key K
N_x	Nonce generated by principal x
P_x	Ciphersuite offer by principal x
$x\|y$	x concatenated to y
PMS	Pre-Master Secret
M	Concatenation of all previously exchanged messages between BigAlice and the gateway

3.3   Case 1: The Security Gateway Is Partially Trusted

In this case, the security gateway GW supports the remote terminal (BigAlice) and the sensor network (TinyBob) in sharing a secret, though without possessing it. First of all, BigAlice sends a Client Hello message that contains its identifier, the SessionID, a ciphersuite offer and a nonce (1). This message is encrypted with K symmetric key and forwarded by GW to TinyBob (2). This latter replies with a Server Hello message including its identifier, the SessionID, a nonce, a ciphersuite counteroffer and its ECDH public values (3). GW keeps the ECDH values for itself and transmits to BigAlice a Server Hello message containing the SessionID and TinyBob's identifier, nonce and cyphersuite counteroffer. It also conveys its own certificate and a certificate request to BigAlice (4). Hence, BigAlice responds with its certificate, its ECDH public values and a newly generated nonce (gateway authentication nonce, $N'_{BigAlice}$), both encrypted with GW public key (recovered from GW certificate) and a signature of its ECDH public values, TinyBob's nonce and identifier (5). The gateway authenticates BigAlice and recovers its ECDH public values and the "gateway authentication nonce". It ciphers this latter and TinyBob's ECDH public elements, with BigAlice public key and transmits the ciphertext to BigAlice (6). The fact that the gateway could decipher the "gateway authentication nonce" and send it back to BigAlice, authenticates the gateway. Likewise, it sends to TinyBob, BigAlice's ECDH public values and a hash of all previously exchanged messages between the gateway and BigAlice, all being encrypted by K (7). Finally, TinyBob and BigAlice can communicate directly and exchange "Finished" messages (8, 9) where

$$Finished = H(R, M) \text{ where } R = PRF(DHK, N_{BigAlice}, N_{TinyBob}),$$
$$DHK \text{ being ECDH agreed key.}$$

BigAlice sends its "Finished" message to TinyBob encrypted with BigAliceMasterKey. Likewise, TinyBob sends its "Finished" message to BigAlice encrypted with TinyBobMasterKey.

$$BigAliceMasterKey = KeyGen(ID_{BigAlice}, N_{BigAlice}, N_{TinyBob}, R)$$
$$TinyBobMasterKey = KeyGen(ID_{TinyBob}, N_{BigAlice}, N_{TinyBob}, R) \text{ (figure 4)}.$$

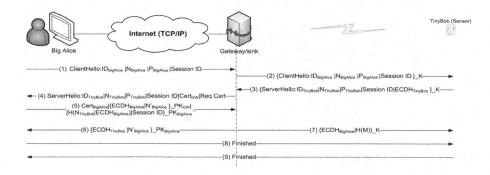

Fig. 4. The gateway is partially trusted

3.4   Case 2: The Security Gateway Is Fully Trusted

In this case, all the communication between TinyBob and BigAlice can be seen in the clear by the gateway. Client and Server Hello messages are identical to previous case (messages 1-4), except for the third message which do not contain TinyBob's public Diffie-Hellman elements. Once Client and Server Hello messages exchanged, BigAlice generates a symmetric pre-master secret (PMS). It responds to the gateway with its certificate, PMS and TinyBob's nonce encrypted with GW public key (recovered from GW certificate) and a signature of PMS, TinyBob's nonce and identifier. Big Alice adds a "Finished" message (5) where :

$$Finished = H(R, H(M)) \text{ where } R = PRF(PMS, N_{BigAlice}, N_{TinyBob})$$

Once the "Finished" message received from BigAlice, the gateway generates a nonce, a Client-read-key and a Client-write-key:

$$Client - write - key = KeyGen(ID_{BigAlice}, N_{BigAlice}, N_{TinyBob}, R)$$
$$Client - read - key = KeyGen(ID_{TinyBob}, N_{BigAlice}, N_{TinyBob}, R)$$

Then, the gateway encrypts these three elements with K and transmits the cyphertext to TinyBob (6). TinyBob decrypts the cyphertext and sends back a hash of its identifier and the nonce generated by the gateway (7). Finally the gateway sends BigAlice a "Finished" message (8) (figure 5).

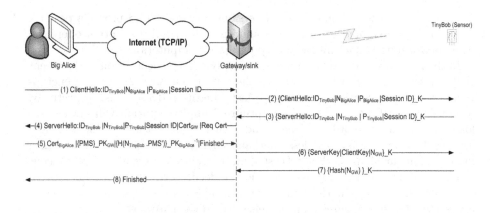

Fig. 5. The gateway is fully trusted

4   Performance Evaluation of Tiny 3-TLS

We have emulated our protocol from the sensor side by means of Avrora for the analysis of the execution time. Avrora (Beta 1.6 version released in July 2005) is an AVR (Advanced Virtual Risc) Simulation and Analysis Framework developped by the UCLA Compilers Group. It provides some information (time consumption, sleep period, energy consumption) about the application downloaded on a sensor. It emulates the code processing on a MICA2 sensor. MICA2 uses a 7,37 Mhz single processor board (MPR2400CA) with 128 KB of EEP-ROM for instructions and 4 KB for data. The application is written in Nesc for TinyOS 1.x.

In this paper we aimed at limiting the number of computations made by the sensors, specially public key cryptography. In the case where a gateway is fully or at least partially trusted (i.e trusted for authentication), this latter can help decreasing the burden on sensors. Indeed, there are few cases where the gateway is unknown or publicly available. Sizzle [4] is an end-to-end security architecture for low power devices. This solution is the closest of the objectives of our architecture. There are few differences between the both solutions and the following table illustrates the advantages and the drawbacks, in terms of computation, of our two use cases (Partially and Fully trusted) compared to [4] proposition.

Table 2. Comparison of Partially and Fully trusted use cases with Sizzle[4]

Tiny 3-TLS version	Partially trusted	Fully trusted
Tiny 3-TLS additional operations	- 1 symmetric encryption - 1 symmetric decryption	- 1 symmetric encryption - 1 symmetric decryption
Sizzle [4] additional operations	- 1 signature verification	- 1 Diffie-Hellman shared key generation - 1 signature verification - "Finished" messages calculations

In comparison with "Sizzle", both versions of Tiny 3-TLS protocol perform one additional symmetric encryption and one additional decryption operation while performing less asymmetric cryptographic computations.

In the Partially Trusted Gateway use case, symmetric decryption of the Client Hello message sent by the gateway to the sensor (message 2) and the encryption of the sensor response (message 3) last 44,8 ms and 156,8 ms, respectively. A signature verification, even in an optimized implementation will always last longer by at least two orders of magnitude. This confirms the fact that Partially Trusted Gateway scenario is less time and energy expensive than Sizzle. In a more obvious fashion, the Fully Trusted Gateway use case is also advantageous in terms of time and energy consumption. Indeed, both symmetric encryption and decryption of Client Hello messages last 44,8 ms. Besides, the most costly operation, that is key agreement, is delegated to the gateway.

5 Security Analysis and Formal Validation

AVISPA Security Analyser:
In order to analyze the security of Tiny 3-TLS, we used Automatic Validation of Internet Protocols and Application (AVISPA) tool, a security protocol analyzer [2]. AVISPA uses a High Level Protocol Specification Language (HLPSL) [9] to describe security protocols and specifying which security goals are achieved by a given one. HLPSL is an expressive and straightforward language, based on the work of Lamport on Temporal Logic of Actions [12]. Communication channels are represented by the variables carrying different properties of a particular environment. We have used OFMC [11] tool since it provides support for specific algebraic properties, in our case the exponential operator used for Diffie-Hellman key agreement in the first case. We correctly compiled our HLPSL model and validated Tiny 3-TLS. The output of the analyzer is provided in table 3.

The Attacker Model:
We have used Dolev-Yao intruder model [10] in which all communications with the intruder are synchronous. In other words, the intruder is in full knowledge of all messages to and from the honest participants. In this model, the attacker can not lead physical attacks against legitimate entities, however, it can participate to the protocol, generating its own messages, replaying old messages and eavesdropping on communications between the different entities. Though, we test our protocol against replay, identity theft, information leakage and man in the middle attacks.

In both cases, the output shows that the security goals are reached after the validation process and that the protocol is safe (that is no attack threatening the specified goals was found). These goals are 1) Mutual strong authentication between BigAlice and GW,and 2) secrecy of Client-write-key and Client-read-key.

Table 3. OFMC output of AVISPA security analyzer

Partially trusted	Fully trusted
% Version of 2005/06/07	% Version of 2005/06/07
SUMMARY	SUMMARY
SAFE	SAFE
DETAILS	DETAILS
BOUNDED_NUMBER_OF_SESSIONS	BOUNDED_NUMBER_OF_SESSIONS
PROTOCOL	PROTOCOL
GOAL	GOAL
as_specified	as_specified
BACKEND	BACKEND
OFMC	OFMC
COMMENTS	COMMENTS
STATISTICS	STATISTICS
parseTime: 0.00s	parseTime: 0.00s
searchTime: 25.21s	searchTime: 4.87s
visitedNodes: 5206 nodes	visitedNodes: 1499 nodes
depth: 13 plies	depth: 11 plies

6   Conclusion and Future Work

In this paper, we proposed Tiny 3-TLS, an extension to TLS handshake that helps establishing end-to-end tunnels between nodes in a wireless sensor network and an external remote terminal. Contrary to other propositions, we rely on the sink node as an intermediate for trust establishment, since it is a fundamental entity in any network architecture that includes sensors.

Depending on the trust model of the sink node, we designed two versions of the protocol with the objective of relieving as far as possible the low-capacity node, that is the sensor, from the burden of costly cryptographic operations and the transmission of their results. Another design challenge was to introduce as few new messages as possible. The resulting protocol, in both versions, does not introduce any change in TLS handshake implementation from the client side.

Finally, we formally validated the new protocol using an automatic protocol analyzer, AVISPA. We are currently implementing the whole protocol and we will consider in future work the dissemination of the generated keys to other sensors of the cluster and network in order to support one-to-many communication security based on TLS.

Acknowledgment

This paper describes work undertaken in the context of the research project IST-MAGNET. MAGNET Beyond is a continuation of the MAGNET research project (www.ist-magnet.org). MAGNET Beyond is a worldwide R&D project within Mobile and Wireless Systems and Platforms Beyond 3G. It will introduce new technologies, systems, and applications that are at the same time user-centric and secure. MAGNET Beyond will develop user-centric business model concepts for secure Personal Networks in multi-network, multi-device, and multi-user environments. It has 30 partners from 15 countries, among these highly influential Industrial Partners, Universities, Research Centers, and SMEs.

References

1. http://compilers.cs.ucla.edu/avrora/, the Avrora project homepage.
2. http://www.avispa-project.org/, the AVISPA project homepage.
3. Watro, R., Kong, D., Cuti, S., Gardiner, C., Lynn, C., Kruus, P.: *TinyPK: Securing Sensor Networks with Public Key Technology*. In ACM Workshop on Security of Ad Hoc and Sensor Networks, October 2004.
4. Gupta, V.,Millard, M., Fung, S., Zhu, Y., Gura, N., Eberle, H.,Shantz, S.C.: *Sizzle: A Standards-based end-to-end Security Architecture for the Embedded Internet*. In Third IEEE International Conference on Pervasive Computing and Communications, March 2005.
5. Masmoudi, K., Hussein, M., Afifi, H., Seret, D.: *Tri-party TLS Adaptation for Trust Delegation in Home Networks*. In IEEE International Conference on Security and Privacy for Emerging Areas in Communication Networks, September 2005.
6. Dierks, T., Rescorla, E.: *The Transport Layer Security (TLS) Protocol - Version 1.1*. IETF RFC 4346, April 2006.
7. Koblitz, N.: *Elliptic Curve Cryptosystems*. Mathematics of Computation, 48:203-209, 1987.
8. Miller, V.: *Uses of Elliptic Curves in Cryptography*, In Advances in Cryptology, CRYPTO'85, LNCS 218, Springer-Verlag, pp. 417-462, 1985.
9. Chevalier, Y. et al.: *A High-Level Protocol Specification Language for Industrial Security-Sensitive Protocols: www.avispa-project.org*
10. Dolev, D. and Yao, A.:*On the Security of Public-Key Protocols*. IEEE Transactions on Information Theory, 2(29), 1983.
11. Basin, D., Modersheim, S. and Viganno, L.: *OFMC: A Symbolic Model-Checker for Security Protocols*. International Journal of Information Security, 2004.
12. Lamport, L.: *The temporal logic of actions*. ACM Transactions on Programming Languages and Systems, 16(3):872923, May 1994.
13. *Wireless medium access control and physical layer specifications for low-rate wireless personal area networks*. IEEE Standard, 802.15.4-2003, May 2003. ISBN 0-7381-3677-5
14. http://www.ist-magnet.org, IST MAGNET-Beyond project homepage.
15. IEEE Std. 802.1X-2004, Standards for Local and Metropolitan Area Networks: Port Based Network Acces Control.

Impact of Pseudonym Changes on Geographic Routing in VANETs

Elmar Schoch[1], Frank Kargl[1], Tim Leinmüller[2],
Stefan Schlott[1], and Panos Papadimitratos[3]

[1] Ulm University, Media Informatics Institute
{elmar.schoch,frank.kargl,stefan.schlott}@uni-ulm.de
[2] DaimlerChrysler AG, Group Research
Tim.Leinmueller@DaimlerChrysler.com
[3] École Polytechnique Fédérale de Lausanne
panos.papadimitratos@epfl.ch

Abstract. Inter-vehicle communication is regarded as one of the major applications of mobile ad hoc networks (MANETs). In these so called vehicular ad hoc networks (VANETs) security and privacy are crucial factors for successful deployment. In a scenario, where each vehicle would have a unique identifier, eavesdroppers could easily accumulate location profiles.

As a solution approach, several authors suggest using changeable pseudonyms as temporary vehicle identifiers. If a vehicle changes its pseudonym from time to time, long-term tracking can be avoided. However, as we show in this paper, changing identifiers has detrimental effects on routing efficiency and increases packet loss.

So, designers of VANET systems need to aim for a balance between privacy protection on the one and performance on the other hand. The results of this paper provide advise on how to achieve this balance.

1 Introduction

Vehicular ad hoc networks – often called VANETs – are one of the most promising application scenarios for mobile ad-hoc networks.

With the advent of car-to-car communication, both passenger safety and driving comfort can be improved significantly. A car detecting an icy road could inform follow-up vehicles and thereby prevent accidents. If an accident occurs anyway, inter-vehicle communication could support emergency relief units to reach the accident site faster by warning drivers blocking the road ahead or preemption of traffic lights. Regarding driving comfort, inter-vehicle communication could serve to exchange traffic flow information for improved navigation or intelligent adaptive cruise control.

Several research initiatives (e.g. projects like Fleetnet [1] or CarTALK [2]), both in Europe and the U.S., have already produced results in the investigation of vehicular ad hoc networks. For instance, geographic routing has been selected as routing scheme due to its compliance with application needs and its good performance under extremely dynamic network conditions [3].

L. Buttyan, V. Gligor, and D. Westhoff (Eds.): ESAS 2006, LNCS 4357, pp. 43–57, 2006.

Ongoing work is now taking the next steps. One step is the effort to define common standards among car manufacturers, resulting in initiatives like the Car2Car Communication Consortium (C2C-CC) [4] and the Vehicle Safety Communication Consortium (VSCC) [5]. Another important step is the research on security and privacy issues of VANETs, because consumers will definitely not accept attackable systems in their cars nor the ability to trace their itinerary. In Europe, the SEVECOM project [6] is specifically dedicated to that.

The importance of privacy is illustrated in Figure 1. Because both geographic routing as well as many VANET applications make extensive use of position information, locations of vehicles are constantly exposed on the wireless communication channel. For instance, several VANET routing and application protocols use beacon messages that are broadcasted periodically, containing the current position and perhaps also speed or other vehicle information. While the dissemination of these data usually does not cause any problem when considering only a single moment, information and place, the combination of several data over time and at different places can uncover privacy relevant information.

As an example, large petroleum companies may have an interest in detecting the routes which (potential) customers travel throughout the day. Using this knowledge, they could plan new petrol stations or adapt prices based on customer behavior. In order to gather these data, they would simply install C2C-ready communication devices at their petrol stations[1] and collect the beacons sent out by all cars that carry VANET equipment. Using information gathered from electronic payment at petrol stations, these companies might even link cars to individual persons and start targeted advertisement for specific customer groups.

Whereas this scenario may have only a modest impact on the privacy of each individual[2], other scenarios with a more severe background seem far more threatening. Government agencies could easily control where people go with their cars in a much more complete and reliable fashion as it is possible with video surveillance and automatic image recognition. Likewise, private investigators could track and trace cars easily through the cities by following the cars in 100 meters distance which is equivalent to placing a radio beacon on the car.

One has to consider, that these location profiles may be accumulated over years and that you might become a suspect of a crime, just because your car was detected near a crime scene three months ago. This may also allow behavior profiles, e.g. your boss may be interested in the fact that you visit the hospital twice a month.

Previous work such as [7,8,9,10] suggests the use of randomly changing identifiers – so called pseudonyms – to prevent this kind of privacy intrusions. While it is still possible to collect data, associating it with identities over time gets much more complicated if node identifiers are used only for a short period of time.

However, when changing pseudonyms a number of new problems arise:

- *Traceability due to context*
  A vehicle may be tracked despite of regular pseudonym changes because of certain circumstances. For instance, if the car changes its pseudonym while

---

[1] Depicted as circles in the figure.

[2] But it may have an influence on gas prices we have to pay.

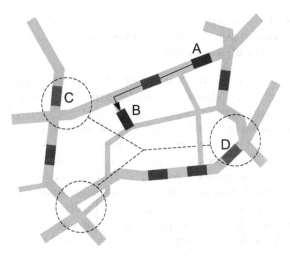

Fig. 1. Passive eavesdropper records beacons and/or application messages at important places and vehicle A tracks way of vehicle B

very few other vehicles are around, linking old and new pseudonym is rather simple by tracing its trajectory using beacons [7]. Similarly, if a car uses changing pseudonyms daily and is parked on the same reserved parking slot each day, the pseudonyms can also be related easily.

– *Traceability due to cross-layer influence*
 Changing the pseudonym on one communication layer does not make sense if protocols on other, non-encrypted layers also use identifiers. In this case, node pseudonyms could be linked by the identifiers of other communication layers. So, changing pseudonyms must be coordinated between layers.

– *Security implications*
 Anonymity has also drawbacks. Many security schemes that want to protect MANETs from selfish or malicious nodes propose mechanisms where these misbehaving nodes are first detected and then excluded from the network. With pseudonyms, misbehaving nodes can evade this exclusion by simply creating a new identity. Preventing this is a hard problem.

– *Problems with application protocols*
 There are applications that need a long-term communication relationship between the involved parties. Examples include any type of file-transfer or interactive chat-sessions. Often, these protocols have an explicit session layer which controls authentication, association, stream control and similar issues. When identifiers change, it can become very complex and expensive to re-establish the session, as partners need to be re-authenticated[3], some data may need to be replayed, etc.

– *Impact on communication protocols*
 In most communication protocols, identifiers play a vital role. For example, beaconing is an important service for geographic routing as well as some

---

[3] See [11] for a potential solution.

applications that deal with context-awareness in VANETs. While high frequency of changing pseudonyms improves privacy, it also complicates the design of communications protocols.

In this paper, we focus on the last aspect. Because geographic routing relies on stable identifiers of neighboring nodes, frequent pseudonym changes disturb proper routing functionality.

Changing the pseudonym once a day may be enough to prevent long-time tracking, but will not prevent an private investigator from following a car throughout the day. There are also applications where the car is needed to identify itself or to its communication partner, e.g. when you do electronic payment of tolls and the money is collected using bank transfers. Once this has happened, your movement profile for the whole day can be directly linked to your identity.

On the other hand changing the pseudonym only once every night while the car is parked at home in the garage has surely no significant influence on communication performance or on-going sessions.

On the other hand, changing the pseudonym every 10 milliseconds might increase privacy protection but will surely render most communication useless, as no node will be able to send you a packet as a reply to a previous packet you send earlier.

This paper analyzes the effects of privacy-enhancement mechanisms on the functionality of position-based routing protocols that forward packets hop-by-hop to the destination. In contrast to topology-based protocols, position-based routing is well suited to the specific characteristics of VANET scenarios [3], e.g. in terms of node mobility and application needs. From a privacy point of view, these protocols have the drawback that they link the position and identity of a node in every beacon message they send.

With our results, we aim at supporting the design of VANET systems that balance between privacy and operative requirements like performance or session stability. In our further analysis, we focus on the performance implications of pseudonym changes. In Section 2, we first describe a theoretical analysis of potential causes for packet loss and expected effects on routing. Later in Section 3, we support these findings by means of simulations. Before we finally summarize and conclude our results in Section 5, we give a short overview on related work in Section 4.

2   Effects of Pseudonym Changes on Geographic Routing

2.1   Routing Approach

We have based our analysis on the Cached Greedy Geocast (CGGC) routing protocol [12] which has been developed as part of the Fleetnet project. With CGGC, nodes periodically announce their identifier and current location using beacon messages. Nodes broadcast beacons every b seconds to all neighbors within reception range. Based on the information contained in beacons, nodes build up neighbor tables. Table entries expire after t_o seconds and are removed from the table afterward.

If a node m generates a packet or receives one for forwarding, it searches its neighbor table for the node which is located closest to the destination:

$$min(d(n, dest)) \; \forall n \in NT$$

where NT stands for neighbor table, $dest$ is the node identifier of the destination node, n is a node entry in the neighbor table, and $d(n, dest)$ is the Euclidean distance between n and $dest$.

If no such node is available (i.e. all $d(n, dest) >= d(m, dest)$ with m being the own node identifier), then the node simply stores the packet in a packet cache until a suitable neighbor becomes available due to node movement.

2.2   Analysis of Effects

For the analysis, we make the basic assumptions that beacons and data packets are sent at fixed intervals, but without any synchronization between each other. Likewise, nodes change pseudonyms at a fixed rate which is also not synchronized to the other intervals.

Data packets and beacons are sent as simple datagrams, there are no higher layer retransmission mechanisms (e.g. TCP) in place. This is a reasonable assumption, as most multi-hop applications which disseminate messages in VANETs work this way.

Let b be the beacon interval in seconds (e.g. $1s$), p be the packet interval (e.g. $2s$), and c be the pseudonym change interval (e.g. $10s$).

For simplicity, we further assume $c > t_o$, i.e. there is at most one pseudonym change per beacon timeout interval. Changing pseudonyms more frequently is usually not reasonable. Further, we assume that $b \leq p$, because many VANET applications send simple information or warning messages at rather long intervals, so this assumption seems reasonable. However, we will also shortly discuss the $b > p$ case at the end.

Figure 2 shows an excerpt from a VANET scenario. Node m has created or received a packet for forwarding which is destined for node o. n is the the neighbor node with the smallest Euclidean distance to o and would be selected as next hop. n periodically broadcasts beacons with its identity and position which m uses to update its position table. But what happens when n changes its identity to n'?

m still has n in its neighbor table and might send packets to n for forwarding. n' will however ignore these packets, because otherwise packets sent to n would be resent by n' so both identities could easily be correlated. Therefore such packets will get lost.

We are now interested in the percentage of packets that may get lost due to a pseudonym change in contrast to a similar scenario without pseudonym change. Figure 5 shows the potential cases and the respective probabilities.

Multiplying the probabilities for each path that leads from the root to a leaf where packets are lost and adding up the results gives us the overall probability

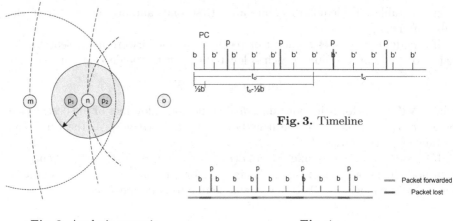

Fig. 3. Timeline

Fig. 2. Analysis scenario   **Fig. 4.**

of packet loss or in other words the expected percentage of packets that will be lost due to pseudonym changes. The result is that $\frac{t_o}{2c}$ of all packets will get lost.

We now explain the probability tree in detail from top to bottom.

Is a packet affected by pseudonym change? Looking at Figure 3, we see that only packets that follow a pseudonym change (PC) can be affected by this PC. One t_o interval after the last beacon with the old pseudonym (b) has been sent, this information will be removed from the neighbor table and only information from beacons containing the new pseudonym (b') will be available to node m. As the last beacon (b) was sent on average $b/2$ before the pseudonym change and as the t_o interval starts from this point on, the average timeframe for affected packets is $t_o - \frac{b}{2}$. Considering the whole time between two pseudonym changes, $\frac{t_o - \frac{b}{2}}{c}$ of all packets will be affected on average. The other $1 - \frac{t_o - \frac{b}{2}}{c}$ packets will be delivered regularly.

Is a packet the first packet after PC? For the first packet after each pseudonym change, there are two alternatives: either the packet p is sent before the next beacon b' or is is sent after the next beacon b'. In the first case, there is no information available on the new pseudonym n' and the packet will be definitely lost. In the second case, the fate of the packet depends on the node movements, as we will see in the next step.

In Figure 4, we explain how to calculate the probability of first receiving a packet before a beacon. We still assume $b \leq p$. Depending on the parameters b and p, there is a varying amount of "complete" beacon intervals within each packet interval, on average $\lfloor \frac{p}{b} \rfloor$. When the pseudonym change happens inside one of these intervals, we will definitely receive another beacon before the next packet.

The "rest" in front and at the end of the packet interval has a varying length which depends on the offset of b at the beginning of the p interval. Depending on this offset, this "rest" ranges between zero and two beacon intervals. On average, it will be one beacon interval, as the packet sent always divides one

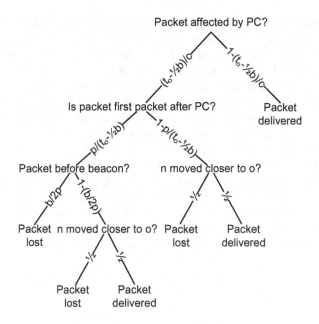

Fig. 5. Loss probability tree

interval which then contributes to the "rest" of the previous and next packet interval.

The relative amount of time of one beacon interval compared to one packet interval is $\frac{b}{p}$. On average, half of this time is located at the beginning of the packet interval and half of the time at the end. Only when the pseudonym change happens in the part the end of a packet interval, the packet is sent without a preceding beacon and the packet is lost (see Figure 4). The probability of loosing a packet because of this reason is therefore $\frac{b}{2p}$.

Has n moved closer to o while changing pseudonyms? For all packets that are affected by a pseudonym change and that are sent after a beacon with the new pseudonym (b') has been received, the following situation applies: the sending node has both information on n and n' in the neighbor table. As the sending node m cannot link n and n', it will simply select the forwarding node based on its routing metric, i.e. the node which is closer to the destination o. Let $d(n,o)$ be the Euclidean distance between n and o. We assume that node n can move in the radius r within one beacon time as shown in Figure 2.

The last beacon before pseudonym change reported position p_n, the next beacon after pseudonym change reports position $p_{n'}$). As m cannot correlate n and n', it assumes that there is an known node at position p_n and another node at position $p_{n'}$. If $d(n',o) < d(n,o)$, the new node will be preferred, otherwise m will try to send its packets to the previously known node.

If $d(n',o) < d(n,o)$, the packet will be received and forwarded, if $d(n',o) > d(n,o)$ the packet will not be received and gets lost. If $d(n',o) = d(n,o)$, m randomly selects one of the two nodes, which gives a 50% chance of success or loss.

If o is far away ($d(n, o) \gg 1$), the circle around n with radius r is divided in two halves, where all positions on the left are further away from o and all positions on the right are closer to o. Assuming random node movement of n, the chance of packet loss because of movement is therefore estimated to be $\frac{1}{2}$.

One might object that node n might even move to a position outside of transmission range of m and packets will then be lost with 100% probability. As this case can however occur with or without pseudonym change and packets sent to n are not received at the new position $p_{n'}$ anyway, the packet is lost, no matter if there is a pseudonym change or not. Since we are only interested in additional packet loss due to pseudonym change, this case will be neglected here.

Of course, movements of other nodes in the neighborhood of m might also change the potential forwarding node. This effect is also not considered here as it also happens independent of pseudonym change at the same rate.

If we now go back to the probability tree in Figure 5 we need to add the multiplied probabilities of all paths leading to a leaf node where packets get lost:

$$
\begin{aligned}
P_{loss} &= \frac{t_o - \frac{b}{2}}{c} \frac{p}{t_o - \frac{b}{2}} \frac{b}{2p} + \\
&\quad \frac{t_o - \frac{b}{2}}{c} \frac{p}{t_o - \frac{b}{2}} (1 - \frac{b}{2p}) \frac{1}{2} + \\
&\quad \frac{t_o - \frac{b}{2}}{c} (1 - \frac{p}{t_o - \frac{b}{2}}) \frac{1}{2} \\
&= \frac{t_o}{2c}
\end{aligned}
$$

What is interesting to see is that the loss probability is independent of the packet send rate and the beacon rate, but instead depends only on the relation between neighbor cache timeout and pseudonym change rate.

This result is valid only for our assumptions where $b \leq p \leq t_o \leq c$. Using a similar reasoning we can also show that for $b \geq p$, the loss probability is

$$
P_{loss} = \frac{b^2 - c^2 + 4bp + 2t_o b}{4bc}
$$

As you can see, in this case the situation gets more complex and all four parameters influence the loss probability.

In the next section, we will now present the results of simulations that analyze the effects of pseudonym changes on the packet delivery rate.

3   Simulation Results

The analysis in the previous section clearly points out which effects may occur when pseudonyms are changed. To estimate the order of magnitude of these effects on geographic routing, we conducted simulations with the network simulator ns-2, version 2.29 [13].

Table 1. Short overview on simulation parameters

Parameter	Value
Number of nodes	100
Length of square node field	1000 – 4000m
Max. node velocity	10 – 50 m/s
Pause times	0.0 s
Mobility model	Random Waypoint
Link-/MAC layer	IEEE 802.11b
Wireless transmission range	250 m
Number of sent messages	500
Pseudonym change interval p	5 – 60 s
Simulation time	120 s
Simulation runs	20
Beacon interval b	1 s
Neighbor cache timeout t_o	6 s

In these simulations, nodes are equipped with the previously described greedy-based geographic routing layer. Besides, every node changes its pseudonym with a defined frequency that is randomly jittered within $\pm$ 5 seconds. After having changed its pseudonym, just packets addressed to the node's new identifier are accepted. Pseudonym change and beaconing intervals are completely independent, which means that there is no extra beacon after the pseudonym change. Both settings help keeping privacy - accepting packets for the old addresses or sending a beacon immediately after the pseudonym change would cut location privacy to some extent.

As data traffic, messages are generated and sent from randomly selected source nodes to random destinations using the described geographic routing protocol. This leads to larger distances between sender and destination when the network field size is increased. Moreover, packets are sent as geo-anycast, which assures that a destination is reachable regardless of changing identifiers. Detailed simulation settings like network topology, node mobility and composition are summarized in Table 1.

3.1   Basic Impact of Pseudonym Changes

A straight-forward measurement to quantify influences on routing is given by the number of packets that reach their destination. This delivery ratio directly reflects the performance of the routing protocol. Figure 6 shows the decrease in delivery ratio that is caused by pseudonym changes in relation to routing with stable identifiers, which is marked in the graph by the value ∞ as pseudonym change interval . Main insights of Figure 6 are on the one hand that delivery performance almost reaches the level without any identifier change when the interval is 60 seconds. On the other hand, a change interval of about five seconds seriously decreases delivery ratio. For instance, in the network with $2000m \times 2000m$ field size, geographic routing usually delivers over 60% of all messages,

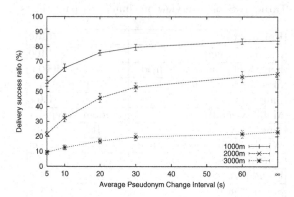

Fig. 6. Packet delivery ratio with influence of pseudonym change at different frequencies and network sizes

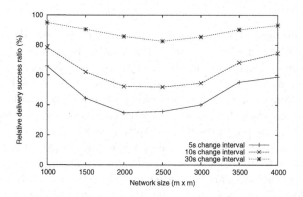

Fig. 7. Reduction of packet delivery ratio with pseudonym change compared to normal forwarding (100%) in dependence of network size and pseudonym change frequency

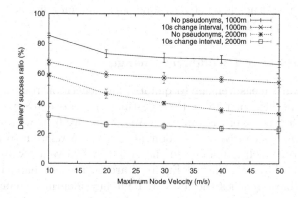

Fig. 8. Packet delivery ratio with different node velocities and both with and without pseudonym changes

whereas only little more than 20% reach their destination when nodes change their identifieres every five seconds.

3.2 Influence of Node Density

Another observation from Figure 6 is the fact that networks with higher node density (like $1000m \times 1000m$) can cope better with pseudonym changes. In this configuration, the additional packet loss is less than 30%, but over 40% in case of the $2000m \times 2000m$ sized field. Figure 7 gives a more detailed insight of the influence of node density. It shows the relation between successfully delivered packets when using changing pseudonyms in contrast to permanent identifiers. As we can see, even with a pseudonym change frequency of $30s$, packet delivery ratio may decrease almost 20%. The fact that there is a peak decrease at about $2000m$ to $2500m$ field side lengths is due to decrease of delivery ratio without changing identifiers when node density gets low ($\sim 20\%$ at $3000m \times 3000m$, see also Figure 6). Therefore, only packets with short trip reach their destination in low-density networks anyway and thus are also likely to face no pseudonym change, too.

Regarding privacy, changing the pseudonym only every 30 seconds may perhaps be a too long time already. Though such a change interval surely avoids being tracked in a global scope, an attacker following another vehicle may be able to figure out into which direction the haunted vehicle has turned off at an intersection. On the other hand, re-identifying the tracked car after it has actually changed its pseudonym could be a difficult task for the attacker if the pseudonym change is done carefully.

3.3 Influence of Node Velocity

Node velocity is a crucial parameter in VANETs. Geographic routing has shown to cope well with this requirement [14]. As depicted in Figure 8, when using pseudonyms, delivery success ratio does not decrease much with higher node velocity. Interestingly, this contrasts to the decrease of successfully delivered packets when routing can rely on stable node identifiers. Particularly in the scenario with lower node density ($2000m \times 2000m$), delivery ratio decreases notably from 60% to 30%, whereas the difference with $10s$ pseudonym change interval is only about 10% between $10m/s$ and $50m/s$ maximum node velocity. Hence, the effect of changing pseudonyms decreases with higher node velocities.

3.4 Comparison with Theoretical Analysis

The loss probability of $\frac{t_o}{2c}$ that we found in the analysis in section 2 is independent of beacon and packet intervals. As this is a result that one might not expect, we explicitly verified it in our simulations. Figure 9 shows the packet delivery ratio with different values for p, c, b and t_o. Though single result values differ about 5%, at large, the graph confirms that b and p are not relevant for loss probability. Besides, also the order of magnitude of losses coheres with the analytical result.

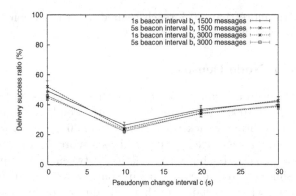

Fig. 9. Packet delivery ratio at different pseudonym change intervals, with varied beacon intervals and message numbers

Taking a look at Figure 7, we see that the loss due to pseudonym change corresponds to on average 50% with $c = 5s$, 30% with $c = 10s$, and $5 - 10\%$ with $c = 30s$. Table 2 compares this to the expected results using our formula $P_{loss} = \frac{t_o}{2c}$.

As a summary, we can conclude that we have a good correspondence of simulation findings and analytical results which both support our claim that pseudonym changes can lead to a significant reduction in routing performance under certain circumstances. It is interesting to see that the packet and beacon rates do not influence this loss.

3.5   Improvement with MAC/LL Callback

The basic reason why packets get lost is because they starve out in link layer interface queues due to neighbors that are no more available. Therefore, applying a direct callback mechanism from link layer to routing layer is likely a method to overcome the problem of outdated neighbor table entries due to pseudonym change. In an enhancement of our simulation implementation, we tested this mechanism in conjunction with pseudonym changes. Thus, the link layer informs the geographic routing about unreachable neighbors immediately after a transmission failed and passes back the packet. The routing then takes up the packet again, determines the next hop the packet was originally sent to and removes it from its neighbor table. After the update, the packet is re-enqueued for routing.

Figure 10 depicts the aggregated number of MAC callbacks that occurred during simulations. In consistence with the previous results, most link failures

Table 2. Comparison of analytical results with simulation findings

c	Simulation	Analytical
5s	$\approx 50\%$	$P_{loss} = \frac{5s}{2*5s} = 50\%$
10	$\approx 30\%$	$P_{loss} = \frac{5s}{2*10s} = 25\%$
30	$\approx 5 - 10\%$	$P_{loss} = \frac{5s}{2*30s} = 8,3\%$

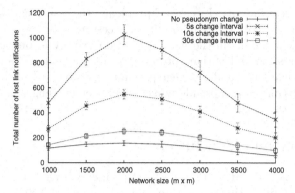

Fig. 10. Aggregated number of lost link notifications

occur in mid-sized networks. More importantly, the simulation results also show that the MAC callback mechanism is able to reduce the performance decrease almost to zero even with pseudonym change frequency of 5s.

Unfortunately in reality, wireless links usually are rather unstable. Thus, if a node removes a neighbor immediately after a single transmission failed, links to neighboring nodes may be removed though they are only temporarily unavailable. To meet this problem, direct MAC callback has to be used carefully, e.g. only after a set of retries.

4   Related Work

With progressing research on VANETs, the quest for privacy has emerged as a crucial factor. Several authors, for instance Hubaux et al. [15] or Dötzer in [8], addressed that topic. They argue, that cars are personal devices that are usually kept for a rather long time and even innocent looking data may become privacy-relevant when evaluated over a longer period of time. Therefore, they propose to use changing pseudonyms as temporary identifiers to preserve privacy. In [15], Hubaux et al. also review entropy as a metric to quantify the effectiveness of pseudonym changes. In [16], Sampigethaya et al. take up the idea of selecting certain nodes as mix nodes. All nodes that belong to one cluster communicate only through their mix node and thus manage to stay private.

On the other hand, [8] also states that vehicles are expected to work reliably, implying that applications of inter-vehicle communication have to face this requirement as well. Unfortunately, from the point of view of security, detection and exclusion of malicious nodes usually relies on the ability to identify nodes. Thus, there is a clear tradeoff between security and privacy. For example, as Golle et. al stated in [7], higher pseudonym change frequency leads to smaller margins for detection and correction of malicious behavior.

The proposed solution to the problem in [8] is to deploy a trusted third party, that issues a limited number of pseudonyms per vehicle and records the corresponding, real identity. In case of problems, the issuer can withdraw the pseudonyms and disclose the real identity if necessary.

Further work was done in the field of location privacy in pervasive computing. In [17], Beresford and Stajano propose so-called mix-zones to overcome the linkability problem when nodes change pseudonyms arbitrarily. Schlott et al. investigate attacks on random pseudonym change schemes using some side channel information in [18].

5 Summary and Conclusion

In this paper, we focused on the effects of pseudonym changes on the performance of geographic routing that is intended to be used in VANETs. The analysis shows, where pseudonym changes affect routing procedures and result in packet losses. Both analytical results and simulation confirm serious performance decreases in case of less dense network connectivity and high pseudonym change intervals ($< 30s$).

We suggest introducing a callback mechanism which informs the routing about failed transmissions. The routing can then cope better with pseudonym changes. On the other hand, such a callback mechanism needs to be implemented carefully because links are rather unstable in highly dynamic ad hoc networks like VANETs.

In conclusion, our work shows that operational and privacy requirements need to be balanced in VANETs. This can be achieved by choosing appropriate pseudonym change intervals and implementing a "soft" callback from link layer, for instance if a transmission failed several times.

Currently, both simulation and analysis focus on the case where beacons are sent more often than data packets ($b < p$) because we estimate this to be very important for many eSafety applications. We are now about to also investigate the opposite case with $b > p$.

These results will help us to develop a privacy protection mechanism for VANETs, which is one of the objectives of the SEVECOM project.

Acknowledgements

Parts of this work have been carried out in contribution to the SEVECOM project [6] that is supported by the European Commission e-Safety initiative under contract no. IST-027795. We also would like to thank Matthias Gerlach for his comments.

References

1. Franz, W., Wagner, C., Maihöfer, C., Hartenstein, H.: Fleetnet: Platform for inter-vehicle communications. In: Proc. 1st Intl. Workshop on Intelligent Transportation, Hamburg, Germany (2004)
2. CarTalk 2000 Project. http://www.cartalk2000.net (2004)

3. Mauve, M., Widmer, J., Hartenstein, H.: A survey on position-based routing in mobile ad-hoc networks. IEEE Network **1** (2001) 30–39
4. Car2Car Communication Consortium. (http://www.car-to-car.org/)
5. US Vehicle Safety Communication Consortium. (http://www-nrd.nhtsa.dot. gov/pdf/nrd-12/CAMP3/pages/VSCC.htm)
6. SEVECOM - Secure Vehicle Communications Project. (http://www.sevecom. org/)
7. Golle, P., Staddon, D.G.J.: Detecting and correcting malicious data in vanets. In: Proceedings of the First ACM Workshop on Vehicular Ad Hoc Networks (VANET), Philadelphia, USA (2004)
8. Doetzer, F.: Privacy issues in vehicular ad hoc networks. In: Workshop on Privacy Enhancing Technologies, Cavtat, Croatia (2005)
9. Aijaz, A., Bochow, B., Dötzer, F., Festag, A., Gerlach, M., Kroh, R., Leinmüller, T.: Attacks on inter vehicle communication systems - an analysis. In: Int'l Workshop on Intelligent Transportation (WIT). (2006)
10. Raya, M., Hubaux, J.P.: The security of vehicular ad hoc networks. In: Proc. of Third ACM Workshop on Security of Ad Hoc and Sensor Networks (SASN 2005), Alexandria, USA (2005)
11. Schlott, S., Kargl, F., Weber, M.: Re-identifying anonymous nodes. In: International Workshop on Location- and Context-Awareness (LoCA 2006), Dublin, Ireland (2006)
12. Maihöfer, C., Eberhardt, R., Schoch, E.: CGGC: Cached Greedy Geocast. In: Proc. 2nd Intl. Conference Wired/Wireless Internet Communications (WWIC 2004). Volume 2957 of Lecture Notes in Computer Science., Frankfurt (Oder), Germany, Springer Verlag (2004)
13. ns 2, N.S. http://www.isi.edu/nsnam/ns/ (2004)
14. Füssler, H., Mauve, M., Hartenstein, H., Käsemann, M., Vollmer, D.: A comparison of routing strategies for vehicular ad hoc networks. Technical Report TR-3-2002, Department of Computer Science, University of Mannheim (2002)
15. Hubaux, J.P., Čapkun, S., Luo, J.: The security and privacy of smart vehicles. IEEE Security and Privacy **4** (2004) 49–55
16. Sampigethaya, K., Huang, L., Li, M., Poovendran, R., Matsuura, K., Sezaki, K.: Caravan: Providing location privacy for vanet. In: Proceedings of Embedded Security in Cars (ESCAR). (2005)
17. Beresford, A.R., Stajano, F.: Location privacy in pervasive computing. IEEE Pervasive Computing **2** (2003) 46–55
18. Schlott, S., Kargl, F., Weber, M.: Random ids for preserving location privacy. (2005)

Identification in Infrastructureless Networks

Gina Kounga and Thomas Walter

DoCoMo Communications Laboratories Europe GmbH,
Landsberger Strasse 312,
80697 Munich, Germany
{kounga,walter}@docomolab-euro.com

Abstract. Confidential communications require entities to mutually authenticate and establish secure communication channels, where the latter requires secret keys to be established between entities. Both —mutual authentication and secure communication— can be achieved by non–revoked public key certificates. However, in infrastructureless networks —such as ad hoc networks—, online trusted third parties (TTP) may not be present that can distribute the required information to verify the revocation status of a certificate. This can prevent confidentiality from being provided. In this paper we define a protocol which permits nodes in an ad hoc network without a shared secret key and without guaranteed access to a TTP, firstly, to mutually authenticate and, secondly, to verify the revocation status of a certificate.

1 Introduction

Many scenarios require confidential communications. In a military application, for instance, some officers from the same coalition —but not necessary from the same country or the same army— may need to exchange some strategic information. Similarly, during a trade fair, some business partners from different companies may need to exchange confidential information. In these scenarios, communicating parties need to mutually authenticate and establish secure communication channels. Public key certificates are a means to achieve this, provided the revocation status of a certificate can be validated. A valid certificate binds a principal's identity to a public key and must not have been revoked [1, 2]. And, once a certificate has been revoked it should not be used anymore. In order to allow an entity to verify the revocation status of a certificate, traditional solutions rely on online third parties such as certificate revocation list (CRL) [1] repositories or online certificate status protocol (OCSP) [2] responders. If up–to–date revocation information is available then this would prevent an attacker A that may have compromised P's certificate from impersonating P.

However, ad hoc networks possess some properties which make access to and distribution of revocation information not always possible. First, nodes are forwarding packets by multi–hop communications. Since nodes are free to move, the connectivity between source and destination nodes can be disrupted at anytime. This prevents nodes from having a guaranteed access to updated revocation

L. Buttyan, V. Gligor, and D. Westhoff (Eds.): ESAS 2006, LNCS 4357, pp. 58–69, 2006.

status information when needed. Second, the movements of nodes may cause network partitions such that a revocation request broadcasted by the legitimate owner of a certificate may not reach the entire network. Then, nodes are not able to make the difference between the legitimate owner of a certificate and an attacker. Under such conditions, nodes have no guarantee that by sending a message encrypted with the public key Pub_P contained in a certificate $Cert_P$, the message will only be decrypted by the legitimate P. Different approaches [3,4,5] are proposed to provide public key based entity authentication in ad hoc networks. However, they require nodes to issue certificates while they may not be able to verify the identity of nodes that request certificates [3,4,5] or they do not permit nodes to know certificates' revocation status [3].

In this paper we propose a solution based on an extension to the X.509 certificate [1] that permits to verify that a certificate is used by its legitimate owner even when there is no online TTP. This implicitly permits nodes to know that a certificate has not been revoked by its legitimate owner and that it is valid. Our solution is defined for mobile devices controlled by human–beings. It is not designed for mobile devices, such as sensors, that operate without any human intervention. In our approach, each node P has a certificate $Cert_P$ which contains the value $S_P = m^{x_P} mod\ n$, where x_P is a secret key generated with one of P's biometric traits or from a pass–phrase. x_P is not stored by P. It must be re–generated whenever it is needed from a capture of P's biometric trait or from the right pass–phrase. Solutions such as [6] have been defined in the literature to generate a same key from different captures of a given biometric trait. Here we focus on the case where x_P is generated from a biometric trait. Since such a trait is permanent, unique and hard to re–produce [7,8], it stays valid in fixed or ad hoc networks. So, when P is in an ad hoc network, any verifier node V can verify that P is the legitimate owner of $Cert_P$ by verifying that P knows x_P. Our solution permits P to prove the knowledge of the private key $Priv_P$ associated with the public key contained in $Cert_P$ as well as the knowledge of the secret key x_P without neither disclosing x_P nor disclosing the biometric trait used to generate it. Once V knows that $Cert_P$ is valid, it can use it to establish a session key with P. For these reasons, our solution provides entity authentication and confidentiality. The established session key may be used to exchange confidential messages or for some later authentication. So it may not be needed to run again the protocol defined here to authenticate a node that has already been authenticated in the past.

The paper is organized as follows. In section 2 we present the attacks against entity authentication. Then, in section 3 we study the related work. We define our approach in section 4 and define our solution in section 5. We discuss its security in section 6 and conclude our work in section 7.

2   Attacks Against Entity Authentication

An attacker may pretend it is another node in order to read some confidential messages. To achieve that it can use different attacks that are described in [9,10] as follows:

- **Impersonation during the certificate issuance process**
  An attacker can request a certificate for another identity than its legitimate one. If no mechanism is defined to detect the attack or/and to invalidate the issued certificate, the attacker is always able to use the issued certificate to impersonate the legitimate owner of the corresponding identity;
- **Replay attack**
  An impersonation or other deception involving use of information from a single previous protocol execution, on the same or a different verifier;
- **Reflection attack**
  An impersonation attack involving sending information from an ongoing protocol execution back to the originator of such information;
- **Chosen–text attack**
  An attack on a challenge–response protocol wherein an adversary strategically chooses challenges in an attempt to extract information about the claimants long–term key;
- **Forced delay**
  A forced delay occurs when an adversary intercepts a message, and relays it at some later point in time.

Some counter–measures can be taken to avoid the previous attacks. These are presented in table 1 as they are listed in [10].

Table 1. Identification protocol attacks and counter–measures

Type of attack	Principles to avoid attacks
Replay	Use of challenge–response techniques; use of nonces; embed target identity in response.
Reflection	Embed identifier of target party in challenge–response; construct protocols with each message of different form (avoid message symmetries); use of uni–directional keys.
Chosen–text	Use of zero–knowledge techniques; embed in each challenge response a self–chosen random number (confounder).
Forced delay	Combined use of random numbers with short response time–outs; timestamps plus appropriate additional techniques.

3   Related Work

Different approaches are proposed in the literature to provide public key based entity authentication in ad hoc networks. In [3, 4] entity authentication is provided with self–generated certificates signed by a distributed virtual certification authority (CA). At network initialization, nodes get shares of a virtual CA's private key. Later, to obtain the virtual CA's signature on their certificates nodes must request valid partial signatures from a given threshold of nodes. These approaches avoid the existence of a single point of failure in the network. However, they do not define any identity proofing process [9] to guarantee that identities contained in certificates are valid. Another issue is that in [3] no solution is proposed to verify whether a certificate has been revoked or not. This may cause nodes to use invalid certificates to authenticate a communicating party. In [4] the monitoring of neighbors is used to detect misbehaving nodes whose certificates must be revoked. However, it may be difficult to define the behaviour of a compromised node. For this reason, there may be situations where nodes are falsely accused. In [5] nodes that do not know each other in advance can authenticate with a chain of valid certificates, i.e. a chain of certificates with a valid user–key binding and which are neither expired nor revoked. Certificates are issued by neighbors which have some reasons to believe that a public key belongs to a given node. Nodes may have, for instance, exchanged their public key through a side channel. However, it may be difficult in most cases to have a clear picture of the ad hoc network membership [11]. Therefore, nodes may not have in advance the required information to validate a user–key binding during the certificate issuance process. For this reason, nodes may not be able to issue valid certificates while they are in the ad hoc network. Solutions proposed in [3,4] are exposed to impersonation during the certificate issuance process. However, because [3,4,5] leave the details of the authentication protocol open the other mentioned attacks do not apply.

For our solution we exploit undeniable signature introduced in [12,13]. Undeniable signature is a zero–knowledge protocol which permits an entity P to prove to an entity V that it has generated the digital signature $S = m^x mod\ n$ on the message m with its private key x. That private key is associated to the public key g^x —with g a public value. The characteristic of an undeniable signature is that it can not be verified without the signer's cooperation. This is because P must prove that it has generated S by raising to the multiplicative inverse of x, the challenge, that V sends in message (2) —cf figure 1.

Remark 1. In figure 1 and in the rest of the document, the challenge and the response to the challenge are computed modulo n, with n a large prime as defined in [12].

4 Approach

4.1 Problem Reformulation

The lack of infrastructure and the possible existence of partitions in ad hoc networks do not guarantee that entities are always reachable that are able to distribute updated revocation status information. Therefore, the only principal that is always able to know whether a certificate is being revoked or not is its legitimate owner. Good practice of public key encryption [14] recommends not to use a public/private key pair after it has been revoked —especially after a key compromise. This makes it realistic to consider that if the legitimate owner of a certificate is still using its certificate, it means that this legitimate owner has not revoked its certificate. Then the problem of identifying whether a certificate

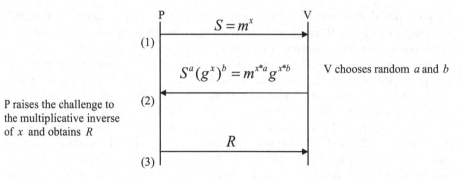

Fig. 1. Undeniable signature scheme

has been revoked or not can be solved by identifying whether one is interacting with the legitimate owner of a certificate or not.

4.2   Choices

Defining a Two–Factor Authentication Solution

To identify the legitimate owner of a certificate we bind a secret to each certificate that is only known by the individual that was issued the certificate. That secret is not stored in the mobile device. Then, in the ad hoc network, the individual must prove the validity of his certificate by proving the knowledge of the bound secret. Many reasons explain this choice among which the important ones are the following two:

- The more factors are used in an authentication solution, the stronger that solution is [9]. Our solution adds one factor to the traditional certificate based authentication solution;
- To prove the validity of a certificate, it is required to prove the knowledge of a secret that is not stored in the mobile device and that is only known by the legitimate owner of the certificate. Therefore, an attacker is not able to use a compromised key pair for impersonation. This is true even if the attacker has stolen the mobile device.

Different means can permit an individual to prove the knowledge of a secret that is not stored in his device:

- The secret can be derived from a password or pass–phrase that the individual has to enter each time he has to prove the validity of his certificate;
- The secret can be based on a biometric trait that the individual has to capture each time that he has to prove the validity of his certificate.

Biometric traits present the advantage that they are unique, hard to reproduce and that individuals do not have to retain them. This is why we chose to use biometric traits for our solution. One may discuss this choice by arguing that it may be awkward to require individuals to intervene each time that an authentication process needs to be run. However, users are already used to it and already accept it: they accept to enter their personal identification number each time they have to use their credit card, they accept to enter their transaction authentication number for each new online banking operation, etc.

Running an Identity Proofing Process in the Fixed Network
As discussed in section 3, with self–generated certificates nodes are free to generate certificates containing any identity. Therefore, nothing permits to know with which entity a secure communication channel is established. Since in ad hoc networks, nodes may not be present that have the means to validate identities of entities that request some certificates, we chose to issue certificates in the fixed network before nodes enter any ad hoc network. Verifying principals' identities before certificate issuance is a requirement that is not always met as discussed in [15]. However, there are some situations where this verification can be done efficiently. For instance, when individuals register at a network provider they usually have to present paper credentials. These paper credentials can be used to run some identity proofing processes before issuing certificates that bind valid identities into certificates. The access to a fixed network is required at registration for certificate issuance. However, afterwards nodes may run independently of the CA and the fixed network as represented in figure 2(b).

 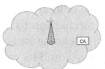 

(a) Certificate issuance during registration in the fixed network

(b) Entity authentication in the ad hoc network

Fig. 2. From registration to entity authentication

5 Identification Protocol

In this section, we detail the mechanisms used during certificate issuance —cf figure 2(a)— and entity authentication —cf figure 2(b).

5.1 Certificate Issuance

P captures a sample of its biometric trait and uses it to generate its secret key x_P. Then, P computes $S_P = m^{x_P} \bmod n$, with n and m both public values defined by CA. When it is done, P sends a request to CA that contains, among other things —e.g. its public key, its identity ID_P and S_P —cf. figure 3. CA verifies that ID_P is P's real identity and checks in its archive that S_P is not bound to

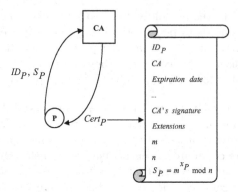

Fig. 3. Certificate request and issuance

a previously issued certificate. If all the verifications are correct, then CA issues to P the certificate $Cert_P$ which contains, among other fields, ID_P, S_P, n and m. n and m are included in the certificate to permit P to be authenticated by a node whose certificate was not issued by CA.

5.2   Authentication Process and Confidential Communication

When P and V want to mutually authenticate in an ad hoc network, they ex-change the messages detailed in figure 4. Here we only detail how V authenticates P, since P uses the same mechanism to authenticate V.

P initiates the process by sending its session identifier sid_P, a challenge m^{a_P}, a Diffie–Hellman public key g^{y_P} and its certificate $Cert_P$. sid_P, m^{a_P} and g^{y_P} are sent signed with P's private key $Priv_P$. It provides integrity and also permits to bind sid_P and g^{y_P} to $Cert_P$. After V has received the message (1), it verifies the signature contained in it. If it is correct, V knows that the message was sent by a node which currently knows the private key $Priv_P$ associated to the public key Pub_P contained in $Cert_P$. However, to verify that $Priv_P$ is currently used by the legitimate owner of $Cert_P$ V sends the message (2). The structure of the message is the same as in message (1) and contains the challenge m^{a_V} that P can only answer correctly if it is able to generate x_P from a capture of its biometric trait. After P has received message (2), it verifies the signature it contains. If it is valid, P captures its biometric trait and re–generates the secret key x_P. Then, it raises the received challenge to x_P and obtains $m^{a_V * x_P}$ as answer to V's challenge. P also calculates the Diffie–Hellman session key $g^{y_P * y_V}$. This key is used to compute $MAC_{g^{y_P * y_V}}(Pub_V, m^{a_V * x_P})$, a message authentication code (MAC) generated on V's public key Pub_V and the answer to V's challenge. This MAC constitutes the proof that P is the legitimate owner of $Cert_P$. Then, P sends the message (3) to V. When V receives the message (3), V first verifies that the session IDs contained in it are the same as in messages (1) and (2). If it is the case, V checks the validity of the received proof. For that, V raises the value S_P contained in $Cert_P$ to a_V. V obtains $m^{x_P * a_V}$. Then it computes the

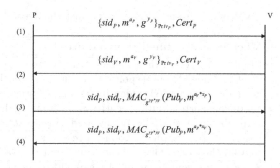

Fig. 4. Protocol for mutual authentication in ad hoc networks

Diffie–Hellman session key that it uses to generate a MAC on its public key and on $m^{x_P * a_V}$. V obtains $w = MAC_{g^{y_P * y_V}}(Pub_V, m^{x_P * a_V})$. To finish, V compares w with the proof it has received in message (3). If they are equal, then it is sure that node P is the legitimate owner of $Cert_P$ and that $Cert_P$ has not been revoked. V can use $Cert_P$ to establish a shared secret key with P that could be used for the exchange of confidential messages.

6 Discussion

6.1 Security of the Identification Protocol

When the legitimate owner of a certificate revokes it, it wants to prevent any other entity from using that certificate. By specifying that V must only use P's certificate $Cert_P$ if P is the legitimate owner of $Cert_P$, we guarantee that V only uses $Cert_P$ if it has not been revoked by its legitimate owner. With our solution, it is still possible to determine that a certificate is valid even when no revocation information is available in the ad hoc network for the following reason: the legitimate owner of a certificate is the only one which is able to generate a valid answer to a received challenge by a capture of its biometric trait. Therefore, even when an attacker has stolen a mobile device, it is not able to impersonate its legitimate owner and even with no connectivity to a fixed network, the validity of a certificate can be checked. So we achieve node authentication and certificate validation in the same protocol run.

The security of our solution also relies on the fact that it is computationally hard for an attacker to find the correct answer to the challenge from a sent proof since that proof is generated from a MAC computed with a Diffie–Hellman session key. Breaking the proof requires to be able to revert a value generated with a cryptographic one–way hash function and to solve the discrete log problem [16]. These are two problems that are computationally hard to solve. Since our solution relies on [12], it also possesses the same security properties as those proved in [12]. Some other mechanisms are defined to protect against the attacks identified in section 2. These are presented in table 2 and are as follows:

Table 2. Mechanisms used to avoid attacks against the defined protocol

Type of attack	Mechanisms defined to avoid attacks
Replay	Proof generated with a challenge–response technique; Target identity embedded in response through the public key contained in the proof; Knowledge identifying uniquely the source and target during current authentication process embedded in response through the Diffie–Hellman key used to generate the proof.
Reflection	During a given authentication process, a message received that contain the same values as the values sent is invalid.
Chosen–text	Self–chosen random numbers embedded in each challenge–response.
Forced delay	Short response time–outs are used.

- **Impersonation during the certificate issuance process**
  Certificates are issued by a CA from the fixed network, that has the means to verify that the identity claimed by an entity that requests a certificate is valid and is its legitimate identity. This avoids impersonation during the certificate issuance process.
- **Replay attack**
  Nodes must use, at each authentication process, session identifiers, challenges, and Diffie–Hellman public keys that are different from those they used in the past. This can easily be done if nodes choose at each new authentication process some values —session identifiers, challenges, Diffie–Hellman public keys— that are greater than those they have sent at the previous one. This will only require nodes to store the values they used at the previous authentication process. This makes that the proof generated by a node is always different from one authentication process to another one. It prevents replay attack from succeeding.
- **Reflection attack**
  During a given authentication process nodes must not accept a message (1) or (2) —cf. figure 4— that contains the same values as those they have sent during the current authentication process.
- **Chosen–text attack**
  The proof is generated with a Diffie–Hellman session key that depends on a secret value chosen by the source and a secret value chosen by the target.
- **Forced delay**
  Nodes can use short response time–outs to avoid this attack.

The use of a biometric trait to generate x_P may introduce a revocation problem. Indeed, like private keys, an attacker is able to compromise x_P over time, for this reason, the certificate lifetime must be a period during which an attacker is not able to break the corresponding public key and is not able to break x_P. When the certificate lifetime is over, the associated value x_P must not be used anymore for entity authentication. However, since x_P is generated from a biometric trait that is by definition permanent, an individual is not able to generate a different x_P. To solve this problem, nodes may use a random value along with their biometric trait to generate x_P. That way, a given node is able to generate different keys from a same biometric trait.

6.2 Enabling Authentication with Certificates Issued by Different CAs

In ad hoc networks, not all nodes have certificates issued by the same CA. So it may be needed that our solution can also be used between nodes whose certificates were issued by different CAs. When certificates are issued by the same CA, that CA is able to verify that the value S_P contained in the certificate is unique by verifying in its archive that no certificate was previously issued that contains the same value. However, if certificates are issued by many CAs, this check is not sufficient. It becomes necessary to also check that S_P has not been used in a certificate issued previously by another CA. This may require that each CA contacts all the CAs that it trusts in order to make the previous verification. A simpler solution may be:

- To use the same function on each mobile device for the generation of strong encryption keys from the capture of biometric traits: since individuals have unique biometric traits, the capture of a biometric trait is always different from an individual to another one and keys generated by applying a same function on captures from different individual are always different;
- That different CAs specify different values for the m used to generate the challenges and to generate S_P.

6.3 Open Issues

Here, we do not consider the case where a certificate is revoked by a CA because of administrative reasons such as a change of organization. Indeed, when no connectivity to a fixed network is available or when no node is present, which knows that a given entity has left an organization, there is no solution to detect the previous case of revocation. However, even when an entity has moved or changed organization, its previous identity still uniquely designates it. So depending on the information that must be transmitted, the impossibility to determine whether a certificate has been revoked by a CA for administrative reasons may not be a concern. The main concern here, is to guarantee that, while they are in an ad hoc network, nodes are always able to establish secure communications with the intended entity.

7 Conclusion

Many scenarios, such as confidential communications between soldiers in a battlefield or between business partners during a trade fair, require nodes to mutually authenticate and establish secure communication channels. Non–revoked public key certificates permit that. In ad hoc networks, the lack of infrastructure and the possible existence of network partitions do not guarantee updated revocation information are available that can permit to evaluate the validity of a certificate. This can prevent confidentiality from being provided. In this paper we have proposed a solution which relies on certificates issued in fixed networks and which bind a secret key generated with nodes' biometric traits to their certificates. That secret key is not stored by nodes. They must re–generate it from a capture of their biometric trait in order to prove they are the legitimate owners of their certificates. This permits to identify that a certificate has not been revoked even when no updated revocation information is available in the network. It also permits nodes which do not share a secret key in advance to mutually authenticate and establish secure communication channels even when no connectivity to a fixed network or an online TTP is available.

Acknowledgments

The authors would like to thank Chris Mitchell for his comments on this work. They also would like to thank the anonymous reviewers for their suggestions and remarks that helped to improve the quality of the paper.

References

1. Housley, R., Polk, W., Ford, W., Solo, D.: Internet X.509 Public Key Infrastructure Certificate and Certificate Revocation List (CRL) Profile. RFC 3280 (Proposed Standard) (2002) Updated by RFC 4325.
2. Myers, M., Ankney, R., Malpani, A., Galperin, S., Adams, C.: RFC 2560: X.509 Internet Public Key Infrastructure Online Certificate Status Protocol – OCSP (1999)
3. Zhou, L., Haas, Z.J.: Securing Ad Hoc Networks. IEEE Network **13**(6) (1999) 24–30
4. Luo, H., Zefros, P., Kong, J., Lu, S., Zhang, L.: Self–securing Ad Hoc Wireless Networks. In: Seventh IEEE Symposium on Computers and Communications (ISCC '02). (2002)
5. Capkun, S., Buttyán, L., Hubaux, J.P.: Self–Organized Public–Key Management for Mobile Ad Hoc Networks. In: Proceedings of the ACM International Workshop on Wireless Security (WiSe). (2002)
6. Dodis, Y., Reyzin, L., Smith, A.: Fuzzy extractors: How to generate strong keys from biometrics and other noisy data. In: Eurocrypt. (2004)
7. Prabhakar, S., Pankanti, S., Jain, A.: Biometric recognition: security and privacy concerns. In: IEEE Security and Privacy Magazine. Volume 1. (2003) 33–42
8. Newton, E.M., Woodward, J.D.: Biometrics: A technical primer. The RAND organization (2001)
9. Burr, William E., Dodson, Donna F., Timothy Polk, W.: Electronic authentication guideline. NIST Special Publication 800–63 Version 1.0.1 (2004)
10. Menezes, A.J., van Oorschot, P.C., Vanstone, S.A.: Handbook of applied cryptography. CRC Press, Boca Raton, Florida (1996)

11. Papadimitratos, P., Haas, Z.J.: Secure routing for mobile ad hoc networks. In: Proceedings of the SCS Communication Networks and Distributed Systems Modeling and Simulation Conference (CNDS 2002), San Antonio, TX, USA (2002)

12. Chaum, D., van Antwerpen, H.: Undeniable signatures. In: CRYPTO '89: Proceedings on Advances in cryptology, New York, NY, USA, Springer–Verlag New York, Inc. (1989) 212–216

13. Chaum, D.: Zero–knowledge undeniable signatures (extended abstract). In: EUROCRYPT '90: Proceedings of the workshop on the theory and application of cryptographic techniques on Advances in cryptology, New York, NY, USA, Springer–Verlag New York, Inc. (1991) 458–464

14. Barker, E., Barker, W., Burr, W., Polk, W., Smid, M.: Recommendation for Key Management - Part 1: General(Revised). NIST Special Publication 800–57 Version 1.0.1 (2006)

15. Ellison, C., Schneier, B.: Ten Risks of PKI: What You're Not Being Told About Public–Key Infrastructure. Computer Security Journal **16**(1) (2000) 1–7

16. Diffie, W., Hellman, M.E.: New Directions in Cryptography. IEEE Transactions on Information Theory **IT–22**(6) (1976) 644–654

Two's Company, Three Is a Crowd: A Group-Admission Protocol for WSNs

Joao Girao and Miquel Martin*

NEC Europe Ltd.
Kurfuersten Anlage 36
69115 Heidelberg
Germany
{joao.girao,miquel.martin}@netlab.nec.de

Abstract. Once a wireless sensor network (WSN) is stable and has been running for a while, sensors start to fail due to hardware problems, battery exhaustion or even due to their physical destruction. In any case, the administrator of the network may wish to replace the damaged nodes with new ones to reinforce the coverage area. In this paper we make use of an out of band channel (OOB) to bootstrap an authenticated symmetric key. The protocol ensures that the new sensor nodes are currently part of the region covered by the network before negotiating sensitive key material and making them a part of the system and its operations. We describe a novel approach to group admission for wireless sensor networks using an OOB secure channel and perform a security evaluation over this protocol.

1 Introduction

Wireless Sensor Networks (WSNs) are considered by many to be a new hot research topic where the focus lies on solving the problems of routing, clustering, security, etc... with the minimum amount of processing and message transmissions. More than that, WSNs are different from other types of networks due to their unique traffic patterns, topology and restricted functionality.

Applications cover a wide scope, ranging from monitoring of environmental data (e.g. quality control in farming), accident prevention on the road, animal tracking, and even people in border controls, as well, as a number of military applications.

Some security protocols in WSNs make use of symmetric keys which are dynamically assigned [1]. These keys are usually agreed on during a bootstrap phase which may or may not be considered attacker free. The problem appears when, after the network has been stable for quite some time, the owner wishes to add

---

* The work presented in this paper was supported by the European Commission within the STReP UbiSec&Sens of the EU Framework Program 6 for Research and Development (IST-2004-2.4.3). The views and conclusions contained herein are those of the authors and should not be interpreted as necessarily representing the official policies or endorsements, either expressed or implied, of the UbiSec&Sens project (http://www.ist-ubisecsens.org) or the European Commission.

L. Buttyan, V. Gligor, and D. Westhoff (Eds.): ESAS 2006, LNCS 4357, pp. 70–82, 2006.

more nodes to the sensor network. Since most protocols assume some common knowledge, such as a key shared with the reader or a pool of keys distributed amongst the nodes, they cannot be extended, since most times this knowledge disappears from either the network or the owner side. Even in case the knowledge is still present, the cost of programming custom made sensors creates a scalability and cost issues.

For the class of sensors considered in this paper, we assume that radio transmission is two orders of magnitude more expensive than computations, in terms of power consumption. Therefore, message transmission is to be minimized, since it is the main reason for the network's limited life span.

We provide a simple and feasible mechanism with which nodes may be added to a sensor network by creating a common base of knowledge, using an Out of Band channel (OOB), which is used by a sensor to prove to its neighbors it is spatially part of the network and vice-versa. This protocol can be used with a number of different OOB channels and is flexible in its operation, allowing for its application in many different key distribution schemes.

Although there has been a number of papers and work related to security in WSNs, the problem of group admission, or rather, of adding new sensors to a pre-existing sensor network, has not been throughly addressed.

Our motivation stems from protocols such as [2], [1], [3], [4] and [5], where extending the network becomes complex and impractical.

In [1] and [3] the problem appears when adding new nodes: so that an attacker cannot retrieve information on keys which are not being used between the communicating nodes, but which might be used somewhere else in the network, these keys should be erased from the sensor's. After this, one cannot add more nodes and expect to get the deployment-time probability that two nearby nodes share a key. The case is similar in [4] and [5] where the master key should be erased from the sensors after the individual keys are agreed upon, or an attacker might obtain this key and break the system. Inherent to all these protocols, including [2], is that whatever method we choose, we must first re-program all the new nodes to contain information about the network. When buying new nodes where we simply want to extend small parts of the network, this process will become expensive and impractical.

Several other papers have looked at how OOB channels and human interaction can be used to enhance security protocols. In [6] the author describes the pairing problem where two nodes have contact for the first time and wish to exchange a strong secret having only the usual wireless channel and a very low bandwidth, authenticated channel. This problem statement also defines our scenario. In [7], the authors automate the OOB channel by using visual mechanisms and a camera in order to reduce the actual human interaction. [8] formalizes multi-channel protocols design and presents a number of variations on [9] and [7] with different security objectives.

Contribution: In this paper we propose a protocol using an Out of Band channel (OOB) that bootstraps a group key which is used amongst the new sensors and the sensors which belong to the network to prove these are valid sensors and in the area covered by the OOB. This protocol can be used to extend or reinforce certain parts of the network by allowing other sensors to join in.

Organization: In the next section, section 2, we discuss the network and attacker models, after which we define clear security objectives we intend to cover by the protocol described in section 3. The following section 4 proposes different OOBs according to their applicability. The scheme itself is proposed in section 5 and the security analysis of the scheme in section 6. Finally, we end our contribution with a discussion on performance and our conclusions in sections 7 and 8.

2   Network and Attacker Models

In this section we will derive a network model consistent with the problem space and a threat model based on the characteristics of the network and application considered in this paper.

2.1   Network Model

We consider a network composed of sensors, $S_i \in \mathcal{S}$ and readers, $R_i \in \mathcal{R}$. Although we make no assumptions on the traffic patterns which occur between these entities, we assume it is possible to have bi-directional communication between the sensors.

We term neighbor of S_j ($N_i \in \mathcal{N}_{S_j}$) the sensor nodes within radio range of S_j and, since we consider the radio to be symmetrical, the sensor S_j is itself a neighbor of each of its N_i.

While the description above is true for the radio channel, we further extend this model to comprise an out of band channel, which is secure by nature. This channel has different characteristics from the radio channel in that it's unidirectional but can still be considered as a broadcast medium scoped in range. The sensors are always at the receiving end and the insertion entity, I, is the sender.

2.2   Attacker Model

Sensors are meant to be cheap and therefore may not comprise a tamper resistance unit. With this in mind, the sensors are subject to attacks which consist in capturing the actual sensor and reading its memory. Solutions which consist of using a unique key are therefore excluded due to the security risk of having a network wide key stored in easy to capture nodes.

There are a few solutions which deal with the key distribution problem in such networks. Most of them ([1], [3]) consider a pool of initial keys which are used to find a common key with the neighbors or a common key ([4], [5]), which should be erased once the bootstrapping phase finishes. In the first case it is required to either program the pool of keys in the new sensors or even impossible to find the common ground on which to build a security association. Programming a pool of keys in new sensors may also prove unfeasible for most commercial applications since it adds complexity on the side of the buyer and the storage of the initial pool of keys.

Our attacker wishes to add sensors of his own in the sensor network. His motivation is either to provide false readings, eavesdrop or simply discover the keys used by the neighbors' sensors. He has physical access to the network location and, unless supervised, may interfere with any network protocol by either using the radio channel or physical means.

It is not our aim to consider denial of service (DoS) attacks, although some importance is given on how to protect the OOB channel from such attacks.

3   Security Objectives

There are two main security objectives to be fulfilled by this protocol:

1. Provide a mechanism for the nodes in a network to recognize new sensor nodes as valid, in the absence of a pre-shared secret or trust relationship, but using a seed provided by an external actor over a secure channel.
2. Design a key agreement protocol that adds the new nodes into the network, by bootstrapping the network key with the authentication information received in the previous step.

4   Out of Band Channel

In communications, an Out Of Band Channel refers to a separate, dedicated channel, different from that used in normal transmissions. In the scope of WSN's, we consider the normal traffic of the network to be "in-band", and propose an external channel to transmit a key that bootstraps the in-band channel security.

The bootstrap key is transmitted over the OOB channel to both the nodes we want to add, and the ones already in the network. Because these two groups of nodes have not yet established any security relation the key must be sent in the clear.

For this reason, the OOB channel must have a reduced scope that ensures only the intended nodes can receive it. We achieve this by choosing an OOB channel which is geographically confined by nature, and therefore assume it to be secure. Some possible examples of such an OOB channel follow:

- *Light beam:* A device like a flash light is turned on and off intermittently. The nodes apply a preset sampling to their light sensors and extract a binary sequence from the light intensity. The scope is limited to the flash light beam spot. Figure 2 illustrates this scenario.
- *Buzzer:* A sound emitting device with a clearly defined output spectrum broadcasts a series of short tones. The nodes use a microphone and a pass-band filter to extract binary sequences from the sound (in the case of an on/off buzzer) or longer sequences if the buzzer emits multiple tones. The scope is limited to the hearing range of the listening device.

- *Local measurement:* The nodes use a predefined function to extract a key from their measurements. For instance, temperature sensors use the range of their reading (e.g. between 30 and 33 degrees) to infer the secret used to bootstrap the key.
- *Vibration measurement:* The old and new nodes are held in a container and shook together (possible shook in the hand). The resulting vibration is interpreted as a key, as explained in [10].

All of these channels use one or more sensors already present in the sensor node to read bit stream from their environment. Because of power saving and security concerns, listening for the OOB message and renegotiating the network keys should not be done constantly. In our approach, nodes already present in the network receive a message from the sink, which triggers the OOB channel monitoring and renegotiation. New nodes are only activated when we are prepared to deliver the OOB message. Section 4.1 illustrates a practical situation where sensors are added using a flashlight as OOB.

Certain applications might have more stringent security requirements, which render our OOB security insufficient; In a possible attack scenario, the attacker plants nodes next to the already existing ones. As we add new sensors and initiate the key bootstrap, the infiltrated sensors have access to the OOB message and can potentially become part of the network. In such cases, the delivery of the OOB message should be done using methods are specific to the channels nature. The easiest way would require a container which confines the channel, since only those nodes which we choose to put into the container could see the message. In the flash light example, one could pick up some of old nodes and hold them in the hand together with the new ones, or inside a dark bag, together with the new ones; this way, the OOB message would only reach our new nodes and our trusted hand picked old nodes).

In the container confined method, the new nodes are assumed to be trusted, but one must carefully choose the old nodes. If any old node is a disguised attacker node, it would gain access to the network. For this reason, we recommend delivering the OOB message in a container that holds any number of new nodes, and only one old node. If the old node already belonged to the network, the key bootstrap will succeed. If, on the other hand, it was an attacker node, the new sensors will never access the WSN, since the attacker node does not have access to it either, and thus can not act as a bridge. When using a single old node, all new nodes must initially communicate through it for the purposes of bootstrapping the key, but once the nodes are securely in the network, further keys can be negotiated, eliminating the single point of failure.

Finally, it is important that the rate at which sensors sample the OOB channel is comparable to the frequency of the changes in the OOB medium. In the flashlight example, sampling frequency should be comparable to the switch-flick rate of the flashlight, and the duration of the message would be given by this rate and the key size.

4.1 Example Secure OOB Channel

Let us analyze the specific case of the light beam. The network owner has decided to increase node density in a given area, and so, purchases a number of
blank sensors. Without any further pre-configuration, he activates the nodes
and scatters them in the desired area, as seen in Fig. 1. Next, he sends a message through the sink, requesting the old nodes to monitor the OOB channel. He can now transmit the key using a normal flashlight: flicking the switch
on and off at random intervals generates variations in the light intensity perceived by the nodes, which is, in turn transformed into a binary sequence,
which will be used as bootstrap key (see Fig. 2). Since the owner can visu-
ally verify whether someone is watching and whether an attacker is interfering
with the process, the channel can be said to be protected against eavesdroppers
and man-in-the-middle attacks. It is therefore private and provides message
integrity.

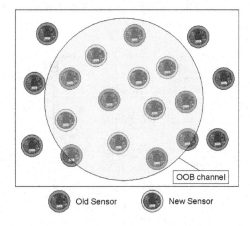

Fig. 1. Sample network and OOB channel coverage

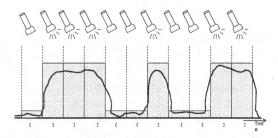

Fig. 2. Shared secret over a secure out of band channel using a flash light

5   The Scheme

Once the OOB channel has been used to securely establish a shared secret, the protocol ensures that the secret is known by the several entities and makes use of this small short-lived key to bootstrap the key agreement protocol. We make use of a combination and variation of two well known protocols: MANA [9] and SPEKE [11].

In the following protocols we consider the interaction between Alice (A) and Bob (B) and then extrapolate for the case of n sensors. For the examples considered, the process is the same whether the sensor is new or was already part of the network so any sensor may either take the role of Alice or Bob. In case the sensors already know each other, the protocol is unnecessary.

5.1   The Toolbox

MA-3. The Manual Authentication Protocol (MANA) [9] allows two devices to pair by allowing a user to input a shared password in both devices, as seen in Fig. 3.

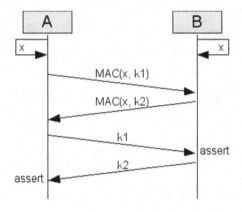

Fig. 3. MA-3

The shared input is used to generate two commitments, one by Alice and the other by Bob, on two pseudo-random numbers, $\{k_1, k_2\} \in \mathbb{Z}$. First the commitments, in this case $MAC(x, k_1)$ for Alice and $MAC(x, k_2)$ for Bob, are exchanged. Once both parties have received the commitment they can open the commitment by sending k_1 and k_2 respectively. Since x is never sent over the wire, it can be used to confirm the commitment and the short-lived key and one-time nature of the protocol ensures its security even with small $|x|$. The typical size for the shared secret x, recommended by the authors of MANA, is on the order of 20 bits.

SPEKE. Simple Password Authenticated Exponential Key Exchange (SPEKE) [11], and also depicted in Fig. 4, is a key agreement protocol which describes a

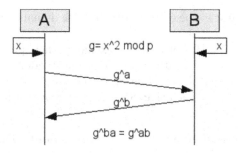

Fig. 4. SPEKE

way to use a shared secret to bootstrap an authenticated Diffie-Hellman (DH) [12] key exchange.

Let x be a member of $\mathbb{Z}$ and $\mathbb{Z}_p$ a multiplicative group where p is prime, then $g = x^2 \bmod p$ is a generator for a subgroup of the multiplicative group.

We then use g and $\mathbb{Z}_p$ as the parameters for the DH key exchange such as g^a is the public parameter for Alice, g^b the public parameter for Bob, with both pseudo-random numbers $\{a, b\} \in \mathbb{Z}$, and $s = g^{ba} = g^{ab}$ the shared secret resulting from the exchange.

Since g is secret, x acts as a shared secret which bootstraps an authenticated DH. Please note that, contrary to the previous scheme, x musn't be a small value. It should be in the range of 80 bits.

5.2   Our Contribution

SPEKE with ECDH. This variation of the SPEKE protocol simply makes use of an Elliptic Curve Diffie-Hellman (ECDH) [13] since our main concern is the size of the operands. In this case, the secret is not used to determine a generator of the group but rather used a secret multiplier of the DH agreed key. The secret itself is never transmitted on the wire. An illustration of the scheme can be seen in Fig. 5.

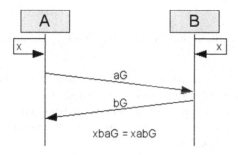

Fig. 5. EC-SPEKE

Let G be a generator in the elliptic curve E with domain parameters T known to all parties.

As in the usual EC-DH, both parties exchange their public parameters aG, for Alice, and bG, for Bob, with a and b pseudo-random numbers in $\mathbb{Z}$. The resulting secret becomes the combination of the previously shared secret $x \in \mathbb{Z}$ with the EC-DH exchange such that $S = xbaG = xabG$ is the agreed key known only by Alice and Bob.

Group Admission and Shared Secret Agreement. This protocol focuses on the communication between the introducer, I, the old, S, and the new, S^*, sensor nodes. I acts like the trusted party to both sides which bootstraps the security association between old and new nodes.

As a first step, I, S and S^*, agree on a common OOB channel. The characteristics of this channel must conform to the ones proposed in section 4, so that we may consider the channel secure. Once the channel is established, I distributes a shared secret to both S and S^* sensors, simultaneously. This small shared secret, x, will be the basis for the steps that follow.

S^* and S sensors will broadcast a commitment to a $k_s G$ value, where $k_s \in \mathbb{Z}$ is random and G a generator for a previously agreed, and secure in terms of ECDLP, elliptic curve E. The resulting value is a random point in E. Finally, the commitment which is broadcasted can be calculated as $\text{MAC}(x, k_s G)$.

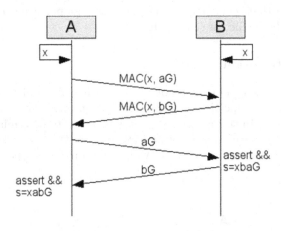

Fig. 6. Group Admission with Key Agreement

Once all commitments have been sent[1], all sensor nodes will open their commitments by sending their values $k_i G$. When these values are received, the commitment is confirmed and, if valid, an entry for that particular sensor node is created in memory. The entry will contain the id of the sensor and the authenticated shared key $s = xk_s k_i G$.

---

[1] This can be achieved by simply setting a timer and ignoring further commitments once a node's commitment has been opened.

The aforementioned scheme, depicted in Fig. 6, ensures that the shared secret s is authenticated via the trusted third party I. Please note that the algorithm is symmetric for S and S^* and in principle either can commit to their value first.

Algorithm 1. Scalable Algorithm for Group Admission with Key Agreement

---

1: S: Receive $x \in \mathbb{Z}$ from OOB channel.
2: $S \rightarrow N_i$: $\text{MAC}(x, k_s G)$
3: $N_i \rightarrow S$: $\text{MAC}(x, k_i G)$
4: $S \rightarrow N_i$: $k_s G$
5: **for all** $i \in \{N_1, N_2, \cdots, N_n\}$ **do**
6:    **if** don't know N_i yet **then**
7:      $N_i \rightarrow S$: $k_i G$
8:      Assert $\text{MAC}(x, k_i G)$
9:      Store, for N_i, $x k_s k_i G$
10:   **end if**
11: **end for**

Algorithm 1 uses the protocol defined above, and depicted in Fig. 6, in an environment with several sensors.

6 Security Analysis

In this section we briefly summarize the security of the protocols on which our proposal is based and then show that the combination of these protocols does not hinder the security level of the scheme. This is not a security proof but rather work in the direction of the proof.

The security of the DH key agreement protocol is based on the discrete log problem. While exponentiation is still considered as a one-way function, or in the case of ECDH the difficulty of inverting a point multiplication, the strength of the agreed key can be correlated to the underlying primitive. The choice of the parameterization of the group and selection of the generator still play important roles in the overall security of the system since the discrete log problem does not apply equally to all groups and the selection of the generator might reveal partial information. All these issues are addressed in [12] and [13].

Since we are using ECDH, it is also important to note that this is a relatively new area and, although we can consider the ECDLP to hold, it might be this is proven solvable in the future. The security level of the resulting key is dependant on this. The DLP in general, and also the ECDLP, are mathematical NP-hard problems and therefore we can achieve *provable security*.

SPEKE is also provable secure since it is based on the same mathematical assumptions as the DH protocol and we can further infer to the security level of EC-SPEKE which is based on ECDH.

The MANA protocol, as also described in [14], is computationally secure. The one-time use of the commitment and key link the attack to a very short time window which allows for short keys. Furthermore, the fact the commitment is only open once both sides have committed to their values disallows a man-in-the-middle attack. Since we use the MANA protocol in the same way, and if we consider that the result of the first point multiplication in the ECDH is a pseudo-random value which falls under the random oracle model (in the sense it cannot be predicted), then the authentication part of our protocol should supply the same security properties as the MANA protocol.

We can therefore divide the key agreement component of our protocol, which should be provable secure, and the authentication part of the protocol, which should be computationally secure. The overall security of this protocol takes the shape of the weakest of its components and, our protocol, should be computationally secure.

It is important to note that no assumptions can be made about this protocol until a formal security analysis of the protocol, which instantiates the line of thought provided in this section, is performed.

Note: Once the commitment is opened, an attacker can easily brute-force the value of the secret key x, since we assume it's size is around 20 bits[2]. However, the importance on the security of this value is limited in time since we only require that it is kept secret from the time the commitments are sent to the point at which they are revealed. Once this phase has passed, the secrecy of x is no longer required. x is added to the agreed key only as a way to link the weak authentication key with the final key. In the case where the protocol is extended to multiple parties, all parties should commit to their values prior to the first open message. This will ensure the security of the protocol still holds true.

7   Performance and Discussion

In [15] the authors provide promising results on the calculation of point multiplication in EC with the same micro-controller as that used in most commercial sensors. Although these results are not acceptable for continuous use in the network, they are quite reasonable for one-time use both in terms of computation intensity, power consumption and time, making this a viable solution.

Also in terms of bandwidth the scheme fits the WSN scenario. The transmission size of the commitments can be as short as 8 bytes, using UMAC-64 [16], with a reasonable security level. The transmission of the opening of the commitments is of one point. If we assume a 163 bit ($\approx$ 20 bytes) generator point to use as base for the ECDH, we would need 21 bytes (which fit 164 bits) to transmit the point. In the overall, both these values fit in one packet of all packet formats so far proposed for sensor networks (so far the lower bound has been a previous proprietary TinyOS [17] Medium Access Control (MAC) protocol with 29 bytes payload).

7.1   Discussion

During the OOB example we suggested that the channel be applied directly to the network. Although this is possible and one way to perform the protocol,

---

[2] It would take an attacker on average 2^{19} tries to obtain the value of x, which is perfectly feasible.

it is not very secure. To minimize the risk of an attacker introducing nodes in the network before the procedure, as a means to authenticate his nodes at the same time as new nodes are added, we suggest that the introducer I captures a small number of already authenticated nodes, which he chooses one by one, and performs the procedure using those nodes and the new ones in a controlled environment. In more practical terms, should the number of sensors be small, we can even foresee that I simply picks up a sensor from the same area that he wishes to replenish and puts all the sensors, new and old, on his hand, where he performs the procedure.

8 Conclusion

In this paper we present a mechanism to extend a sensor network by using an OOB channel to convey a short secret which is then used to authenticate a key agreement protocol. We show how this scheme is theoretically secure and feasible for implementation under the restrictions of the sensor nodes.

We believe this protocol to be generic enough to be applied with a number of encryption and authentication protocols.

References

1. Pietro, R.D., Mancini, L., Mei, A.: Random key-assignment for secure wireless sensor networks. In: 1st ACM Workshop on Security of Ad Hoc and Sensor Networks (SASN'03). (2003) 62–71
2. Perrig, A., Szewczyk, R., Wen, V., Culler, D., Tygar, J.D.: SPINS: Security protocols for sensor networks. Wireless Networks **8** (2002) 521–534
3. Chan, H., Perrig, A., Song, D.: Random key predistribution schemes for sensor networks. In: IEEE Symposium on Security and Privacy. (2003)
4. Zhu, S., Setia, S., Jajodia, S.: Leap: efficient security mechanisms for large-scale distributed sensor networks. In: CCS '03: Proceedings of the 10th ACM conference on Computer and communications security, New York, NY, USA, ACM Press (2003) 62–72
5. Lai, B., Kim, S., Verbauwhede, I.: Scalable session key construction protocol for wireless sensor networks (2002)
6. Hoepman, J.: The ephemeral pairing problem. In: 8th Int. Conf. Finantial Cryptography, Key West, FL, USA (2004)
7. McCune, J.M., Perrig, A., Reiter, M.K.: Seeing-is-believing: Using camera phones for human-verifiable authentication. In: SP '05: Proceedings of the 2005 IEEE Symposium on Security and Privacy, Washington, DC, USA, IEEE Computer Society (2005) 110–124
8. Wong, F.L., Stajano, F.: Multi-channel protocols. In: Proceedings of Security Protocols Workshop, LNCS (2005)
9. Gehrmann, C., Mitchell, C.J., Nyberg, K.: Manual authentication for wireless devices. Cryptobytes **7** (2004) 29–37
10. Holmquist, L., Friedemann, M., Schiele, B., Alahuhta, P., Beigl, M., Gellersen, H.: Smart-its friends: A technique for users to easily establish connections between smart artefacts. Lecture Notes in Computer Science **2201** (2001) 116

11. Jablon, D.: Strong password-only authenticated key exchange. Computer Communication Review, ACM SIGCOMM **26** (1996) 5–26
12. Diffie, W., Hellman, M.E.: New directions in cryptography. IEEE Transactions on Information Theory **IT-22** (1976) 644–654
13. Research, C.: Standards for efficient cryptography, SEC 1: Elliptic curve cryptography (2000) Version 1.0.
14. Laur, S., Asokan, N., Nyberg, K.: Efficient mutual data authentication using manually authenticated strings. Research Report in the IACR ePrint archive (2005) http://eprint.iacr.org/2005/424.
15. Gura, N., Patel, A., Wander, A., Eberle, H., Shantz, S.: Comparing Elliptic Curve Cryptography and RSA on 8-bit CPUs. Cryptographic Hardware and Embedded Systems (CHES) (2004) 119–132
16. Black, J., Halevi, S., Krawczyk, H., Krovetz, T., , Rogaway, P.: Umac: Fast and secure message authentication. In: Advances in Cryptology - CRYPTO '99. Lecture Notes in Computer Science. Volume 1666. (1999) 216–233
17. Hill, J., Levis, P., Madden, S., Woo, A., Polastre, J., Whitehouse, C., Szewczyk, R., Sharp, C., Gay, D., Welsh, M., Culler, D., Brewer, E.: TinyOS: http://www.tinyos.net (2005)

So Near and Yet So Far: Distance-Bounding Attacks in Wireless Networks

Jolyon Clulow, Gerhard P. Hancke, Markus G. Kuhn, and Tyler Moore

Computer Laboratory, University of Cambridge
15 JJ Thomson Avenue, Cambridge CB3 0FD, United Kingdom
firstname.lastname@cl.cam.ac.uk

Abstract. Distance-bounding protocols aim to prevent an adversary from pretending that two parties are physically closer than they really are. We show that proposed distance-bounding protocols of Hu, Perrig and Johnson (2003), Sastry, Shankar and Wagner (2003), and Čapkun and Hubaux (2005, 2006) are vulnerable to a guessing attack where the malicious prover preemptively transmits guessed values for a number of response bits. We also show that communication channels not optimized for minimal latency imperil the security of distance-bounding protocols. The attacker can exploit this to appear closer himself or to perform a relaying attack against other nodes. We describe attack strategies to achieve this, including optimizing the communication protocol stack, taking early decisions as to the value of received bits and modifying the waveform of transmitted bits. We consider applying distance-bounding protocols to constrained devices and evaluate existing proposals for distance bounding in ad hoc networks.

1   Introduction

Distance-bounding protocols are specialized authentication protocols that determine an upper bound for the physical distance between two communicating parties [1]. They aim to prevent attackers from pretending that the prover is closer to the verifier than is actually the case. Distance-bounding protocols have been suggested for application in access control tokens (e.g., contact-less smartcards that open doors), to prevent *relaying* attacks where a local attacker relays a challenge to a distant token that returns a valid response. Distance bounding is an integral aspect of many secure localization or positioning proposals where the location of nodes is inferred from their communication [2].

Such knowledge is useful for mapping the topology of the network and for geographically aware routing algorithms [3]. Therefore, distance bounding has also been proposed as a protective measure for wireless networks, where relaying attacks (in this context also known as *wormhole* attacks) could be used to circumvent key establishment and routing protocols [4,5,6] if an adversary tunnels messages across the network using a low latency, out-of-band channel [5,7]. This emulates nodes at either end of the wormhole being closer than they actually are.

L. Buttyan, V. Gligor, and D. Westhoff (Eds.): ESAS 2006, LNCS 4357, pp. 83–97, 2006.

Distance bounding provides a mechanism for a node to determine whether another node is a genuine neighbor, that is, physically located within its communication radius. Neighbors are in a position of trust and integral to the correct operation of a wireless network. Confidentiality and authentication are achieved using keys shared between neighbors and it is through neighbors that nodes communicate with the rest of the network. Neighboring nodes also serve as intermediaries when path keys are established between two nodes that do not share a pre-assigned key. Finally, it is the neighbors of a node that can best detect when it is compromised and that are typically used in revocation, reputation or voting schemes. Masquerading as a neighbor therefore provides the basis for mounting attacks on routing, key establishment and revocation.

We consider the secure implementation of distance-bounding protocols in ad hoc, wireless networks. We observe that typical transmission formats and modulation techniques introduce latencies, which the adversary can reduce substantially, allowing him to appear closer to the verifier than his actual position. Similarly, the symbol detection mechanism of a receiver can be optimized to provide an early indication of received bits. This provides a "head start" but increases the possibility of transmission errors. It is also possible for an adversary to extract timing advantage from bit transmission by delaying to the last possible moment and then broadcasting at a significantly higher power level. While this does create a different waveform, receivers that integrate the signal over the whole period and decode the symbol based on the area under the waveform will see the same outcome. These attack strategies highlight additional security-critical requirements that distance bounding implementations must meet.

Section 2 provides some background to distance-bounding protocols. We then discuss possible attacks on time-of-flight distance-bounding protocols and present general principles for secure distance bounding in Section 3. Section 4 reviews some proposals to apply distance-bounding techniques in ad hoc and sensor networks and comments on their security. The appendix relates our insights to existing sensor-mote technology.

2   Background

Distance and location measurement has countless applications, most notably in navigation and construction. In wireless networks, we aim to infer the location of potentially mobile devices using existing communication channels. This prompts consideration of distance bounding and secure localization protocols.

Secure location services provide relative or absolute location of nodes within the network [8,9]. This requires not only the ability to calculate distances or angles, but also collaboration between multiple nodes, including 'anchor' or base station nodes that provide trusted reference location information [2]. Secure location services can leverage the existence of multiple nodes or base stations to cross reference, repeat and verify measurements to defend against malicious behavior [10,11,12,13,14].

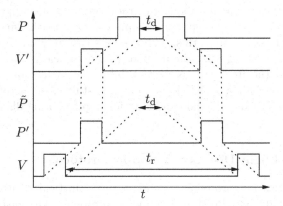

Fig. 1. Relay attack with slow medium: The vertical axis indicates node position. The attacker places a fake prover P' and verifier V' near the genuine verifier V and prover P, respectively. V' and P' communicate over a speed-of-light channel, while P and V use a slow speed-of-sound channel. A challenge issued by V is relayed by P' and V' much faster, and therefore received by P prematurely. The same may happen for the response. V measures a reduced round-trip time t_r and calculates, based on the assumed propagation speed and P's processing delay t_d, an artificially close position $\tilde{P}$ for P.

By contrast, distance bounding only involves two parties, a prover and a verifier, and allows the verifier to place an upper bound on the physical distance to the prover. Unlike secure location services, distance bounding relies exclusively on the protocol and communication medium to ensure security. Thus the requirements are more stringent.

Location-finding techniques generally use one of the following three basic methods:

- **Received Signal Strength (RSS):** Uses the inverse relationship between signal strength and distance to estimate the distance to other nodes [15].
- **Angle-of-Arrival (AoA):** Examines the directions of received signals to determine the locations of transmitters or receivers.
- **Time-of-Flight (ToF):** Measures elapsed time for a message exchange to estimate distance based on the communication medium's propagation speed.

The first two approaches are usually disqualified from security applications since attackers can easily alter received signal strength, by either amplifying or attenuating a signal, and angle-of-arrival, by reflecting or retransmitting from a different direction. This leaves only time-of-flight as a possible mechanism for secure location finding. Both radio frequency (RF) and ultrasound channels have been used in location systems. Since the propagation speed of sound is six orders of magnitude slower than light, the acoustic channel makes it easier to obtain high spatial resolution using simple hardware. However, ultrasound is vulnerable to a relay attack where messages are forwarded over a faster communication medium, as shown in Figure 1.

In contrast, the propagation speed of radio waves in air approaches the in-vacuum speed of light. Thus it resists simple relay attacks since information cannot propagate faster than this. The attacker can only make a node appear further away by blocking a legitimate node's communication and sending a delayed version to the intended receiver. While implementation on constrained devices can be a challenge, RF is already an established medium for mobile communication. So it is an ideal candidate for implementing distance-bounding systems.

2.1   Time-of-Flight Distance-Bounding Protocols

'Timed authentication protocols' are early, unsophisticated attempts to construct time-of-flight based distance-bounding protocols. The basic idea is to execute a challenge-response authentication protocol under a very tight time-out constraint. For example, a verifier V transmits a random n-bit nonce $N_V \in_R \{0,1\}^n$ to the prover P, who replies with a message-authentication code $h_K(N_V)$, where h is a keyed pseudo-random function and K is a shared secret. Numerous protocols have been proposed using different constructions for pseudo-random functions keyed with shared secrets, public-key mechanisms, or trusted third parties. Examples in the literature include [5,16].

Conventional authentication protocols suffer from a common failing: it is not practical to implement the necessary time-out accurately enough over normal communications layers. The transmission time for full data packets and processing delays prevent such protocols from achieving the timing accuracy required.

In contrast, protocols specifically designed for distance-bounding applications do not transmit entire data packets. Rather, they operate at the bit level by recording individual bit-arrival times. We now review several such protocols.

Bit stream with timed reception: These protocols assume that both the verifier and the prover share a common, trusted, high-precision time base (e.g., secure GPS receivers). The verifier sends out random bits $C_1, C_2, \ldots, C_n$ at times $t_1, t_2, \ldots, t_n$ (where $t_i = t_0 + i \cdot t_p$). The prover receives at its antenna input the bit values $C_1', C_2', \ldots, C_n'$ at times $t_1 + \Delta t, t_2 + \Delta t, \ldots, t_n + \Delta t$. It then replies with a message-authenticated data packet

$$\{t_0 + \Delta t, C_1', C_2', \ldots, C_n'\}_K.$$

The verifier checks the message-authentication code of this packet with the shared key K and verifies that $C_i = C_i'$ for at least $k > \frac{n}{2}$ different values $i \in \{1, \ldots, n\}$, where k and n are security parameters. Finally, the verifier checks whether $\Delta t \le d/c$, where d is the upper bound for the distance and c is the speed of light. Setting $k < n$ allows for some transmission errors. (For brevity, we omit here technical details on how both sides agree *a priori* or *a posteriori* on $t_0 + \Delta t$.)

Duplex bit streams: In the absence of a common trusted clock, the class of protocols just outlined can be extended to transmit random data in both directions simultaneously [1]. The verifier sends C_i at $t_i = t_0 + i \cdot t_p$ as before, which the prover again receives at times $t_i + \Delta t$, but now the prover also sends random bits R_i in the opposite direction at times $t_i + \Delta t$ (e.g., on a different radio frequency), which the verifier receives at times $t_i + 2\Delta t$ as R_i'. The prover finally transmits a message-authenticated data packet

$$\{C_1', C_2', \ldots, C_n', R_1, R_2, \ldots, R_n\}_K.$$

The verifier checks the message-authentication code with key K, then verifies that $C_i = C_i'$ and $R_i = R_i'$ for at least $k > \frac{n}{2}$ different values $i \in \{1, \ldots, n\}$, where k and n are security parameters, and finally checks whether $\Delta t \leq d/c$. Instead of authenticating for each received value C_i' the corresponding time, in this variant, the prover authenticates what it sent out in the other direction at the time of receiving C_i'.

In both protocols, the prover can easily cheat, either by lying about $t_0 + \Delta t$ or by sending R_i before receiving C_i'. Therefore, these protocols can only defend against third-party attackers that do not have access to the shared secret key K. Such cheating can be made more difficult if R_i is not simply an unpredictable random bit, but is calculated as a function of C_i'. It is important that the processing time is minimized to reduce the uncertainty of the distance-bounding process. Therefore, the function $g(i, C_i') \mapsto R_i$ must be easy to implement with only a few gate delays. Two such approaches have been described in the literature.

Bitwise XOR with pre-commitment: Both the verifier and prover first generate random bit strings $C = (C_1, C_2, \ldots, C_n)$ and $M = (M_1, M_2, \ldots, M_n)$, respectively. The prover commits to M (e.g., by transmitting a collision-resistant message authentication code $h_K(M)$). The verifier then sends one C_i after another, which the prover receives as C_i'. It then instantly replies with a bit $R_i = C_i' \oplus M_i$, which is calculated by XOR-ing each received challenge bit with the corresponding bit of M. Finally the prover reveals M and authenticates C'. The commitment on M is needed to prevent the prover from sending a random bit R_i early and then setting $M_i = C_i' \oplus R_i$ after receiving C_i'. Authenticating C' keeps attackers from sending fake C_i bits prematurely to the prover to learn bits of M_i for responding early to the verifier.

This construction first appeared in the Brands-Chaum protocol [1] and has inspired a number of variants [7,12,13]. As was pointed out in [17], this protocol can tolerate bit errors in the transmission of the C_i and R_i as long as the C' received and the M applied are afterwards transmitted over an error-corrected channel. The verifier can then accept the response if $R_i' = C_i \oplus M_i$ for at least k_1 bits i and $C_j' = C_j$ for at least k_2 bits j, where $k_1, k_2 > \frac{n}{2}$ and n are security parameters.

Pre-computed table lookup: The verifier generates a random bit string $C_1, C_2, \ldots, C_n$ and a nonce N_V that is sent to the prover. The prover responds with its nonce N_P. Both the prover and the verifier then use the pseudo-random function h and the secret key K in order to calculate two n-bit sequences R^0 and R^1:

$$(R_1^0, R_2^0, R_3^0, \ldots, R_n^0, R_1^1, R_2^1, R_3^1, \ldots, R_n^1) := h_K(N_V, N_P)$$

The prover's reply bit $R_i = R_i^{C_i'}$ to each C_i' received from the verifier is the result of a 1-bit table lookup in R^0 or R^1, selected by the received challenge bit

C_i' (for $1 \leq i \leq n$). The verifier checks whether at least k of the n R_i' bits that it receives match its locally calculated $R_i^{C_i}$ values. The values $k > \frac{3}{4}n$ and n are security parameters. The Hancke-Kuhn protocol [17] presents this strategy, which has the advantage that no further data has to be exchanged once the rapid bit exchanges have taken place.

Accuracy. The accuracy of the distance bound is influenced by the precision or resolution of the timing mechanism, properties of the communication channel including pulse width and bit period t_p, and processing delay t_d between receiving a challenge and sending the response.

Both the bitwise XOR with pre-commitment and pre-computed table lookup classes of protocols are designed to minimize the processing delay t_d. The former achieves this through the use of a fast operation (i.e., XOR) while the latter allows for pre-computation by the prover entirely before the time-critical challenge-response phase begins. In contrast, timed authentication protocols require the online generation of a signature or message authentication code during the timed period. Not only does this introduce an inaccuracy into the distance calculation but a malicious prover with high performance hardware can extract a time advantage by performing these operations faster. The effect is more pronounced and debilitating for constrained devices.

A single-bit exchange provides the highest time (and therefore distance) resolution, as it depends only on propagation time, pulse width and processing delay. Resolution also motivates the proposed use of ultra wideband or similar communications for distance bounding [18,19,20]. These are characterized by short pulse width and are already used in current location systems with resolution in the order of 30 cm [21]. Multiple timed message exchanges may appear inefficient but multiple measurements increase accuracy and confidence.

In contrast, some authors propose timing a single exchange of multi-bit challenge-response messages. For example, Čapkun and Hubaux describe essentially the Brands-Chaum protocol modified to a single message exchange [12,13]. In such systems, the choice of when to start and stop timing affects the resolution since it is now additionally dependent on the number of transmitted bits and the bit period, not just the pulse width. The greatest precision is obtained by timing from the transmission of the last bit of the challenge to the receipt of the first bit of the response. Care must be exercised to ensure that the first response bit depends on the last challenge bit. Čapkun and Hubaux achieve this by reversing the order of the response bits.

Bit Errors. Previously proposed protocols either fail in the event of a single bit error or require additional error correction overhead. This is not ideal in applications where communication errors are likely to occur and it is also vulnerable to a denial of service attack by an active adversary. We shall see later in Section 3 that resilience to noise is important requirement for security. Hancke and Kuhn [17] consider the impact of bit errors on distance-bounding protocols. The authors indicate how protocols can be modified to be resilient by specifying an error threshold.

3   Attacks on Time-of-Flight Protocols

3.1   Threat Model

Honest nodes adhere to their programmed strategy including algorithms for distance bounding. Malicious nodes can eavesdrop any message broadcast by an honest node. A malicious node can communicate with any other attacker-controlled node (via an out-of-band channel) as well as with honest nodes. Attacker-controlled nodes may modify any packet or transmission protocol, inserting or removing chosen identifiers, timestamps and location claims, message payloads and signatures. An attacker may have access to more sophisticated hardware and processing capabilities compared to that of normal devices.

We consider two attacks on distance-bounding protocols. A malicious prover can pretend to be closer to the verifier by responding faster than an honest node could. In a *relay attack*, malicious intermediaries seek to shorten the perceived distance between an honest prover and verifier. We do not consider here the case where a malicious prover colludes with another node that is located closer to the verifier, since a malicious prover can obviously always release all its secret keys to a colluder.

3.2   Guessing Attacks on Packet-Based Challenge-Response Protocols

Single-exchange challenge-response protocols with multi-bit messages are vulnerable to a guessing attack that enables a malicious prover to reduce the apparent distance to the verifier. The attack as applied to Čapkun-Hubaux [12,13] is shown in Figure 2. The key observation is that an adversary can guess the value for the last bit transmitted by the verifier and preemptively transmit a response. With probability $\frac{1}{2}$ the adversary guesses correctly and gains a timing advantage of up to twice the bit period. The advantage gained depends not on pulse width but on the bit period for the channel. So while n single-bit challenges reduce an attacker's chances of guessing the correct response to 2^{-n}, a single n-bit message can be shortened with probability $\frac{1}{2}$. An attacker can tailor his distance improvement according to his likelihood of success: he can shorten by $\Delta d \cdot l$ with probability 2^{-l}, where $\Delta d = 2t_p c$ is the distance traversed during two bit periods. Furthermore, an attacker could exploit this even more if the protocol tolerates a specified threshold of errors. This weakness is present in the distance-bounding protocol proposals of Hu, Perrig and Johnson [5], Sastry, Shankar and Wagner [16], and Čapkun-Hubaux [12,13], and challenges the choice of a timed packet-based challenge-response exchange.

3.3   Exploiting Packet-Level Latencies

The security evaluation of a distance-bounding protocol must also consider ways in which an attacker could reduce any latency introduced by underlying communication layers. Most transmission formats and modulation techniques have

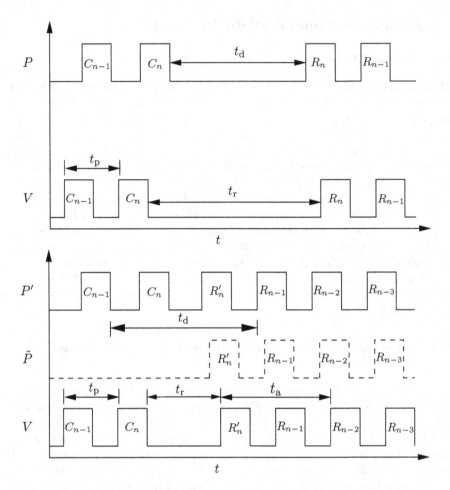

Fig. 2. The top figure shows normal operation of a single-exchange challenge-response protocol with the verifier calculating the distance bound from the measured round-trip time t_r. In the bottom figure, the malicious prover P' guesses the first response bit R'_n and transmits it after receiving challenge bit C_{n-1}. This gives the attacker enough time to calculate and respond with the correct response bit R_{n-1}, as well as all subsequent response bits. This yields timing advantage t_a equal to twice the bit period, so the verifier measures a shorter round-trip time t_r and perceives the prover at location $\tilde{P}$.

been designed for robustness, ease of use, and power efficiency, rather than for minimizing transmission latency of individual data bits. Transmission software usually has to commit to an entire data block several bit times before the block's first data bit is actually transmitted. Likewise, the receiving software can only access its content several bit times after the entire block has been received. In the simplest case, namely the asynchronous byte transmission scheme used on RS-232 lines, data blocks are just eight bits long and only a start and a stop bit are added as overhead. More commonly, data blocks comprise multiple bytes and are

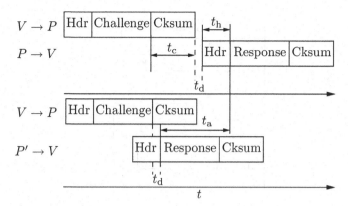

Fig. 3. If the verifier expects the prover to strictly adhere to the communication protocol, an attacker can gain time t_a equal to $t_c + t_h$. Time t_d is required to calculate the response once the entire challenge has been received. The attacker ignores the data trailer and starts calculating its response while preemptively transmitting the header of the return data.

transmitted with synchronization preambles, headers with source and destination addresses and sequence numbers, as well as checksums and packet delimiters (HDLC, Ethernet, etc.). In the most sophisticated transmission schemes, error correcting encoders and decoders may add substantial further delays.

An attacker may not be restricted by the latencies imposed by regular implementations. It is often feasible to design special variant implementations of low-level communication standards, where the value of each data bit can be changed right up to the start of bit transmission, or where the receiving end is notified of each bit's value as it is decoded. An example of this attack is shown in Figure 3. (In practice, an attacker may have to replace a standard communications chip with an entirely software-based design, or an FPGA-based hardware/software codesign, to obtain such a specialized low-latency transceiver implementation economically.)

A possible overclocking attack is also worth noting. In many communication systems, the transmitter has control over the exact bit period t_p, and it is the responsibility of the receiver to recover the exact bit rate by extracting a clock signal embedded with the packet data (e.g., using Manchester coding). Recipients implement a phase-locked loop (PLL) circuit for this purpose, which must be able to tolerate certain deviations from the nominal frequency. An attacker who wants to appear closer may transmit at the maximum bit rate that the receiver's circuit still tolerates, leading to an earlier reception of the entire packet.

3.4 Deferred Bit Signalling

An attacker could also change a bit even after its transmission time has begun or act upon a received bit before its transmission has been completed. In simple modulation schemes, such as amplitude-shift keying (ASK) or frequency

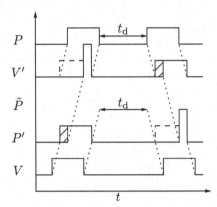

Fig. 4. In this variation of the relay attack the attacker gains time when P' estimates the value of the challenge bit from V early on in the bit period and V' transmits m-times the symbol amplitude to P in the final $\frac{1}{m}$-th of the bit period. The process is then repeated for the response bit, albeit with V' and P' swapping roles.

shift keying (FSK), each bit value is represented on the communication channel through the transmission of one of two different waveforms ("symbols"). Such a symbol might be one of two tones (FSK) or one of two amplitude levels (ASK). The receiver has to decide for each bit, in the presence of background noise, which symbol has most likely been transmitted. It does so by comparing the difference between the received waveform and the waveforms of the two candidate symbols, and integrates these differences over the entire duration of the symbol.

A regular transmitter makes the best use of its limited transmission power by spreading the energy available for each symbol as uniformly over the symbol's transmission time slot as possible (subject to constraints on transition times that bandwidth limitations bring). An adversary's modified implementation, however, may send no energy for $\frac{m-1}{m}$ of the time interval, and then may send the bit value during the final $\frac{1}{m}$-th of the available time, using a more powerful transmitter, with m-times higher amplitude than that used in a regular implementation. For the receiving end, which integrates the energy received over the entire symbol time, the result is the same, but the transmitter can delay committing to a bit's value by $\frac{m-1}{m}$ of a bit time. An example of this attack is shown in Figure 4.

3.5 Early Bit Detection

Likewise, an attacker may use a variant implementation of a receiver that does not wait for the decision of which bit has been received until all energy related to that bit has been received and integrated. If the attacker's receiver has an m-times better signal-to-noise ratio than what a regular receiver really needs, then the attacker's receiver can terminate the integration already with $\frac{1}{m}$-th of the symbol's signal in (after about $\frac{1}{m}$ of the bit's transmission time), while still obtaining an acceptable bit error rate. This way, the attacker can save $\frac{m-1}{m}$ of the symbol's transmission time compared to using a regular receiver. The necessary

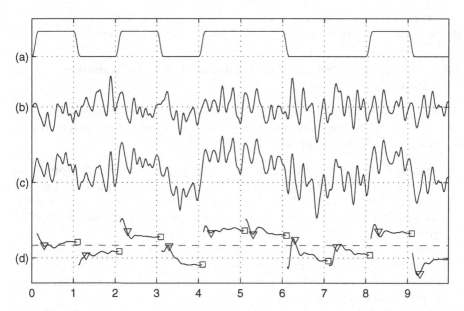

Fig. 5. Early decision decoder example, showing transmitted signal (a), added noise (b), and resulting received waveform (c). Curve (d) shows the result of averaging the received signal from the start of each bit. Squares mark the result of averaging the full bit length, and triangles the result of averaging only the first 20%. The dashed line represents the decision threshold (below: 0, above: 1). This early detection attempt leads only to a single bit error (bit 6) in this example.

m-times better signal-to-noise ratio could be achieved by reducing the distance to the receiver or with an antenna with better directional gain.

Figure 5 demonstrates the operation of a modified decoder in a receiver that was designed to provide an early decision for each bit compared to a conventional decoder. Waveform (a) is the output of the transmitter, which the receiver can see only along with an added noise signal (b), resulting in the received waveform (c). The receiver can achieve the best signal-to-noise ratio by processing (c) with a "matched filter", that is by multiplying the received waveform with the noise-free shape of a transmitted bit and integrating the result. In this example, the bits are represented by nearly rectangular pulses; therefore, the application of a matched filter is nearly equivalent to averaging the signal over the duration of one bit time. Waveform (d) in Figure 5 shows the result of averaging the received signal from the start of the current bit up to the current input value. The little squares show where this averaging process has integrated the whole length of the bit. At these points, the average output best represents the transmitted value and can be compared against the dashed threshold line to decide whether a 0 or 1 was received. To decide earlier, we must use an intermediate value of the average. The triangles on curve (d) show the value after only 1/5 of each bit has been received. These values are 4/5 of a bit time earlier available, but provide only 1/5 of the signal-to-noise amplitude ratio. This example shows a binary amplitude-shift-keying baseband signal in the interest of simplicity, but the principle can equally be applied to modulated complex symbols.

3.6 Principles for Secure Time-of-Flight Distance-Bounding Protocols

With all these attacks in mind, the designer of a distance-bounding protocol should optimize the choice of communication medium and transmission format according to the following principles:

- **Principle 1:** Use a communication medium with a propagation speed as close as possible to the physical limit for propagating information through space-time (the speed of light in vacuum). This excludes not only acoustic communication techniques, but also limits applicability of wires and optical fibers.
- **Principle 2:** Use a communication format in which only a single bit is transmitted and the recipient can instantly react on its reception. This excludes most traditional byte- or block-based communication formats, and in particular any form of error correction.
- **Principle 3:** Minimize the length of the symbol used to represent this single bit. In other words, output the energy that distinguishes the two possible transmitted bit values within as short a time as is feasible. This leaves the attacker little room to shorten this time interval further.
- **Principle 4:** The distance-bounding protocol should be designed to cope well with substantial bit error rates during the rapid single-bit exchange, because the previous criterion may limit the energy that can be spent on transmitting a single bit and conventional error correction is not applicable.

4 Existing Distance-Bounding Proposals

Secure Neighbor Detection. The secure neighbor detection protocol proposed by Hu, Perrig and Johnson [5] is an instance of a timed authentication protocol where the elapsed time during the exchange of signed nonces infers a distance bound.

The protocol has significant processing overhead including hashing and then verifying and signing incoming and outgoing messages. While the authors discuss mechanisms for increasing the efficiency of the signing operations, the associated delay renders the bound inaccurate and unreliable. Furthermore, malicious nodes with higher performance components can extract a time advantage by performing these operations faster. The timing of only one multi-bit message exchange means the protocol is vulnerable to the guessing attack described in Section 3. We also note that the protocol is not robust in the presence of communication errors.

In-Location Verification Protocol. Sastry, Shankar and Wagner [16] propose a timed authentication protocol to verify a prover's claimed physical location l

within a circular region R centered on the verifier. The verifier issues a random challenge N to which the prover responds via a sound channel with $F_k(N)$ where F_k is a pseudo-random function. The verifier accepts this if $l \in R$ and the elapsed time is less than or equal to $d \cdot (c^{-1} + s^{-1})$ where c and s are the speed of radio waves and sound respectively and d is the distance.

Several authors have commented that this proposal is vulnerable due to its use of sound as a carrier, which contradicts Principle 1. We also criticize the use of a single challenge-response message exchange and a delay inducing pseudo-random function.

Čapkun-Hubaux. Čapkun and Hubaux propose a distance-bounding protocol for use in secure positioning [12,13]. They modify the Brands-Chaum protocol by converting it into a single message exchange involving a multi-bit challenge-response.

Again, timing a single message exchange means the protocol is vulnerable to the guessing attack described in Section 3. We also note that the protocol is not robust in the presence of communication errors.

Mutually Authenticated Distance Bounding (MAD). Čapkun, Buttyán and Hubaux propose MAD [7], which modifies the Brands-Chaum protocol to allow both parties participating in the protocol to bound the distance to the other party simultaneously. This protocol does not suffer from the same bounding inaccuracies as those described above. Bits are exchanged over the radio channel; only single bits are transmitted rather than entire messages; no cryptographic operations are performed between timed exchanges. As with the Brands-Chaum protocol, a single bit error causes the protocol to fail; thus it is less suited for noisy channels.

5   Conclusion

In this paper, we have investigated the security of distance-bounding protocols for wireless networks. We have shown that time-of-flight techniques are vulnerable to several attacks: the round-trip time for a single timed multi-bit challenge-response can be reduced by guessing and preemptively transmitting response bits; communication layer protocol latencies can be avoided by the adversary; and time advantage can be extracted by modifying the transmission waveform and through the early detection of symbols. These attacks can be successfully applied to a number of existing proposals for use in ad hoc and sensor networks.

We propose a number of principles to adhere to when implementing distance-bounding systems. These restrict the choice of communication medium to speed-of-light channels, the communication format to single bit exchanges for timing, symbol length to narrow (ultra wideband) pulses, and protocols to error-tolerant versions. These restrictions increase the technical challenge of implementing secure distance bounding.

References

1. Brands, S., Chaum, D.: Distance-bounding protocols (extended abstract). In: EUROCRYPT. (1993) 344–359
2. Karl, H., Willig, A.: Protocols and Architectures for Wireless Sensor Networks. Wiley (2005)
3. Karp, B., Kung, H.T.: GPSR: greedy perimeter stateless routing for wireless networks. In: MOBICOM. (2000) 243–254
4. Hu, Y.C., Perrig, A., Johnson, D.B.: Packet leashes: A defense against wormhole attacks in wireless networks. In: INFOCOM. (2003)
5. Hu, Y.C., Perrig, A., Johnson, D.B.: Rushing attacks and defense in wireless ad hoc network routing protocols. [22] 30–40
6. Karlof, C., Wagner, D.: Secure routing in wireless sensor networks: attacks and countermeasures. Ad Hoc Networks 1(2-3) (2003) 293–315
7. Čapkun, S., Buttyán, L., Hubaux, J.P.: SECTOR: secure tracking of node encounters in multi-hop wireless networks. In Setia, S., Swarup, V., eds.: SASN, ACM (2003) 21–32
8. Werb, J., Lanzl, C.: Designing a positioning system for finding things and people indoors. IEEE Spectrum 35(9) (1998) 71–78
9. Bahl, P., Padmanabhan, V.: RADAR: An in-building RF-based user location and tracking system. In: Nineteenth Annual Joint Conference of the IEEE Computer and Communication Society, IEEE (2000) 775–784
10. Liu, D., Ning, P., Du, W.: Attack-resistant location estimation in sensor networks. In: IPSN, IEEE (2005) 99–106
11. Liu, D., Ning, P., Du, W.: Detecting malicious beacon nodes for secure location discovery in wireless sensor networks. In: ICDCS, IEEE Computer Society (2005) 609–619
12. Čapkun, S., Hubaux, J.P.: Secure positioning of wireless devices with application to sensor networks. In: INFOCOM. (2005)
13. Čapkun, S., Hubaux, J.P.: Secure positioning in wireless networks. IEEE Journal on Selected Areas in Communications: Special Issue on Security in Wireless Ad Hoc Networks 24(2) (2006) 221–232
14. S. Čapkun, M.C., Srivastava, M.: Securing localization with hidden and mobile base stations. Internet-draft, NESL, UCLA (2005)
15. Krumm, J., Horvitz, E.: LOCADIO: Inferring motion and location from Wi-Fi signal strengths. In: First Annual Internationl Conference on Mobile and Ubiquitous Systems: Networking and Services, IEEE (2004) 4–13
16. Sastry, N., Shankar, U., Wagner, D.: Secure verification of location claims. [22] 1–10
17. Hancke, G.P., Kuhn, M.G.: An RFID distance bounding protocol. In: IEEE SecureComm 2005, Athens, Greece, 5–9 September 2005, IEEE Computer Society (2005) 67–73
18. R. Zetik, J.S., Thome, R.: UWB localization – active and passive approach. In: 21st IEEE Instrumentation and Measurement Technology Conference, IEEE (2004) 1005–1009
19. R.J. Fontana, E.R., Barney, J.: Commercialization of an ultra wideband precision asset location system. In: Conference on Ultra Wideband Systems and Technologies, IEEE (2003) 369–373
20. M. Ghavami, L.M., Kohno, R.: Ultra Wideband Signals and Systems in Communication Engineering. Wiley (2004)

21. Ubisense: White papers and datasheets. http://www.ubisense.net (2003–2006)
22. Maughan, W.D., Perrig, A., eds.: Proceedings of the 2003 ACM Workshop on Wireless Security, San Diego, CA, USA, September 19, 2003. In Maughan, W.D., Perrig, A., eds.: Workshop on Wireless Security, ACM (2003)
23. Crossbow Technology: MICA2 mote (2006) http://www.xbow.com/Products/Product_pdf_files/Wireless_pdf/MICA2_Datasheet.pdf.

A   Distance Bounding with Existing Sensor Motes

Depending on the required spatial resolution, the communication requirements for a distance-bounding system can be quite stringent and are likely to exceed the capabilities of standard hardware. The MICA2 [23] mote, to name one illustrative example, has a communication rate of 38.4 kbit/s on its radio channel. In other words, a single bit lasts 26042 ns and is 7.8 km long. This means that the previously described attacks to shortcut the duration of a single bit with special hardware have the potential to manipulate a distance bound by several kilometers, many times the mote's nominal communication radius of 300 m. And this does not even take into account yet any protocol overhead (additional bits added at the start and end of a transmission frame) that the mote hardware relies on. Even if these constraints could be eliminated, the mote's 8 MHz clock still only permits its logic circuits to discriminate time intervals in 125 ns increments at best. In terms of a message round-trip, this still limits the distance resolution to at least 20 m.

For effective distance bounding, such a mote would have to implement a fast distance-bounding channel in addition to its slower standard communication channel. This separate distance-bounding channel would be optimized according to the principles listed in Section 3.6 towards the rapid turnaround exchange of single-bit messages, rather than for maximum range and reliability.

Dynamics of Learning Algorithms for the On-Demand Secure Byzantine Routing Protocol*

Baruch Awerbuch[1], Robert G. Cole[2], Reza Curtmola[1],
David Holmer[1], and Herbert Rubens[1]

[1] Department of Computer Science, Johns Hopkins University, Baltimore, MD, USA
[2] The JHU Applied Physics Laboratory, Laurel, MD, USA

Abstract. We investigate the performance of of several protocol enhancements to the On-Demand Secure Byzantine Routing (ODSBR) [3] protocol in the presence of various Byzantine Attack models. These enhancements include a) modifications to the packet flow rates, b) a network layer retransmission capability and c) Nodal Weighting (in addition to Link Weighting) in the reputation database. These enhancements are meant to improve the learning rate of the protocol. The attack models investigated include previously investigated models [4] and a new and effective attack model, termed the *MAC-Level Attack*. We investigate the protocol enhancements through analytic models and simulation studies. We find that the protocol enhancements improve the learning times of the ODSBR protocol. The Nodal Weighting enhancement specifically helps in the presence of the various colluding Byzantine Attack models investigated.

Keywords: MANET Routing, Security, Byzantine Attacks.

1 Introduction

The Internet has demonstrated itself to be vulnerable to numerous and evolving security intrusions. The growing reliance on wireless networks exacerbates the problem by offering easy access to the communications media. Emergency services and national militaries are planning on the extensive reliance on Mobile Ad Hoc Networks (MANETs) for key communications capabilities. It is imperative that the issues of computer network security be addressed within the core networking protocols building the foundations for MANETs and wired networks.

Much effort into hardening networking protocols concentrates on protection against *Outsider Attacks*. This body of work relies on cryptographic mechanisms to ensure the integrity, authenticity and confidentiality of data. An example of work securing routing protocols with these techniques is [11]. Less work has addressed *Insider (Byzantine) Attacks*. It is assumed *a priori* that the Byzantine adversary has gained access to one or many of the network nodes and therefore has access to the cryptographic keys associated with the compromised nodes.

---

* The full version of the paper is available as a technical report, see [5].

L. Buttyan, V. Gligor, and D. Westhoff (Eds.): ESAS 2006, LNCS 4357, pp. 98–112, 2006.
© Springer-Verlag Berlin Heidelberg 2006

In [3], the On-Demand Secure Byzantine Routing (ODSBR) routing protocol was proposed for MANETs. ODSBR is secure against outsider attacks due to the incorporation of cryptographic mechanisms. Notably, ODSBR is also secure in a well defined sense against Byzantine Attacks. In [4], the stationary, time averaged performance of ODSBR was evaluated through the development of an extensive simulation model. In this paper, we extend the work in [4] by a) proposing several protocol enhancements to the ODSBR protocol and b) analyzing their performance impact on the time dependent convergence of the protocol in the presence of previously studied attacks and in the presence of a new MAC-Level attack. The specific protocol enhancements investigated are packet flow rate adjustments, end-to-end retransmission at the network layer and the addition of a Nodal Weighting component to the reputation database. These enhancements are shown to improve the efficiency of the ODSBR protocol in avoiding Byzantine attackers. In addition to studying previously proposed attacks, we investigate the voracity of a new MAC-Level attacker in disrupting the network performance. In this context we demonstrate the benefit of incorporating the Nodal Weighting enhancement into the ODSBR protocol. We investigate these protocol modifications and the impact of the new attack through analytic modeling and extensive simulation studies. We analyze the protocol enhancements with respect to their impact on the average time it takes the protocol to learn the presence of network adversaries and find non-adversarial paths through the network. In this sense, we investigate the temporal dynamics of the ODSBR protocol.

The rest of this paper is organized as follows: The next section reviews previous, related work. Section 3 overviews the ODSBR protocol. Section 4 lists the various attack models addressed in this paper. Section 5 presents the new protocol enhancements to the ODSBR protocol. Section 6 presents an analytic model of the ODSBR dynamics. Section 7 presents our simulation studies of the protocol enhancements. Section 8 contains conclusions and proposed future work.

2   Previous Work

Notable work investigating the development of protocols which are resilient to Byzantine Attacks include [9] and [15]. [9] provided an analysis of the Byzantine Generals Problem, i.e. reaching consensus in the presence of malicious participants. [15] studied the general problem of hardening the Network Layer of a data network against Byzantine attackers. The analysis of two approaches was presented, one based upon a flooding algorithm for path discovery and one based upon a link state method.

Work on securing MANET routing protocols against Byzantine attacks falls into several categories, i.e., Passive Neighbor Monitoring Methods, Active Monitoring Methods and Active Monitoring with Fault Isolation Methods. The work in [8], [7] and [10] investigated passive methods to monitor the behavior of neighboring nodes in order to detect faulty behavior. In these works, if a neighbor is deemed to be misbehaving, the monitoring node suggests or carries out a path reroute around the faulty neighbor. These methods require that the networks rely on omni-directional antennas and nodes that transmit at a single rate, i.e., no multi-rate systems can be used.

[1] investigated the use of active monitoring capabilities, generally in the form of end-to-end monitoring, in their investigation of novel attack scenarios against TCP flows. The work did not address the issue of identifying the faulty component or avoiding it in the network reroute. [13] and [14] proposed the use of diverse, multi-path routing as a means to secure data transmissions against malicious nodes within a MANET. Here data packets are segmented, redundancy is added, and transmitted over a set of disjoint paths.

Several studies have investigated both active monitoring and fault isolation systems. These are often referred to as 'Reputation-Based' systems, because the nodes maintain a picture of the reliability of each component comprising the network. Notable works in this area are [2] and [3]. In [2], a Byzantine resilient protocol was proposed for a Link State protocol in a wired environment. Their scheme relied on end-to-end monitoring and fault isolation to identify faulty links. In [3], the ODSBR protocol was proposed for the network layer in a MANET.

3   The ODSBR Protocol

ODSBR [3,4] is a point-to-point on-demand secure routing protocol for ad hoc wireless networks, designed to be resilient against a wide range of external and Byzantine attacks. It is based on the observation that no matter what attack and how it is executed, the only threat an adversary can pose is to disrupt packet delivery. Data packets and control packets are coupled together, so that adversaries do not go undetected if they start dropping packets. The protocol assumes that while all the network nodes can be authenticated, only the source can be fully trusted. At the highest level, ODSBR operates using three modules: the *Route Discovery Module*, the *Path Monitoring Module*, and the *Component Weighting Module*.

The *Route Discovery Module* returns the least weight path from the source to the destination based upon a reliability metric that captures past history. The metric is represented by a Component Weighting Table that contains weights of links and is maintained by the source node. The Route Discovery Module relies on an on-demand, double flooding mechanism which is based on a combination of the source digitally signing the flood and per node flood verification. Faulty links have a high weight and are avoided in this process.

The *Path Monitoring Module* monitors the quality of the source-routed path, based on end-to-end acknowledgments for each data packet sent. If the packet loss rate exceeds a prescribed *loss threshold* on a given route, the Path Monitoring Module enters a fault isolation state, in which the source uses an adaptive probing technique to locate faulty links on the path to the destination. The source requires secure acknowledgments from intermediate nodes along the route. The acknowledgments are accumulated using per node timers into a single message back to the source. A fault will be attributed to one of the links adjacent to the adversary. The source then updates the Component Weighting Table and initiates a new route discovery. The loss threshold is tracked by maintaining a *sliding window* which holds the recent history of loss events.

The *Component Weighting Module* maintains the node's current view of the reliability of each component in the network. A component has its weight increased if it is found faulty. The weight of a faulty component is decreased based upon the source's view of successful data packets delivered to the destination over that faulty component.

Together, as long as a fault free path from the source to the destination exists, these three modules bound the number of losses caused by adversaries, even when a majority of the nodes are colluding Byzantine adversaries [3].

4   Attack Scenarios

The ODSBR protocol is resilient to the following Byzantine and non-Byzantine attack scenarios [3]:

False Route Attack where an adversary generates a false route. In ODSBR, the route is built up while the *route_req* packets are flooded through the network. Each node's contribution to the path is appended to the route and an aggregate hash is added which protects against modifications to the list by adversaries.

Incrimination Attack where an adversary tries to incriminate other nodes by tampering with end-to-end acknowledgments. Because of the aggregate integrity mechanism [6] used in ODSBR, a given node on the path is not able to modify an upstream acknowledgment to incriminate the downstream node.

Black Hole Attack where the adversarial node correctly participates in the route discovery protocol, but then behaves errantly during data transport. The ODSBR Path Monitoring Module will discover this behavior and isolate the offending link.

Flood Rush and Worm Hole Attack where the adversarial nodes act to encourage routes to be setup through them and then behave errantly during data transport. Methods include expediting route_req packets to speed delivery of their path information to the source (i.e., Flood Rush) or building tunnels between colluding nodes to imply that shorter paths exist through them to the source (i.e., Worm Hole and Super Worm Hole attacks). The ODSBR protocol will avoid these spurious links. Further, because the ODSBR source node will accept *route_resp* packets with path weights smaller than any prior route_resp packet, Flood Rush attacks are ineffective.

Adaptive Packet Dropping where a Black Hole attacker could adapt its packet dropping behavior as an attempt to defeat the Path Monitoring Module. It is shown in [3] that regardless of the dynamics of the packet dropping algorithm, the ODSBR protocol bounds the total loss rate to a value proportional to the loss threshold employed.

MAC-Level Attack where a pair of protocol passive adversaries with radio repeaters create the perception of numerous false links. Each device monitors its local radio channel and transmits signals down a tunnel to its remote mate. The remote mate then retransmits the signal out onto its local radio channel. The effect is to make all nodes within radio range of one repeater think they are a single hop from all nodes within radio range of the remote mate. This is extremely effective in pulling in routes and can cause severe havoc on network performance. This is a new attack, first analyzed and simulated in this paper.

The resilience of the ODSBR protocol to these various attack scenarios was discussed extensively in [3]. In [4], simulation studies of the ODSBR protocol under various simulated attack scenarios and mobility conditions were presented. It was shown that the performance of the ODSBR protocol is robust against the attack scenarios discussed above. In this paper, we extend the analysis of the ODSBR protocol in the presence of the new MAC-Level attack.

5   ODSBR Protocol Enhancements

We specifically analyze the following protocol enhancements:

Packet Flow Rate Adjustments where we investigate reducing network packet size to achieve increased flow rates and speed protocol convergence. The Path Monitoring Module detects and isolates faulty links based upon counting the number of dropped packets within a specified window. By fragmenting packets at the network layer, the rate of network packets increases and hence the ODSBR fault detection and isolation times would correspondingly decrease.

Network Layer Retransmissions where we investigate the impact of increased packet flow rate due to packet retransmission at the network layer in the event of network packet dropping. A network layer retransmission protocol was suggested in [15] as a means to improve the overall robustness of the network layer against general Byzantine attacks. The ODSBR protocol is an end-to-end acknowledgment protocol with a timeout mechanism to detect path losses. We compliment this acknowledgment protocol by adding packet retransmissions. The default path acknowledgment timeout is 0.5 seconds times the number of hops remaining to the destination node. We implement the retransmission protocol at the source node by keeping track of the number of times a given packet is transmitted to the destination. When the source node either times out or receives a lost packet indication, the source retransmits the packet in the event that it has not been transmitted in excess of $n_{retries}$ times. Thus, the source node effectively increases the packet flow rate by retransmitting each packet up to $n_{retries}$ times in the presence of an adversary.

Nodal Weighting in the Component Weighting Table where we investigate the impact of the addition of Nodal Weighting to the ODSBR component reputation database. We expect that this enhancement will improve the long time-scale convergence of the protocol and improve its ability to search through complex adversarial topologies when looking for good paths through the network. Over long time-scales, learning is the result of building up knowledge of the behavior of the entire network. We were motivated to propose a Nodal Weighting component to the ODSBR reputation database while investigating the impact of the new,

MAC-Level attacker. Hence, we discuss the impact of Nodal Weighting primarily in the context of this new attack model.

We investigate two learning algorithms:

Ln,m,p - where n is the proportional weight given to the path hop count, m is the proportional weight given to the links based upon the fault count, and p is the proportional weight given to the nodes in the path based upon the number of faults summed across all of their links. The L indicates that the respective weighting is increased linearly proportional to the component's fault count. The path weight is given by the sum of the hop, link and nodal weight for each component in the path.

Wn,m,p - where the W indicates that the link weights are proportional to $2^{(number\ of\ faults)}$. Thus, $W1,1,0$ represents the original ODSBR weighting mechanism developed in [3] and reported on in [4]. The notation $W1,1,1$ represents a new learning algorithm we refer to as *Nodal Weighting*. In Nodal Weighting, an additional nodal weight is given to the path weight. The Nodal Weight is developed by summing the link weights of all the links connecting to the node and then multiplying that sum by the proportional weighting factor, p.

6   ODSBR Dynamics

In this section we develop a qualitative model of the dynamics of the ODSBR protocol to better understand the effects of our protocol enhancements. In [5], we present a more thorough discussion of our modeling and its assumptions.

When a source node wishes to establish a data flow, it performs a relatively quick path discovery. Then, the source node begins data transmission to the destination, while performing end-to-end monitoring of the flow. If the route contains one or more adversaries, then the source will detect and isolate a faulty link and perform a reroute. It may go through several reroutes prior to finding a good path through the network. Eventually, the existing path will break due to nodal mobility. Once again the source must perform a path discovery and re-establish a data path. Prior to the path breaking due to nodal mobility, the source node learned about the integrity of some of the links and recorded this information in its Link Weighting Table. This information will reduce the probability of initially hitting a path with an adversary in future path discoveries. This behavior repeats as the protocol switches between monitoring a path and searching for a new good path when the current path breaks due to mobility. This assumes the relative motion of the nodes is slow compared to the response of the path discovery and monitoring functions. If this assumption does not hold, then the ODSBR's Path Monitoring and fault isolation functions will fail to have sufficient time to discover adversarial behavior along the current path.

So, imagine the MANET system stepping through a series of static topology cases. Each static case has a lifetime equal to the mean lifetime of a given path through the network. As the system steps to a new topology state, it inherits the knowledge about the integrity of the links learned from the previous topology cases. Upon entering a new topology, the source node initiates a new

Table 1. Half lives for learning
algorithms

Learning Algorithm	Half Life
Short Time Scale	$t_{1/2} = \frac{2TW}{gR} ln2$
Long Time Scale	$t_{1/2} = \frac{Lr}{v\alpha} ln2$

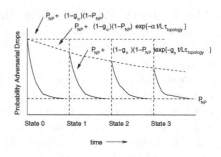

Fig. 1. The model predictions for the long
time-scale dynamics of the ODSBR protocol

route request. Thus two time-scales exist; a short time-scale related to the time required within a static topology for the source node to find a good path and a long time-scale related to the time for a given source node to build up its Link Weight Table. The dynamics of the short time-scale learning are studied within the context of a static topology case. The dynamics of the long time-scale learning are studied within the context of information built up by progressing through the series of static topology cases. The system jumps from state-to-state roughly each $\tau_{topology}$ seconds.

Here we summarize the predictions of this model. For details of the derivations, refer to [5]. Our modeling focuses on estimating the time evolution of the probability of adversarial packet discards. The model suggests that both the short time-scale and the long time-scale evolution of packet discards, and hence the learning times of the ODSBR protocol, converge exponentially. This behavior is illustrated in Figure 1. Table 1 lists the half-life of each of the exponentially decaying terms. Here, $t_{1/2}$ represents the time at which the exponentially decaying function falls to one half its initial value, T is the ODSBR loss threshold, W is the size of the sliding window of loss results, R is the packet rate per flow, r is the radio range, v is the nodal speed, L is the number of links in the network, g is the probability of randomly picking a good (non-adversarial) path in the network, and α is the average number of path faults prior to finding a good path within each "static" topology state.

7   Simulations Studies

In [4] a simulation model of the ODSBR protocol was developed based upon the NS2 simulation tool kit [12]. The attack models discussed in Section 4 were implemented in the simulation. The stationary state, packet discard ratio was reported under various attack scenarios and different nodal speeds. Here we extend the work in [4] by analyzing ODSBR protocol enhancements and the impact of the new MAC-Level attack.

The prominent metric we investigate is the *Probability of Adversarial Packet Discards*, which is the ratio of the packets dropped due to the adversarial behavior of the Byzantine nodes divided by the number of packets injected into the network by the application flows over the given time interval. Our simulation runs are divided up into ten equal time intervals and the adversarial packet discard probability is reported over these ten intervals. Our base case simulation model follows [4] and is comprised of 50 good nodes and 10 adversarial nodes located in a 1000 by 1000 meter grid. The nodes are randomly placed within the grid according to a uniform distribution and move within the grid according to the modified Way Point model [17]. The modified Random Way Point Model is run for 300 seconds of simulation time prior to initiating the traffic flows, protocol modeling and data collection phase of the simulation. Each result represents the average over 30 independent simulation runs. The underlying radio model is that of an 802.11 wireless network with a data rate of 2 Mbps and a radio reception range of 250 meters as determined by a Two Ground Wave propagation model [16]. Ten Constant Bit Rate (CBR) traffic sources are chosen at random over the good nodes. These traffic sources are connected to 10 traffic sinks, also chosen at random over the good nodes excluding the source node. An aggregate load of 0.1Mbps was offered to the network by having each flow send 256 byte packets at an approximate rate of 4.9 packets per second. Each of the ten CBR flows remain active for the duration of the data collection phase of each independent simulation run.

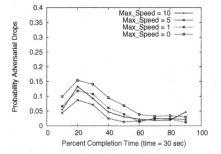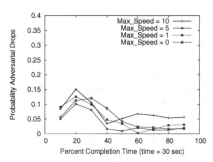

Fig. 2. The convergence of the search algorithms against the BH attack. The LHS plot shows results for Link Weighting and the RHS plot shows results with the addition of Nodal Weighting.

7.1 Short Time Scale Dynamics

Figure 2 shows the temporal behavior of the adversarial packet discard probability for simulation runs of 30 seconds. The two plots show the short term learning of the ODSBR protocol in the presence of 10 randomly placed adversarial nodes running the Black Hole Attack. The Left Hand Side (LHS) plot runs the ODSBR protocol as defined in [3] and [4], while the Right Hand Side (RHS) plot shows the performance of the modified ODSBR protocol which incorporates Nodal Weighting as discussed in the next section. The four separate curves within each plot represent simulation runs with different nodal speeds, i.e., 0, 1, 5 and 10 meters per second. Due to packet buffering and finite route discovery times, there is a startup period in the beginning of the simulation runs. Once initial routes are established and packets begin to flow into the network, the Byzantine nodes running their Black Hole Attack begin to drop data packets. This results in the relatively large peak in the probability of adversarial packet drops in the 3 to 12 second range. As the path monitoring function begins to fault isolate the adversarial links and initiate path reroutes, the probability of adversarial drops begins to decrease in roughly an exponential fashion as predicted by our model of the short time-scale dynamics. The probability of adversarial packet drops will not approach zero due to the the finite probability that no good path exists between a pair of nodes. This is illustrated in the simulation results by observing the zero speed curves.

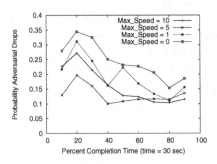 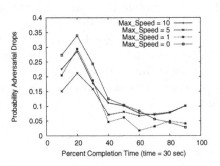

Fig. 3. The convergence of the search algorithms against the BHFSW attack. The LHS plot shows Link Weighting results and the RHS plot show results for combined Nodal and Link Weighting.

Figure 3 shows comparable results for adversaries which are implementing Black Hole with Flood Rush and forming a fully interconnected set of Worm Holes (BHFSW). This is an extremely powerful attack scenario. From the simulations, we see that the ODSBR protocol is reducing the probability of adversarial dropping, however the results are not as good as for the previous attack model due to the topological complexity that the Super Worm Holes introduce. Notice that the Nodal Weighting scheme shows improved performance in the RHS plot.

Our analytic model predicts a short term half-life of roughly $(2TW/Rg)ln2 \approx (2x0.1x100/5x0.4)ln2 = 7$ seconds. The expected time within the static topology state is roughly $r/v \approx 250/(5mps) = 50$ seconds. Hence, these results relate to the short time-scale learning of the ODSBR protocol.

7.2   Increased Packet Flow Rate

Figure 4 shows the simulation results for different packet flow rates. The plot on the LHS gives results for three packet flow rates, i.e., 1 packet per second (pps), 3 pps and 5 pps for a nodal maximum speed of 1 meter per second (mps). The plot on the

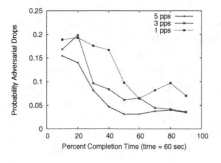 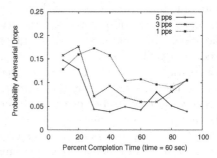

Fig. 4. The impact of packet flow rates for two different mobilities, i.e., 1 mps for the LHS plot and 5 mps for the RHS plot

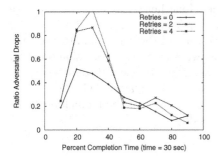 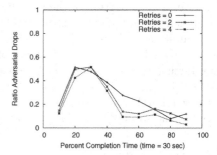

Fig. 5. The impact of packet retransmission on convergence times for 30 second run with and without renormalization

RHS shows the comparable results for a nodal speed of 5 mps. We see that the half-life for the short time-scale convergence increases as the packet flow rates decrease. The increase is not directly proportional to the packet flow rate because the route discovery times have not proportionally changed. Here, the route lifetime for the 1 mps cases (the LHS of the figure) is roughly 250 seconds, while for the 5 mps cases (the RHS of the figure) is roughly 50 seconds. The Route Monitoring lifetime of the ODSBR protocol is expected to be roughly 50 seconds for the slowest packet flow rate of 1 pps. Thus, we expect that the convergence of the learning protocols to be much better in the plot on the LHS than on the RHS. So, the convergence of the 1 pps flow rate with a maximum nodal speed of 5 mps is rather poor. However, the convergence in all cases in Figure 4 improves with increased packet flow rates.

7.3   Network Layer Retransmission

Figure 5 shows the results of the network layer retransmissions on the convergence of the ODSBR protocol. The plot on the LHS presents the raw results from our simulation runs. The three curves on this plot represent the results for an $n_{retries}$ value of 0, 2 and 4, respectively. As the number of retries increases, the maximum peak in the ratio of adversarial discards increases, and in fact exceeds unity. The reason for this is that we are plotting the ratio of the number of adversarial drops in the network divided by the packets sent by the application. Due to the possibility that each application packet is retransmitted, this value can exceed unity. To better visualize the results in the RHS plot, we have scaled the individual curves according to the peak values (the curve for an $n_{retries} = 0$ was left unchanged). As $n_{retries}$ is increased, the convergence half lives decrease, although not as dramatically as one might expect. The application flow rate in these examples is roughly 5 pps. At that rate, the threshold detection and fault isolation time is roughly 7 seconds. The default timeout for the ODSBR protocol is 0.5 seconds times the mean path length. Hence, the route is established and carries quite a few packets prior to the first packet retransmission occurring. Hence, the retransmission protocol is effective in increasing the packet flow rate only over a later portion of the path lifetime. Nonetheless, we do see a decrease in the half-life of the convergence time as $n_{retries}$ increases.

In addition to decreasing the convergence time of the route monitoring time for the ODSBR protocol, the existence of a network layer retransmission protocol may further buffer (or completely mask) the effects of other Byzantine attack models. In [1], a number of novel Byzantine attacks against TCP flows were discussed. Further analysis of network layer retransmissions should include TCP-based traffic sources and additional attack models.

7.4   Nodal Weighting

We first analyze the impact of Nodal Weighting by running a set of simulations on static topologies to assess the behavior and performance of the protocol enhancements in scenarios where the results can be easily explained. Figure 6 shows the static test cases. For each case, the nodes in solid black are participants in the ODSBR routing protocol and the nodes in dashed black represent the two colluding MAC-Level attack nodes. The dashed black line between the two MAC-Level nodes represent the tunnel set up between these colluding nodes. The source node is on the far left of each figure and the destination node is on the far right. Case A has only a single virtual path through the colluding pair. Case B has 3^2 virtual paths due to the fact that 3 good nodes are found within range of each colluding node. Case C has 5^2 virtual paths.

We ran NS2 simulations for each topology case. We measured the time to which the ODSBR protocol first set up a good-route (around the MAC-Level adversaries). Theses results are reported in Table 2.

The results in Table 2 for Case A show good-route discovery times of 75, 30 and 15 seconds respectively for the $L1, 1, 0$, $W1, 1, 0$ and $W1, 1, 1$ algorithms.Notice that the path length for the bad path is 3 while the path length for the good path is 13 hops. Thus the algorithm must weight the bad path by at least an additional 10 points in order for the source node to consider choosing the good path. For the $L1, 1, 0$ algorithm, the source node must discover and fault isolate

Table 2. Learning Times for Test Cases

Case	Weights	Time (seconds)	Search Combinations
A	L1,1,0	75	1
A	W1,1,0	30	1
A	W1,1,1	15	1
B	L1,1,0	680	9
B	W1,1,0	240	9
B	W1,1,1	48	9
C	L1,1,0	1900	25
C	W1,1,0	720	25
C	W1,1,1	72	25

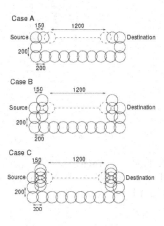

Fig. 6. The test case topologies

the faulty link eleven times in order to increase the weight of the bad path by more than ten points. Given an application flow rate of roughly 5 packets per second, a threshold of 0.1 and a sliding window of 100 packets, then the time to discover and isolate a link is going to be longer than four seconds each round. This, in addition to route discovery times, transmission times, etc. result in a route time of 75 seconds. For $W1,1,0$ weighting, due to the exponential weighting based upon the number of faults, the source only needs to fault isolate the bad link four times in order for the source to increase the bad route length by more than 10 points. This cuts the good path discovery time down by more than half. The $W1,1,1$ algorithm cuts this in half again because of the triple counting of the link faults, once for the nodal weighting of the node on the left side of the link, once for the link weighting and once for the nodal weighting for the node on the right hand side of the link.

For the Cases B and C, the combinations are multiplied due to the number of virtual paths to search. For Case B, where there are nine virtual paths to search, the discovery times have increased by roughly nine times over the results in Case A. For Case C, where there are 25 virtual paths to search, the discovery times have increased by roughly 25 times over the results in Case A. The effectiveness of this attack increases in proportion to the square of the number of nodes within the vicinity of the MAC-Level nodes, i.e., the learning times of the algorithms scale like z^2 where z is the average number of nodes within radio range of the adversaries. Further, the different learning algorithms, i.e., $Ln,n,0$ and $Wn,n,0$, affect convergence times by modifying the constant of proportionality but not by fundamentally changing the z^2 scaling. However, the Nodal Weighting algorithm, $W1,1,1$, in addition decreases the potential number of search options. The learning time for the Nodal Weighting case increases in proportion to the number of nodes z within range of the adversary. This is verified by the simulation results.

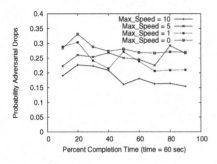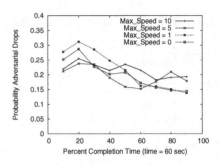

Fig. 7. The convergence of the search algorithms against the MAC-Level attack model. The LHS plot shows Link Weighting results and the RHS plot show results for combined Nodal and Link Weighting.

We now investigate the performance of the Nodal Weighting algorithm within the MANET topology. For these simulations, the long time-scale half-life is predicted to be $(L\tau_{topology}/\alpha)ln2$ where $\alpha \approx (1-g)/g$ (see [5]), L is the number of potential links in the MANET and $\tau_{topology}$ is roughly r/v. Assuming $g \approx 0.8$, $r = 250m$, $v = 5m/s$ and $L = (60)^2/2$, we get roughly 7 hours for the long time-scale learning half-life. This is an extremely long time is due to a) the number of links being proportional to N^2 and b) the random nature of the measurement strategy. Nodal weighting has the potential for effectively reducing L from $N^2/2$ to N. This reduces the long time-scale learning half-life by a factor of 30; reducing the 7 hours to 14 minutes. This is a rather dramatic improvement. It is only possible to reduce this long time-scale learning further by incorporating some form of shared learning between the good nodes in the network. This is a challenging area of study due to the security implications of shared trust in Byzantine environments.

Figures 2 and 3 present the convergence results for the ODSBR short time-scale learning with Nodal Weighting. The plots on the LHS show the results of the W1,1,0 learning algorithm, while the plots on the RHS of the figure show the corresponding results for the W1,1,1 learning algorithm. There appears to be little difference between the convergence of the ODSBR short time-scale behavior between the non-Nodal and the Nodal Weighting algorithms. Clearly the introduction of the W1,1,1 learning algorithm does not adversely affect the ODSBR protocol performance. Nodal Weighting does show improvement for all mobilities in the presence of BHFSW attackers. We expect that this is due to the relatively large number of search paths required of the learning algorithms under this attack model.

Figure 7 shows the simulation results for the MAC-Level attack in the MANET topology. The time duration for these simulation runs is 60 seconds. The plot on the LHS shows the results for mobilities of 0, 1, 5, and 10 mps with ODSBR nodes running the W1,1,0 algorithm. While the plot on the RHS shows the comparable results with ODSBR nodes running the W1,1,1 algorithm. The results for the non-Nodal Weighting algorithm show that the algorithm is having a hard time finding good routes through the network. However, the Nodal Weighting results, on the RHS of the figure, demonstrate an improved trend toward convergence.

8 Conclusions

We investigated the benefits of several ODSBR protocol enhancements through analytic and simulation modeling. Further, we analyzed a new attack model, termed the MAC-Level attacker. Our simulations were performed for a range of network parameters including varying nodal speeds, different Byzantine attack models and different network topologies. These studies demonstrated improved convergence times due to the proposed protocol enhancements. The impact of a network layer retransmission protocol was not as great as we expected due to the relatively large value of the retransmission time outs with respect to the fault isolation times of the ODSBR protocol. However, the incorporation of the Nodal Weighting scheme showed dramatic improvements in searching through complex topologies introduced by the MAC-Level adversarial attack model and hence improved the convergence time performance of the ODSBR protocol.

In future work, we plan on additional studies of the Network Layer Retransmission protocol in carrying TCP traffic and in protecting against other attack models. However, the most notable and challenging future work item is the investigation of methods for good nodes to share information learned with other nodes.

Acknowledgments

We would like to thank Cristina Nita-Rotaru of Purdue University for her advise and comments on aspects of this work. Further, we would like to thank the anonymous reviewers for their insightful comments.

References

1. Aad, I., Hubaux, J.-P. and E.W. Knightly, *Denial of Service Resilience in Ad Hoc Networks*, Mobicom'04, Philadelphia, September 2004.
2. Avramopoulos, I., Kobayashi, H., Wang, R. and A. Krishnamurthy, *Highly Secure and Efficient Routing*, INFOCOM'04, March 2004.
3. Awerbuch, B., R., Holmer, D., Nita-Rotaru, C. and H. Rubens, *An on-demand secure routing protocol resilient to byzantine failures*, ACM Workshop on Wireless Security (WiSe), September 2002.
4. Awerbuch, B., Curtmola, R., Holmer, D., Nita-Rotaru, C. and H. Rubens, *On the Survivability of Routing Protocols in Ad Hoc Wireless Networks*, SecureCom'05, September 2005.
5. Awerbuch, B., Cole, R.G., Curtmola, R., Holmer, D., Nita-Rotaru, C. and H. Rubens, *Dynamics of Learning Algorithms for the On-Demand Secure Byzantine Routing Protocol*, JHU Applied Physics Laboratory Technical Report No. VIC-05-088, November 2005.

6. Boneh, D., Gentry, C., Shacham, H. and B. Lynn, *Aggregate and verifiable encrypted signatures from bilinear maps*, in Proceedings of Eurocrypt'03, 2003.

7. Buttyan, L. and J.P.Hubaux, *Enforcing Service Availability in Mobile Ad-Hoc WANs*, In Proceeding of IEEE/ACM Workshop on Mobile Ad Hoc Networking and Computing (MobiHoc), Boston, MA, USA, August 2000.

8. Hu, Y.-C., Perrig, A. and D.B.Johnson, *Ariadne: A secure on-demand routing protocol for ad hoc networks*, In Proceedings of the Eighth ACM International Conference on Mobile Computing and Networking (MobiCom 2002), September 2002.

9. Lamport, L., Shostak, R. and M. Pease, *The Byzantine Generals Problem*, ACM Transactions on Programming Languages and Systems, Vol. 4, No. 3, July 1982.

10. Marti, S., Giuli, T.J., Lai, K. and M. Baker, *Mitigating routing misbehavior in mobile ad hoc networks*, In Mobile Computing and Networking (MobiCom 2000), September 2000.

11. Murphy, S., Badger, M. and B. Wellington, *OSPF with Digital Signatures*, IETF RFC 2154, June 1997.

12. The Network Simulator - ns2, *http://www.isi.edu/nsnam/ns/*, 2005.

13. Papadimitratos, P. and Z. Haas, *Secure routing for mobile ad hoc networks*, In SCS Communication Networks and Distributed Systems Modeling and Simulation Conference, 2002.

14. Papadimitratos, P. and Z. Haas, *Secure data transmission in mobile ad hoc networks*, In ACM Workshop on Wireless Security (WiSe), 2003.

15. Perlman, R., *Network Layer Protocols with Byzantine Robustness*, MIT Thesis, August 1988.

16. Rappaport, T. *Wireless Communications Principles and Practice*, 2nd Ed., Pearson Education Press (Singapore), 2002.

17. Yoon, J., Liu, M. and B.D. Noble, *Random waypoint considered harmful*, INFOCOM'03, April 2003.

On the Wiretap Channel Induced by Noisy Tags

Julien Bringer and Hervé Chabanne

Sagem Défense Sécurité

Abstract. At CARDIS'06, Castelluccia and Avoine introduce noisy tags to allow key exchange between an RFID tag and a reader. We here show that their protocol leads to a well-known information problem: the wiretap channel. We then make use of works by Thangaraj et al. on the case where the main channel is noiseless and where there are only erasures on the wiretapper's channel to improve previous results on noisy tags. In particular, we show how one can achieve, in a practical manner, perfect secrecy for key exchange in this noisy tags context.

Keywords: RFID, wiretap channel, noisy tags, LDPC codes.

1 Introduction

Securely pairing RFID tags to a reader is a particularly hard challenge due to the cost constrainsts which push to always reduce resources inside RFID tags. A very attractive solution was proposed by Castelluccia and Avoine in [2] as in their protocol the tag behaves like a memory, i.e. only sends a sequence of bits to the reader. Note that, doing so, the protocol is naturally more resistant to side channel attacks, which begin to appear for RFIDs [6].

What makes the simplicity of the protocol by Castelluccia and Avoine possible is the introduction on the reader side of a particular RFID called the noisy tag which allows to add perturbations in the communications between the RFID tag and its reader. This extra noise is controlled by the reader but remains unknown to eavesdroppers.

Following Castelluccia and Avoine, we here improve their protocol by introducing new coding scheme of the informations sent by the RFID tag, leading to perfect secrecy.

In Sect. 2, we recall how noisy tags are used by Castelluccia and Avoine and show that this leads to a well-known problem: a particular wiretap channel. In Sect. 3, we recall results on the classical wiretap channel problem and advances due to Thangaraj et al. on the very case of noisy tags. In Sect. 4, we give some examples to illustrate that perfect secrecy is achievable in a practical manner. Section 5 concludes.

For references on RFID security, we invite the reader to check online references at `http://lasecwww.epfl.ch/~gavoine/rfid`. See also [4] for a recent survey.

L. Buttyan, V. Gligor, and D. Westhoff (Eds.): ESAS 2006, LNCS 4357, pp. 113–120, 2006.

2   Noisy Tags

Quoting Castelluccia and Avoine, the idea of noisy tags comes from a key exchange scheme developped at Bells Telephone Labs during WWII.

Here each reader comes equipped with a special RFID tag: the Noisy Tag (NT). And both the RFID Tag (T) which wants to establish a key with the reader and the Noisy Tag emit bits, simultaneously in order to hide the bits sent by T. Typically, the sequence of bits issued from the Noisy Tag is a pseudo-random sequence of bits, controlled by its associated reader.

We suppose (cf. [2]) that the bit '1' is implemented by a pulse of x mV and that the bit '0' corresponds to a pulse of 0 mV.

- From an attacker's point of view:
    - when T and NT have sent a different bit, he observes x mV in the air and can not distinguish, between T and NT, which one sent the bit '0' and which one sent the '1' : this corresponds to an erasure on the wiretap channel,
    - when both T and NT have sent the same bit, he certainly knows which bit it was as he gets 0 mV, if both T and NT have sent '0', or $2x$ mV if T and NT have sent '1'.
- From the reader's view point, as it knows in advance the sequence of bits produced by NT, at the end, it can retrieve the bits emitted by NT from those which are received and thus obtains the ones issued by T.

This situation which corresponds to the Bit-Based Protocol, Version 1 of [2], can be described as follows (see Fig. 1):

1. there is a noiseless main channel between T and the reader,
2. the attacker gets the information from a Binary Erasure Channel where an erasure has one chance over two to happen.

In Figure 1, BEC$(1 - \epsilon)$ stands for Binary Erasure Channel with a probalility of $1 - \epsilon$ to have an erasure.

Remark 1. *Castelluccia and Avoine introduce three different protocols in [2]. In the last one, to obtain a security level of 2^{80}, an RFID tag T has to send more than one Kbits to establish an 80-bit long key with a reader. The first two ones require that the RFID tag T sends roughly 2 times the key length, but in these protocols, some informations are leaked to the eavesdropper.*

Note that we do not address here (and in [2] neither) the problem of exchanging the same key several times. I.e. we do not consider different executions of the protocol between an RFID tag and readers for establishing the same key across time. We may only consider that the attacker has access to a wiretap modelized as a Binary Erasure Channel BEC$(1 - 1/2)$ if he observes one execution of the protocol, BEC$(1/4)$ if he eavesdrops two executions and so on. The last protocol of [2] - Code-Based Protocol - suffers also from this kind of

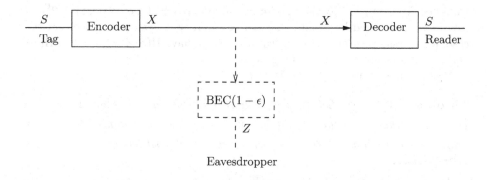

Fig. 1. Wiretap channel with erasure

situation as with only two observations of the same key exchange, an attacker knows exactly which key is emitted by the RFID tag T (even with several noisy tags). Some solution may be envisaged to alleviate this problem. For instance, we may think at a renewal of key material inside RFID tag T after each successful execution of the protocol [5].

3   The Erasure Wiretapper's Channel

The scenario of wiretap channels with erasure, including the one associated to the noisy tags model depicted in Fig. 1, has been studied by Thangaraj et al. [10].

The wiretap channel problem was first introduced by Wyner [11] in 1975. Classicaly, to transmit k-bit messages, a binary linear code C of length n is chosen and each message is associated to a chosen coset of C. More precisely, let

- $n = k + l$,
- $G = (g_1, \ldots, g_l)$ be a generator matrix $l \times n$ of C,
- $h_1, \ldots, h_k$ be k linearly independent vectors from $\{0,1\}^n$, not in C,
- $v = (v_1, \ldots, v_l)$ be a uniformly random l-bit vector,

then a message $s = (s_1, \ldots, s_k)$ in $\{0,1\}^k$ is encoded as

$$x = s_1 h_1 + s_2 h_2 + \cdots + s_k h_k + v_1 g_1 + v_2 g_2 + \cdots + v_l g_l. \tag{1}$$

We will only consider here the case where $(g_1, \ldots, g_l, h_1, \ldots, h_k)$ span the entire space vector $\{0,1\}^n$. Note that with such a construction, the information rate of the communication channel will be $R = k/n$ (i.e. 1 minus the information rate of C).

Given z received by an eavesdropper, if a coset of C contains at least one vector that agrees with $z \in \{0,1\}^n$ in the unerased positions, we say that the coset is consistent with z. Let $N(C, z)$ be the total number of cosets of C consistent with z. For a code C of length n and dimension $l = n - k$, the maximum possible value for $N(C, z)$ is 2^k. If the maximum value is reached, i.e. $N(C, z) = 2^k$, we say that z is secured by C and that perfect secrecy is achieved. Indeed, in this case, for messages from a random variable S, we have $\mathrm{H}(S|Z = z) = k = \mathrm{H}(S)$, i.e. that z does not reveal anything on S.

Now, we have a nice characterization:

Theorem 1 ([7,10]). *Let an $[n, n - k]$ code C have a generator matrix $G = \left(a_1 \cdots a_n\right)$ where a_i is the i-th column of G. Consider an instance of the eavesdropper's observation $z \in \{0, 1, ?\}^n$ with μ unerased positions given by $\{i : z_i \neq ?\} = \{i_1, i_2, \ldots, i_\mu\}$.*

Then, z is secured by C if and only if the matrix $G_\mu = \left(a_{i_1}\, a_{i_2} \cdots a_{i_\mu}\right)$ has maximal rank: $\mathrm{Rank}\, G_\mu = \mu$.

Proof (For the purpose of completeness, we here give the proof from [10]). If G_μ has rank μ, the code C has all 2^μ possible μ-tuples in the μ unerased positions. So each coset of C also has all 2^μ possible μ-tuples in the revealed positions. Hence $N(C, z) = 2^k$.

If G_μ has rank less than μ, the code C does not have all μ-tuples in the μ unerased positions. So there exists at least one coset that does not contain a given μ-tuple in the μ unerased positions, this implies $N(C, z) < 2^k$. □

The main purpose of [10] is to introduce codes that approach secrecy capacity (i.e. the largest k/n for which the objectives of secure and reliable communication is achievable) over some wiretap channels. In particular, for a wiretap channel with a noiseless main channel and a binary erasure channel as the wiretapper's channel (as in Fig. 1, see previous section), the authors of [10] exhibit constructions which allow to reach linear-time decodable codes.

One construction of [10] relies on duals of Low-Density Parity-Check (LDPC) codes (see [3] for details on LDPC codes). They choose an LDPC code $[n, k]$ and use the dual (or equivalently a parity check matrix), which is an $[n, n - k]$ code, as the code C.

LDPC codes are linear codes obtained from sparse bipartite graphs. Consider a bipartite graph with n left (message or variable) nodes and r right (check) nodes. Then forms the binary matrix in which the entry (i, j) is 1 if and only if the i-th check node is connected to the j-th message node in the graph via an edge (see Fig. 2 for an example). This "adjacency" matrix is used as a parity check matrix for an LDPC code.

In [8], the threshold α^* of an LDPC code is introduced. This threshold serves us - following [10] - to bind LDPC codes to the wiretap channel via Theorem 1:

Theorem 2 ([10]). *Let H be a parity-check matrix of an LDPC code with threshold α^*. Then a submatrix formed by selecting columns of H independently with probability ϵ will have full column rank for $\epsilon < \alpha^*$ for large k with high probability.*

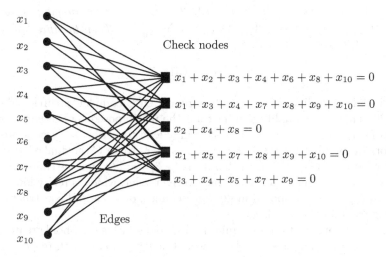

Fig. 2. A bipartite graph of an irregular LDPC code

In other words, a code C which is the dual of an LDPC code has a great chance to be a good candidate for encoding messages over our noisy tag channel provided that $\epsilon < \alpha^*$.

With such a code, the exchange is then the following (see Fig. 1). To reveal its secret s to a reader, the tag sends its encoding value x in the air and the reader retrieves the value of the secret from the string x sent by the tag simply by decoding it.

We therefore must know how much it costs. Now recovering s from x in (1) is an $O(n^2)$ operation (as there are no errors on the main channel because the noisy tag is controlled by the reader), the computation of s is essentially a syndrome computation for C. So to recover s, it is sufficient to multiply x with a matrix. Moreover, this could be improved: [10] gives also designs for linear or almost-linear decodable secrecy codes for the system shown in Fig. 1. Finally, this decoding stage is easily performed by the reader.

4   A Practical Example

In practice, we limit ourselves to a particular class of LDPC codes, the regular codes, where the threshold (in the Binary Erasure Channel) is easily computable. An LDPC code with an underlying bipartite graph for which each message node is connected to exactly j check nodes and each check node involves k message nodes is called a (j, k)-regular LDPC code. It is shown in [1] that we have the following result.

Lemma 1. *Let C be a (j, k)-regular LDPC code and σ the unique positive real root of $P(X) = ((j-1)(k-1) - 1) X^{k-2} - \sum_{i=0}^{k-3} X^i$. Then the threshold α^* of C for the BEC is*

$$\alpha^* = \frac{1 - \sigma}{(1 - \sigma^{k-1})^{j-1}}.$$

In particular, according to [1], a $(3, 4)$-regular LDPC code has a threshold α^* of 0.647426. This is reasonably greater than the 0.5 imposed by the wiretapper's channel in the noisy tag model and so it may lead to perfect secrecy. Moreover, the information rate of a (j, k)-regular code is $1 - \frac{j}{k}$, so for C the dual of this code, the information rate on the main channel is $1 - 3/4 = 1/4$ and one can transmit a 80-bit key long by sending only 320 bits to the reader, which is really lower than in the third protocol proposed in [2]. For instance, one can find constructions of $(3, 4)$-regular LDPC codes in [9].

Many other constructions of regular LDPC codes with a threshold greater than $1/2$ are available, and thus the choice would be easily made with respect to the local constraints. For instance, it could be valuable to increase the information rate if the number of bits has to be lower. For example, a $(4, 6)$-regular code and a $(3, 5)$-regular code have both a threshold around 0.5. As the first one gives a rate of $1/3$ and the second one a rate of $2/5$, it allows to send only 240 bits in the first case and 200 bits in the second case, for a secret of 80 bits. At last, it could also be necessary to increase the threshold if the probabily of erasures (from the attacker's point of view) decreases.

Remark 2. *For the last point, we can also use several noisy tags at the same time to avoid the probability to be too low. Another "trick" is possible: as the reader also knows when a bit is leaked over the wiretapper's channel, then it can have a special command to tell to suspend its communication with the RFID tag T when too many bits have escaped to an eavesdropper.*

Actually, a good thing is that for the RFID tag this coding scheme does not change the implementation but only the length of the vector to store, as the idea is to run the encoding algorithm outside the tag and thus to write directly the encoded value x (and in option the key s, if it is used after the execution of this protocol) in the tag, in order to keep its behaviour like a memory. Hence, the encoding complexity is not a constraint for the tag.

Reusability. We focused on the case where the string x is sent only once, but to consider the impact of repeated observation by an adversary, we have seen mainly three ideas which are summarized below. Of course, to improve efficiency, these solutions should be combined. Note that, as mentioned in Sect. 2, it is possible to simulate repetitions by taking a BEC with a lower probability of erasure.

- First, as in [2], we can increase the number of noisy tags in parallel in order to stay in the same model, for instance to keep a probability of erasure greater than $1/2$. With Q noisy tags, an attacker would need about 2^{Q-1}

repetitions to observe the channel with a probability lower than $1/2$ (i.e. to be in a BEC($1 - \epsilon$) more favourable with $\epsilon > 1/2$).

- A second way is to use a dual code of an LDPC code with an increased threshold in order to retain the result of theorem 2. A possible drawback is that it would decrease the capacity and thus would have a marked effect on the efficiency of the scheme if the adversary can observe many attempts.

- Another point is to update the tag's key after each successful authentication. This option looks more reasonable than the two previous ones, but then it becomes important to create an authenticated channel from the reader to the tag in order to communicate success. Otherwise, the tag could suffer, for instance, a denial-of-service attack in which the attacker communicate success several times to the tag leading to a state de-synchronization between tag and reader.

5   Conclusion

We have shown how, following Thangaraj et al., the use of dual of LDPC codes may allow to achieve perfect secrecy for the noisy tags at low cost. In fact, we have given a solution, where the eavesdropper gets no information on the key from a theoretical point of view, with a cost which compares favourably in terms of communication with the protocols by Castelluccia and Avoine. To be fair, one should notice that it requires more computations on the reader side: at most $O(n^2)$ operations, which seems not critical to us.

The security provided here concerns the passive attackers, a remaining point is to analyse if this wiretap model is sufficient for providing perfect secrecy against active attacks, where the adversary can impersonate either tag or reader in many communication attempts. The above-mentioned problem of dealing with multiple observations is a part of the security analysis to do in order to address all practical security issues. The next step in this direction is to focus ourselves on a well-chosen code and to check its behaviour.

Acknowledgments

The authors wish to thank the anonymous referees for their useful suggestions which helped to improve the presentation of this paper.

References

1. Louay Bazzi, Thomas J. Richardson, and Rüdiger L. Urbanke. Exact thresholds and optimal codes for the binary-symmetric channel and gallager's decoding algorithm A. *IEEE Transactions on Information Theory*, 50(9):2010–2021, 2004.
2. Claude Castelluccia and Gildas Avoine. Noisy tags: A pretty good key exchange protocol for RFID tags. In Josep Domingo-Ferrer, Joachim Posegga, and Daniel Schreckling, editors, *International Conference on Smart Card Research and Advanced Applications – CARDIS*, volume 3928 of *Lecture Notes in Computer Science*, pages 289–299, Tarragona, Spain, April 2006. IFIP, Springer-Verlag.

3. R. G. Gallager. *Low-Density Parity Check Codes*. Number 21 in Research monograph series. MIT Press, Cambridge, MA, 1963.
4. Simson L. Garfinkel, Ari Juels, and Ravikanth Pappu. RFID Privacy: An Overview of Problems and Proposed Solutions. *IEEE Security & Privacy*, 3(3):34–43, 2005.
5. David Molnar and David Wagner. Privacy and security in library RFID: Issues, practices, and architectures. In Birgit Pfitzmann and Peng Liu, editors, *Conference on Computer and Communications Security – ACM CCS*, pages 210–219, Washington, DC, USA, October 2004. ACM, ACM Press.
6. Yossi Oren and Adi Shamir. Power analysis of RFID tags, 2006. http://www.wisdom.weizmann.ac.il/ yossio/rfid/.
7. L. H. Ozarow and A. D. Wyner. Wire–tap channel II. *The Bell System Technical Journal*, 63(10):2135–2157, 1984.
8. Thomas J. Richardson and Rüdiger L. Urbanke. Efficient encoding of low-density parity-check codes. *IEEE Transactions on Information Theory*, 47(2):638–656, 2001.
9. Roxana Smarandache and Pascal O. Vontobel. On regular quasi-cyclic LDPC codes from binomials. In *Proceedings of IEEE International Symposium on Information Theory*, page 274, Chicago, IL, USA, June 27 – July 2 2004.
10. Andrew Thangaraj, Souvik Dihidar, A. Robert Calderbank, Steven W. McLaughlin, and Jean-Marc Merolla. On the application of LDPC codes to a novel wiretap channel inspired by quantum key distribution. arXiv.org, Report cs.IT/0411003, 2004. http://arxiv.org/abs/cs.IT/0411003.
11. A.D. Wyner. The wire–tap channel. *The Bell System Technical Journal*, 54(8):1355–1387, 1975.

On Optimality of Key Pre-distribution Schemes for Distributed Sensor Networks

Subhas Kumar Ghosh

Honeywell Technology Solutions Lab.,
151/1, Doraisanipalya, Bannerghatta Road,
Bangalore, India-560076
Subhas.Kumar@honeywell.com

Abstract. We derive the optimality results for key pre distribution scheme for distributed sensor networks, and relations between interesting parameters. Namely, given a key-pool of size n we derive the optimal value that is jointly achievable for parameters like, Size optimality: using less memory per node - while supporting large network, Connectivity optimality: possibility of establishing secure communication between any two nodes over short path, and Resiliency optimality: large fraction of network remains working under compromise or node capture. We characterize this relation in graph theoretic framework. Our result shows that the desired graph (a combination of network topology graph on which key-share graph is embedded) must have small clique and independent set and must have high expansion properties, in other words Expander graphs are best suited for forming secure networks.

1 Introduction

Security is an important issue in deploying distributed sensor networks (DSN). One of the approaches to establish secure communication is constructing protocol based on pre-distributed keys. Basic model we consider here is key pre-distribution mechanism (**KPS**) as defined by Eschenauer and Gligor [13] (see Section-2). Several extensions and variations can be found in the works of Chan, Perrig, and Song [10], Liu and Ning [17], Du, Deng, Han and Varshney[11], which considers random key pre-distribution mechanism (*randomized*-**KPS**). These works extended the basic random key assignment schemes using conference key distribution schemes of Blom [4] and Blundo et el [5]. A random subset assignment key predistribution scheme, and a hypercube-based key predistribution scheme was studied in [19]. A closest pairwise keys predistribution scheme and a location-based pairwise keys scheme which takes advantage of sensors' expected locations was described in [18].

Under the basic model of key pre-distribution mechanism for a secure sensor network, Çamtepe and Yener [6] considered a deterministic pre-key distribution mechanism (*deterministic*-**KPS**). Çamtepe and Yener's method uses block design techniques in combinatorial design theory. Very similar approaches based on combinatorial design theory are proposed in [16,15] along with probabilistic

L. Buttyan, V. Gligor, and D. Westhoff (Eds.): ESAS 2006, LNCS 4357, pp. 121–135, 2006.

approaches yielding hybrid designs (*hybrid*-**KPS**) to support arbitrary network sizes. Recently Chakrabarti, Maitra and Roy [9] considered combinatorial design followed by a probabilistic merging applied to key pre-distribution in sensor nodes. They used a transversal design to construct a configuration and then used random merging of blocks to form sensor nodes providing flexibility in adjusting the number of common keys between any two nodes.

All previous works derive bounds on properties of the network under respective schemes. However, it is not clear what properties are desired, and what are possible bounds on achievable parameters, as well as their relations. This is precisely what we analyze in this work. In this work we consider both *randomized*-**KPS** and *deterministic*-**KPS** and look at their optimality for three most desired set of parameters, namely, (*i*) using less memory per node - while supporting large network, (*ii*) possibility of establishing secure communication between any two nodes in the network over a short path (possibly $\mathcal{O}(\log n)$, where n is the order of the network), and (*iii*) resiliency under compromise or node capture. In this work we derive optimality results for key pre-distribution scheme, and trade-off relations between parameters.

1.1 Contribution

In this paper, we focus on key pre-distribution problem for DSN. We first define the efficiency and security properties of a key pre-distribution procedure. Then we show how these parameters map to properties of shared key graph combined with network graph. Our main contribution comes from deriving optimality results for key pre-distribution scheme on this combined graph expressed as a function of properties of the resulting graph. We are able to show that if one requires a key pre-distribution mechanism which is both efficient and secure then combined network graph with shared key graph need to have good expansion properties.

1.2 Remainder of This Paper

In section-2 we define some basic terminologies. We describe random key pre-distribution scheme and show how a set system or combinatorial design can be used as a deterministic key pre-distribution scheme. In section-3 we derive optimality results for key pre-distribution scheme. Following which we compare the derived parameters in this work with other known results in section-4.

2 Key Pre-distribution Mechanism

2.1 Randomized KPS

First we describe the random key pre-distribution schemes. Random key pre-distribution scheme works by selecting a *pool of keys* X from some pre-specified *key-space* of size $|X| = n$. Each node is then assigned a random subset of keys generated by sampling X by a fixed number of times l. The idea is that after deployment, any two nodes can initiate communication with the common key if they have one. Thus a *randomized*-**KPS** is defined by a set X and a family of subsets of X, $\mathcal{A} = \{A_1, A_2, \ldots, A_m\}$, where $\forall i, |A_i| = l$ is the size of *key-ring*.

2.2 Deterministic KPS

Now we describe deterministic key pre-distribution schemes. A *set system* or *combinatorial design* $(X, \mathcal{A})$ consists of a finite set X of elements called *points*, $X = \{x_1, x_2, \ldots, x_n\}$, and a family of subsets of X, i.e. $\mathcal{A} = \{A_1, A_2, \ldots, A_m\}$, with $A_j \subseteq X, \forall j : 1 \leq j \leq m$ called *blocks*. If all blocks are of same size, say l, then $(X, \mathcal{A})$ is said to be *uniform design* (of rank l). A set system $(X, \mathcal{A})$ can be used to design a *deterministic*-**KPS** for DSNs as follows. Let us denote the sensor nodes by $\mathcal{U} = \{u_1, u_2, \ldots, u_m\}$. We then identify each block $A_i \in \mathcal{A}$ with one sensor node $u_i \in \mathcal{U}$, and we identify the ground set X as the set of n keys. Then, for $1 \leq j \leq m$, sensor node u_i receives the set of keys in block A_i.

2.3 Vital Parameters

Let $(X, \mathcal{A})$ be a **KPS** (deterministic or randomized). As noted in previous section, several proposals exists for key pre-distribution in DSN, however, with a possible loss in specific cases, one could unify them. Almost all **KPS** has three important design objectives, namely: (1) A pre-distribution of shares, (2) Shared key discovery, and establishing path keys when two nodes do not share a key, (3) Resiliency of the network under node capture. We have already described the step pre-distribution of shares. In shared key discovery phase nodes interact in their neighborhood to assess possible common shares. Hence, possibility of finding a neighbor having common key depends on distribution scheme, as well as network topology. Objective of path key establishment is to have a secure communication link between a pair of nodes which do not share a common key, but through their neighbors with which they have common key they can establish a secure path. For resiliency observe that when a sensor node is compromised all its l keys will become unusable. We need to consider how many secure links will still exist in the network. Assume u_a, u_b and u_c are three nodes sharing a common key. If u_c is compromised then u_a and u_b can no longer communicate, as their only common key is assumed to be compromised now, however they may still be able to establish a path key (with extra communication cost). In sequel we formally define these parameters and conditions under which we say optimality is achieved.

2.4 Optimality Considerations

For any of the above key pre-distribution schemes, parameters we will be interested about are from two directions, *efficiency*, and *security*. Efficiency in fact captures several aspects of the design. First, for every network of size $m > 1$ we must be able to provide a construction using as small share per-node as possible. We capture this in the following definition:

Definition 1. (Share Size Optimal KPS): *A key pre-distribution scheme* $(X, \mathcal{A})$ *with* $|X| = n$, *and* $|\mathcal{A}| = m$, *where the size of each set* $A_i \in \mathcal{A}$ *is* l *will be calld a* (m, l, n)-**KPS**. *For a fixed* $|X| = n$, *a* (m, l, n)-**KPS** *is share size optimal if it achieves minimum* l *and maximum* m.

Few comments are in place about Definition-1. Note that X is identified with the key-pool. Hence, idea of defining optimality with respect to fixed $|X| = n$ and achieving smallest l and maximum m implies supporting maximum size network (m) using smallest share size per node (l). A more constructive definition is indeed possible, where one may require that, given m, l, n and i one can generate the share for ith node A_i efficiently (possibly in time polynomial in $(\log m, l, n)$, however we will not consider the optimality issue from computational perspective in this work.

Second aspect of an efficient design is the ability to form a secure network. As described above this has two objectives, having shared key in the neighborhood, and having path key between any pairs. Two sensor nodes u_i and $u_j \in \mathcal{U}$, share a key if and only if $A_i \cap A_j \neq \emptyset$, and they are neighbors on the network graph. We would like to have at least one node in the neighborhood for a node with which it shares a key.

Condition to ensure the existence of path key between any pair of nodes is slightly complicated. To be able to establish a path key between u_i and $u_j \in \mathcal{U}$ we must have following: Let $P_{i,j}$ be the set of all possible paths between u_i and u_j, then to be able to establish a path key there must be at least one path (denoted by natural sequence of vertices on network graph) $p = u_i u_k \ldots u_j \in P_{i,j}$ such that there is a common key between every consecutive pair of vertices in p. Formally:

Definition 2. (Connectivity Optimal KPS): *Let* $(X, \mathcal{A})$ *be a* **KPS** *(deterministic or randomized). Then we shall call* $(X, \mathcal{A})$ *a* (ϵ, k)-*connectivity optimal* **KPS** *if for any pair of nodes* u *and* v, *the probability that they can establish a path-key over shortest path of length* k *is greater than* ϵ, *where the probability is taken over all pairwise vertices of the network graph.*

Final consideration is the security. Again looking at the key sharing graph and the network graph, we can estimate that any chosen pair of nodes will not have a secure link when a fraction of nodes are compromised in the network.

Definition 3. (Resiliency Optimal KPS): *Let* $(X, \mathcal{A})$ *be a* **KPS** *(deterministic or randomized). Then for* $\gamma, \delta \in \mathbb{R}$ *and* $0 \leq \gamma, \delta \leq 1$ *we shall call* $(X, \mathcal{A})$ *a* (γ, δ)-*resiliency optimal* **KPS** *if with probability greater than* γ *remaining* $(1 - \delta)$ *fraction of the network can establish secure connection even when a* δ *fraction of nodes are compromised.*

Following Table (Table-1) lists the parameters.

3   Optimality of KPS

We have described the set of desired properties of key-pre-distribution scheme for a DSN. Next we will derive the condition that achieves the optimal values for

Table 1. Design Parameters

Parameter	Meaning	Objective
n	Key-pool size	Fixed
m	Network size	Maximize
l	Share size	Minimize
ϵ	Key sharing probability	Maximize
k	Key path length	Minimize
γ	Resiliency	Maximize
δ	Fraction compromised	Maximize

the set of parameters as described in definition-1, definition-2, and in definition-3. In following we shall denote the key sharing graph by $\mathcal{G}$ with a associated set-system $(X, \mathcal{A})$. We shall also by $\mathcal{H}$ denote the network graph of the sensor nodes. Graph $\mathcal{G}$ has vertex set $\mathcal{A}$, and two vertex A_i and A_j are connected by an edge iff $A_i \cap A_j \neq \emptyset$.

Modeling $\mathcal{H}$ is somewhat delicate. Since sensor nodes are randomly deployed in a geographic region, it might appear a random graph might be suitable as a network model. In their work Eschenauer and Gligor [13] considered random graph model and used classical result of Erdös and Rényi [12] on connectivity. Erdös and Rényi model allows one to relate local connectivity(i.e., the probability that two nodes are connected) and the global connectivity (i.e., the probability that the whole network is connected). However, model used in [13], and many other subsequent works on *randomized*-**KPS** has been questioned recently ([14,21]), as most of these works assumed that the underlying physical network is dense enough to enable their key pre-distribution to be effective. This issue can be stated as follows: assuming sensors are deployed in a two-dimensional plane, by placing each node uniformly and independently at a random location, let us also assume that nodes can transmit at various power levels, then a combination of these two factor determines the relation between global vs. local connectivity. As an example, if we assume that the given network is connected - what can we say about the degree of each node?

To characterize $\mathcal{H}$ we will use a result of Xue and P. R. Kumar [22]. Let $\mathcal{S}$ be a unit square in $\mathbb{R}^2$, and suppose n nodes identified with set $V : |V| = m$ are placed uniformly and independently in $\mathcal{S}$. Then $\mathcal{H}$ is the network graph formed when each node is connected to its neighborhood. More precisely, there exists an edge between $u, v \in V$ if when $u \in \mathcal{N}(v)$, where $\forall u \in V, \mathcal{N}(u) \stackrel{\Delta}{=} \{v : (u, v) \in E\}$. We also assume this implies $v \in \mathcal{N}(u)$, in other words we consider undirected network graphs. If $\forall u \in V, |\mathcal{N}(u)| = \phi_m$, then main result by Xue and P. R. Kumar can be stated as:

Theorem 1. [22] :*For $\mathcal{H}(m, \phi_m)$ to be asymptotically connected, $\Theta(\log m)$ neighbors are necessary and sufficient. Specifically, there are two constants $0 < c_1 < c_2$ such that:*

$$\lim_{m \to \infty} \mathbf{Pr}\left[\mathcal{H}\left(m, c_1 \log m\right) \text{ is disconnected}\right] = 1 \text{ and} \tag{1}$$

$$\lim_{m \to \infty} \mathbf{Pr}\left[\mathcal{H}\left(m, c_2 \log m\right) \text{ is connected}\right] = 1. \tag{2}$$

It is possible to choose $c_1 = 0.074$ and $c_2 = 5.1774$, however the critical value of the constant is unknown.

With Theorem-1, when we write $\mathcal{H}$, we will essentially mean $\mathcal{H}(n, \phi_m)$, where ϕ_m is of order $\Theta(\log m)$. Given $\mathcal{G} = (V, E)$ and $\mathcal{H} = (V, T)$ (note, both of them are defined on the same set of vertices), to "embed" $\mathcal{G}$ over $\mathcal{H}$ we consider the product $\mathcal{G} \cdot \mathcal{H}$ - defined as the graph whose vertex set is the Cartesian product $V \times V$ in which vertices (u, v) and (u', v') are adjacent if u, u' are either equal or adjacent in $\mathcal{G}$ and v, v' are either equal or adjacent in $\mathcal{H}$. Observe that when (u, u') has non-empty intersection on $\mathcal{G}$ and (v, v') are adjacent on $\mathcal{H}$, (u, v) and (u', v') has a secure link on $\mathcal{G} \cdot \mathcal{H}$.

3.1   Outline of Proof

Now observe that in order to establish the optimality of the desired parameters, we need to express them in terms of the properties of the graph $\mathcal{G} \cdot \mathcal{H}$. Our proof is based on techniques used in [3] and also following methods and tools used by Alon in [2]. This method (dimension argument) can be described as follows. We wish to bound the size of some finite combinatorially defined set of objects A. To do this, we first map the elements of A to a linearly independent set of vectors in some vector space V. Then we apply the dimension argument: $|A| \leq \dim V$. On this direction we will take following steps:

1. First we will require a common mechanism to represent $\mathcal{G}$ and $\mathcal{H}$. We will do this by considering a subspace of the space of polynomials in m variables over $\mathbb{R}$. A representation of a graph of order m over such subspace is an assignment of a polynomial f_v to each vertex v along with a point of evaluation of the polynomial c_v in $\mathbb{R}^m$ to each vertex such that $f_v(c_v) \neq 0$ but if $(u, v) \in E(G)$ then $f_v(c_u) = 0$. To combine $\mathcal{G}$ and $\mathcal{H}$ we consider the Tensor product of corresponding vector spaces which represents $\mathcal{G}$ and $\mathcal{H}$, and obtain a combined graph as tensor product $\mathcal{G} \cdot \mathcal{H}$.

2. Once we have a representation of the graph $\mathcal{G} \cdot \mathcal{H}$ we derive the desired parameters expressed in terms of the vector space representing $\mathcal{G} \cdot \mathcal{H}$. A simple proposition suggests that in order to ensure any two node have a secure key-path, they must be in same connected component of the product graph $\mathcal{G} \cdot \mathcal{H}$.

3. We consider $\mathcal{G} \cdot \mathcal{H}$ as a d-regular undirected graph (we justify this choice). Now we observe that a graph is connected iff its second largest eigenvalue of the adjacency matrix λ_2 is greater than 0 (first eigenvalue λ_1 is same as the degree d), and $\lambda_1 > \lambda_2$.

4. This characterization allows us to choose l optimally so that the graph $\mathcal{G} \cdot \mathcal{H}$ is connected, and based on which we derive other parameters.

3.2   Combining Graphs

In following to present our results, we first provide a geometric view of the combined key sharing graph $\mathcal{G}$ and network graph $\mathcal{H}$. Let $G = (V, E)$ be a graph of order m and let $\mathcal{F}$ be a subspace of the space of polynomials in m variables over $\mathbb{R}$. A representation of G over $\mathcal{F}$ is an assignment of a polynomial $f_v \in \mathcal{F}$ to each vertex $v \in V$ along with an assignment of a point $c_v \in \mathbb{R}^m$ to each $v \in V$ such that following two conditions hold:

1. For each $v \in V$, $f_v(c_v) \neq 0$.
2. If $(u, v) \in E(G)$ then $f_v(c_u) = 0$.

We need few notations first. Let $[n] = \{1, 2, \ldots, n\}$. With each set $A_i \subseteq [n]$ we associate its characteristic vector $v_i = (v_{i1}, v_{i2}, \ldots, v_{in}) \in \mathbb{R}^n$ where $v_{ij} = 1$ if $j \in A_i$ and $v_{ij} = 0$ otherwise. For $x, y \in \mathbb{R}^n$, let $x \cdot y = \sum_{i=1}^{n} x_i y_i$ denote their standard inner product.

Lemma 1. *Key-sharing graph $\mathcal{G}(m, l, n)$ has a representation over $\mathcal{P}$, where $\mathcal{P}$ is a subspace of the space of polynomials in n-variables of degree at most $l - 1$ over $\mathbb{R}$.*

Proof. Let $(X, \mathcal{A})$ be the **KPS**. $\mathcal{G}$ has vertex set $V(\mathcal{G})$ where each $v \in V(\mathcal{G})$ can be identified with a subset $A_i \subseteq X$, and $|A_i| = l$. Let $A_1, A_2, \ldots, A_m$ be the vertex set of $\mathcal{G}$. By construction, in the vertex set of $\mathcal{G}$, between vertex A_i and A_j there is an edge iff $|A_i \cap A_j| \neq \emptyset$. Using notations defined above clearly we have $v_i \cdot v_j = |A_i \cap A_j|$, where v is the characteristic vector of set A. For $i = 1, \ldots, m$, for each $A_i \in \mathcal{A}$ let us define the following polynomials $P_i(x_1, \ldots, x_n)$ on n variables:

$$\forall i : 1 \leq i \leq m, P_i(x_1, \ldots, x_n) \overset{\Delta}{=} \prod_{k=1}^{l-1} \left(\sum_{j \in A_i} x_i - k \right)$$

For each set A_i let us assign polynomial P_i and a point $c_i = v_i$, the characteristic vector of the set A_i to vertex i. Clearly,

$$\forall i : 1 \leq i \leq m, P_i(c_i) \neq 0, \text{ and}$$
$$\forall i, j : 1 \leq i \neq j \leq m, \text{ and } A_i \cap A_j \neq \emptyset, P_i(c_j) = 0.$$

Let p_i be the multilinear polynomial obtained from the standard representation of P_i as a sum of monomials by using, repeatedly, the relations $x_i^2 = x_i$. Since the vectors $c_i = v_i$ have $\{0, 1\}$ coordinates, $p_i(c_j) = P_i(c_j)$ for all A_i and A_j, and graph $\mathcal{G}$ has a representation over $\mathcal{P}$, where $\mathcal{P}$ is a subspace of the space of polynomials in n-variables. Also observe that the degree of multilinear polynomial $\deg(p_i) \leq l - 1$, completing the proof. $\qquad \square$

For a graph $G = (V, E)$ define neighborhood graph $NB(G)$ as: $\forall i \in V(G)$ let $\mathcal{N}_i = \{j : (i, j) \in E(G)\}$, then $NB(G) = (V_{NB}, E_{NB}) : V_{NB} = \{\mathcal{N}_i\}_{\forall i \in V(G)}$ and $(\mathcal{N}_i, \mathcal{N}_j) \in E_{NB} \iff \mathcal{N}_i \cap \mathcal{N}_j \neq \emptyset$.

Lemma 2. *Let* $\mathcal{H}(m, \phi_m)$ *be a network-graph, then* $NB(\mathcal{H}(m, \phi_m))$ *has a representation over* $\mathcal{Q}$, *where* $\mathcal{Q}$ *is a subspace of the space of polynomials in* m-*variables of degree at most* $\phi_m - 1$ *over* $\mathbb{R}$.

Proof. Recall, ϕ_m is the cardinality of neighborhood for every vertex $i \in V(\mathcal{H})$, and observe that for the graph $\mathcal{H}$ to be disconnected, following must hold:

1. $\forall i \in V(\mathcal{H}), |\mathcal{N}_i| = \phi_m$, and
2. There exists at least two connected component $H_1 = (V_1, E_1)$ and $H_2 = (V_2, E_2)$, such that $V(\mathcal{H}) = V_1 \cup V_2$, $V_1 \cap V_2 = \emptyset$, and $E(\mathcal{H}) = E_1 \cup E_2$.

For each vertex $i \in V(\mathcal{H})$ define neighborhood of i as the set A_i. For the neighborhood of each vertex $1 \leq i \leq m, \mathcal{N}_i$ let us define the following polynomials $Q_i(y_1, \ldots, y_m)$ on m variables:

$$\forall i : 1 \leq i \leq m, Q_i(y_1, \ldots, y_m) \triangleq \prod_{t=1}^{\phi_m - 1} \left(\sum_{j \in \mathcal{N}_i} y_j - t \right)$$

For each set $\mathcal{N}_i$ let us assign polynomial Q_i and a point $d_i = v_i$, the characteristic vector of the set $\mathcal{N}_i$. Lemma follows using similar argument as above considering space of multilinear polynomials q_i of degree $\deg q_i \leq \phi_m - 1$. □

Lemma-2 is for the neighborhood graph of $\mathcal{H}$. While we need to show that $\mathcal{H}$ has a similar property. Following lemma asserts that.

Lemma 3. $\mathcal{H}(m, \phi_m)$ *has a representation over* $\mathcal{Q}$ *iff* $NB(\mathcal{H}(m, \phi_m))$ *has a representation over* $\mathcal{Q}$ *and* $\mathcal{H}(m, \phi_m)$ *is connected, moreover* $\mathcal{Q}$ *is a subspace of the space of polynomials in* m-*variables of degree at most* ϕ_m *over* $\mathbb{R}$.

Proof. By Lemma-2, $NB(\mathcal{H}(m, \phi_m))$ has a representation over $\mathcal{Q}$ as

$$\left\{ \prod_{t=1}^{\phi_m - 1} \left(\sum_{j \in \mathcal{N}_i} y_j - t \right), d_i : i \in V(\mathcal{H}) \right\}$$

Then we can represent $\mathcal{H}$ over $\mathcal{Q}$ by considering

$$\left\{ Q'_i = y_i \cdot \prod_{t=1}^{\phi_m - 1} \left(\sum_{j \in \mathcal{N}_i} y_j - t \right), (0, 0, \ldots, 1, \ldots, 0)^T + d_i : i \in V(\mathcal{H}) \right\}$$

for ith vertex in $V(\mathcal{H})$, only ith entry of the vector $v'_i = (0, 0, \ldots, 1, \ldots, 0)^T$ is 1 and other entries are 0. Observe that $Q'_i(v'_i + d_j) \neq 0 \iff i = j$. Also, polynomials are defined over the space $\mathcal{Q}$ and have degree at most ϕ_m. □

Lemma-1 and Lemma-3 provides a characterization of the graphs $\mathcal{G}$ and $\mathcal{H}$ as a vector space of polynomials $\mathcal{P}$ and $\mathcal{Q}$ over the same field, and we can combine them now considering the space spanned by the polynomials $p(x_1, x_2, \ldots, x_n) \cdot q(y_1, y_2, \ldots, y_m)$ where $p \in \mathcal{P}$ and $q \in \mathcal{Q}$ using *tensor product* $\mathcal{P} \otimes \mathcal{Q}$ of the two vector spaces. We have the following lemma.

Lemma 4. *[2]: Let $\mathcal{G} = (V, E)$ and $\mathcal{H} = (V, T)$ be two graphs. Assume $\mathcal{G}$ has a representation $\{p_v (x_1, x_2, \ldots, x_l), c_v : v \in V\}$ over $\mathcal{P}$ and $\mathcal{H}$ has a representation $\{q_u (y_1, y_2, \ldots, y_r), d_u : u \in V\}$ over $\mathcal{Q}$, where $\mathcal{P}$ and $\mathcal{Q}$ are spaces of polynomials over the same field $\mathbb{R}$. Then $\{p_v \cdot q_u, c_v d_u : (v, u) \in V \times V\}$ is a representation of the graph product of $\mathcal{G}$ and $\mathcal{H}$ as $\mathcal{G} \cdot \mathcal{H}$ over $\mathcal{P} \otimes \mathcal{Q}$, where $c_v d_u$ denotes the concatenation of c_v and d_u.*

Proof. Observe, for every $((u, v), (u', v')) \in V \times V$,

$$p_v \cdot q_u (c_{v'} d_{u'}) = p_v (c_{v'}) \cdot q_u (d_{u'}).$$

Product is non-zero when $c_v d_u = c_{v'} d_{u'}$ and it is zero when $((u, v), (u', v'))$ is an edge. Hence this is indeed a representation of $\mathcal{G} \cdot \mathcal{H}$ over $\mathcal{P} \otimes \mathcal{Q}$.   □

3.3 Expressing Parameters by Properties of Product Graph

While, we have a characterization of the graph $\mathcal{H}$ to be connected by Theorem-1, we need to establish such criteria for the graph $\mathcal{G} \cdot \mathcal{H}$ in terms of ϕ_m and l. Observe that, by Theorem-1, choosing ϕ_m we can ensure connectivity of the network graph $\mathcal{H}$ and also there exists a choice of l (though smallest l which will ensure connected graph might not be trivial to derive) which ensures the connectivity in key-sharing graph $\mathcal{G}$, we need to establish a condition on the product graph $\mathcal{G} \cdot \mathcal{H}$ such that any two node can establish a secure key-path. Following proposition provides a necessary condition for that.

Proposition 1. *Let $\mathcal{H}$ be the network graph and let $\mathcal{G}$ be the key-sharing graph. On $\mathcal{H}$ any two vertices u and u' can establish a secure key path $p = uu_1 \ldots u_k u'$ such that there is a common key between every consecutive pair of vertices in p iff product graph $\mathcal{G} \cdot \mathcal{H}$ has a connected component $T = V_T, E_T$ and vertices (v, u) and (v', u') such that both $(v, u), (v', u') \in V_T$.*

Proof. Proof of this proposition is straightforward. First note that a connected component of a graph induces a partition on its vertex set. Now, between two vertices (v, u) and (v', u') on the product graph there is an edge, iff (v, v') is an edge in $\mathcal{G}$ and (u, u') is an edge in $\mathcal{H}$. Extending it for path is simple and we omit it.   □

We can use the simple proposition for choosing ϕ_m (we will do that as per Theorem-1), with a bound on l so that $\mathcal{G} \cdot \mathcal{H}$ is connected. However, to make things simpler, we would like the graph $\mathcal{G} \cdot \mathcal{H}$ to be d-regular, for some $d > 0$. Recall, a graph G is d-regular when every vertex in G has exactly d neighbors. Justification for this choice can be found in the following proposition:

Proposition 2. *For every integer $m, d > 0$, if there exists a graph on m vertices with average degree $\delta (G) = d$, then there exists a d-regular graph G' which is at least as much optimal (connectivity, and resiliency) as much G is.*

Proof. Let G' be a d-regular graph which is (ϵ', k')-connectivity optimal, and (γ', δ')-resiliency optimal. We need to show that for any G with average degree

$\delta\left(G\right) = d$, such that G is (ϵ, k)-connectivity optimal, and (γ, δ)-resiliency optimal. Then when $k = k'$ we have $\epsilon \leq \epsilon'$. Similarly, when $\delta = \delta'$ we have $\gamma \leq \gamma'$.

Connectivity:

$$
\begin{aligned}
\epsilon &= \mathbf{Pr}_{u,v \in G} \left[\exists \text{ a path of length } k \text{ between } u, v\right] \\
&= \mathbf{Pr}_{u,v \in G} \left[(u, v) \in E\left(G^k\right)\right] \\
&= \mathbf{Pr}_{u,w \in G} \left[(u, w) \in E\left(G^{\lceil k/2 \rceil}\right)\right] \mathbf{Pr}_{u,w \in G} \left[(w, v) \in E\left(G^{\lfloor k/2 \rfloor}\right)\right] \\
&= \left(\mathbf{Pr}_{u',v' \in G} \left[(u', v') \in E\left(G\right)\right]\right)^k \\
&\leq \left(\mathbf{Pr}_{u',v' \in G'} \left[(u, v) \in E\left(G'\right)\right]\right)^k \leq \left(\mathbf{Pr}_{u,v \in G'} \left[(u, v) \in E\left(G'^k\right)\right]\right) \leq \epsilon'
\end{aligned}
$$

Where, the third line follows by considering the probability that there exists a $t < k$ and a vertex w such that $(u, w) \in E\left(G^t\right)$ and $(w, v) \in E\left(G^{k-t}\right)$, and repeating it ($G^r$ is the rth power of G, where every r length path in G is an edge in G^r). Inequality follows from the fact that $\mathbf{Pr}_{u,v \in G} \left[(u, v) \in E\left(G\right)\right] \leq \mathbf{Pr}_{u,v \in G'} \left[(u, v) \in E\left(G'\right)\right]$, by noting a regular graph induces uniform probability distribution and G has average degree equal to d. A similar result can be obtained for resiliency. $\qquad\square$

Now our objective is to choose a bound on l so that graph $\mathcal{G} \cdot \mathcal{H}$ is connected. We have $\phi_m = \Theta\left(\log m\right)$ and we will assume that the combined graph is regular, and we are sure by Proposition-2 that this will not be any loss of generality.

Lemma 5. *If $\phi_m = \Theta\left(\log m\right)$ and $l \geq \mathcal{O}\left(1\right)$ then graph $\mathcal{G} \cdot \mathcal{H}$ is a (m, d, λ)-connected graph with number of vertice $m = \left(en/l\right)^l$, degree $d = 2l \log en/l$, and expansion ratio $1 - \lambda$.*

Proof. We first present a result for a graph $G = (V, E)$ of order m which is d-regular, and then extend it to our graph $\mathcal{G} \cdot \mathcal{H}$. Let A_G be the $m \times m$ symmetric adjacency matrix of a graph G. A_G is real and symmetric, and has m real eigenvalues which we denote by $\lambda_1 \geq \lambda_2 \geq \ldots \geq \lambda_m$. An associated orthonormal system of eigenvectors are $v_1, \ldots, v_m$ with $A v_i = \lambda_i v_i$. Note that $\lambda_1 = d$, and it is obtained for all one vector $\mathbf{1}$. Note that eigenvalues are closely related to connectedness of a graph. A graph is connected iff $\lambda_1 > \lambda_2$.

Let $S \subset V\left(G\right)$ be a subset of the vertex set. A cut of G is $S \subset V\left(G\right)$ such that $\left|E\left(S, \bar{S}\right)\right| = e\left(S, \bar{S}\right) = 0$, where for any $S \subset V\left(G\right)$ by $\bar{S}$ we denote the set $V \setminus S$, and $E\left(X, Y\right)$ denotes the set of cross edges between $X, Y \subset V\left(G\right)$. We note that a graph is connected iff it has no cuts.

Consider vector $\mathbf{v} = \left|\bar{S}\right| v_S - \left|S\right| v_{\bar{S}}$, where $v_X \in \{0, 1\}^m$ denotes the characteristic vector of set X. Clearly $\mathbf{v} \perp \mathbf{1}$, and

$$
\|\mathbf{v}\|^2 = \left|\bar{S}\right|^2 |S| + |S|^2 \left|\bar{S}\right| = \left|\bar{S}\right| |S| \left(|S| + \left|\bar{S}\right|\right) = m |S| \left|\bar{S}\right|
$$

Also,

$$
\mathbf{v} A \mathbf{v}^T = 2 \left(\left|E\left(S\right)\right| \left|\bar{S}\right|^2 + \left|E\left(\bar{S}\right)\right| |S|^2 - |S| \left|\bar{S}\right| \left|E\left(S, \bar{S}\right)\right|\right)
$$

As, G is d-regular so substituting $2\,|E\,(S)| = d\,|S| - |E\,(S,\bar{S})|$ and $2\,|E\,(\bar{S})| = d\,|\bar{S}| - |E\,(S,\bar{S})|$, we obtain:

$$\mathbf{v}A\mathbf{v}^T = md\,|S|\,|\bar{S}| - m^2\,|E\,(S,\bar{S})|$$

This allows us to compute λ_2 by computing the *Rayleigh quotient*:

$$\lambda_2 \geq \frac{\mathbf{v}A\mathbf{v}^T}{\|\mathbf{v}\|^2} = d - \frac{m\,|E\,(S,\bar{S})|}{|S|\,|\bar{S}|} \geq d - 2\,|E\,(S,\bar{S})|\,/\,|S|, \text{ with } |S| \leq m/2$$

Now observe that we have $\lambda_1 = d > \lambda_2 \geq d - 2\,|E\,(S,\bar{S})|\,/\,|S|$, in order to ensure that the graph is connected. Hence for every $S \subseteq V\,(G)\,, |S| \leq m/2$, we must ensure that the term $2\,|E\,(S,\bar{S})|\,/\,|S|$ is away from 0, but less than d. Define

$$h\,(G) \overset{\Delta}{=} \min_{S:|S|\leq m/2} |E\,(S,\bar{S})|\,/\,|S|.$$

as the expansion ratio of graph G. Define a graph G with $\lambda_2/d \leq \lambda : \lambda < 1$ as (m, d, λ)-graph G. We have following claim:

Claim. If $\mathcal{G}$ is an (m, d_g, λ_g)-graph and $\mathcal{H}$ is an (m, d_h, λ_h)-graph, then $\mathcal{G} \cdot \mathcal{H}$ is an $(m^2, d_g d_h, \max\,(\lambda_g, \lambda_h))$-graph.

Proof. Considering the normalized adjacency matrix of graph $\mathcal{G}$ and $\mathcal{H}$ and observing that normalized adjacency matrix of graph $\mathcal{G} \cdot \mathcal{H}$ is the tensor product of these two matrices. Thus eigenvalues are pairwise products of eigenvalues of $\mathcal{G}$ and $\mathcal{H}$. Largest eigenvalue is thus $\mathbf{1} \cdot \mathbf{1}$, and second largest eigenvalue must be either $\mathbf{1} \cdot \lambda_h$ or $\lambda_g \cdot \mathbf{1}$.   □

To obtain a bound on l we must relate $h\,(\mathcal{G} \cdot \mathcal{H})$ to l. By the last paragraph, it will sufficient for us to consider $\mathcal{G}$ as an (m, d_g, λ_g)-graph with $\lambda_g \geq \lambda_h$. Let d be the degree of $\mathcal{G} \cdot \mathcal{H}$, and choose $d_g = d/d_h = d/\log m$, note that this choice is feasible by Lemma-4. Thus we have $h\,(\mathcal{G} \cdot \mathcal{H}) \geq d\,(1 - \lambda_g)\,/2\log m$. On the other hand if $l < n/2$ size subsets of $[n]$ are chosen, then degree of any vertex on $\mathcal{G}$ can be at most

$$\sum_{i=1}^{l-1} \binom{n}{i} \leq l\left(\frac{en}{l}\right)^l$$

We can possibly support large network (i.e. have a large m) if we allow large degree, but our objective will be to have a low degree graph with good expansion ratio. This implies d must be of order $\mathcal{O}\,(\log m)$. This gives us the (m, d, λ)-connected graph with number of vertices $m = (en/l)^l$, degree $d = 2l\log\,(en/l)$, and expansion ratio $1 - \lambda$, when $l = \mathcal{O}\,(1)$.

               □

3.4   Optimality Results

Now we establish bounds on the desired parameters. Intuitively, on the product graph $\mathcal{G} \cdot \mathcal{H}$ vertices can establish secure link directly (resp. by a key path) if they have an edge (resp. they are in same connected component). Notice that all vertices that belongs to a clique on product graph $\mathcal{G} \cdot \mathcal{H}$ has pair-wise secure link. Thus cliques on this graph ensure more number of secure connectivity. On the other hand when a vertex is compromised, all other vertices belonging to the same clique are also compromised, thus larger independent set ensures more resiliency. This seems contradictory - but not so, when graph has small cliques and many of them. Concretely, if there is no small set S for which $\mathcal{G} \cdot \mathcal{H} \setminus S$ has one very large component and many small ones then both requirements are met. In other words we show that graph having neither large clique, nor large independent set are best for product graph $\mathcal{G} \cdot \mathcal{H}$ if they also have good expansion ratio. We note the following fact (known as Expander Mixing Lemma) implying large expansion ratio implies the graph is nearly random:

Lemma 6. *Let $G = (V, E)$ be a d-regular graph. Then for all $S, T \subseteq V(G)$:*

$$\left| |E(S,T)| - \frac{d\,|S|\,|T|}{m} \right| \leq \lambda_2 \sqrt{|S|\,|T|}. \tag{3}$$

Now we need to answer the following question concerning definition-2: for a randomly chosen pair of vertices u and v, what is the probability that they have a path of length k.

Lemma 7. *Let $\mathcal{G} \cdot \mathcal{H}$ be a $\left((en/l)^l, 2l \log (en/l), \lambda \right)$ graph, then corresponding* **KPS** *is $(\mathcal{O}(\log n), \mathcal{O}(1))$ - connectivity optimal.*

Proof. The distance $d(u, v)$ between vertices u and v in a graph $G = (V, E)$ is the length of the shortest path between them. The diameter of G can be defined as $\max_{u,v} \{d(u,v)\}$. Also $B(u, r) = \{v : d(u, v) \leq r\}$, is the ball or radius r around u. We claim that an (m, d, λ)-graph G has diameter $\mathcal{O}(\log m)$. This follows from fact that $|B(u, r)| > m/2$ for every vertex u and some $r \in \mathcal{O}(\log m)$. This, in turn follows from G's expansion properties. Namely, we show that $|B(u, r + 1)| > (1 + \epsilon) |B(u, r)|$ for some fixed $\epsilon > 0$ as long as $|B(u, r)| \leq m/2$. We have by Lemma-6 that $|E(S, S)| / |S| \leq d \cdot (|S|/m + \lambda)$ for every set S. Therefore, $|E(S, \bar{S})| / |S| \geq d \cdot ((1 - \lambda) - |S|/m)$. But S has at least $|E(S, \bar{S})|/d$ neighbors outside of itself, so the claim follows with $\epsilon = 1/2 - \lambda$.

Now to compute connectivity parameter, we note following:

$$\mathbf{Pr}_{u,v} [u \text{ and } v \text{ has path of length } k \leq \mathcal{O}(\log m)] \geq \mathcal{O}(1)$$

$\square$

Similarly, for resiliency:

Lemma 8. *Let $\mathcal{G} \cdot \mathcal{H}$ be a $\left((en/l)^l, 2l \log (en/l), \lambda \right)$ graph, then corresponding* **KPS** *is $(\delta/(1 - \lambda) l \log n, \delta)$-resiliency optimal for all $\delta > 0$.*

Proof. It is sufficient to estimate the probability of the size of a cut on the product graph $\mathcal{G} \cdot \mathcal{H}$, i.e.:

$$\mathbf{Pr}_{u,v} \left[u, v \text{ has path when } \delta \text{ fraction of nodes are compromised } \right] \geq$$
$$\mathbf{Pr}_{u,v} \left[u, v \text{ is in different component when } \delta m \text{ nodes are removed } \right] =$$
$$\mathbf{Pr} \left[\delta m \text{ is a minimum cut } \right] = \frac{\delta m}{md \left(1 - \lambda \right)}$$

□

Finally, we combine these to obtain the following theorem:

Theorem 2. *There exists a* **KPS** *with*
n size key-pool, $m = \mathcal{O} \left(n^l \right)$ size network, $l \geq \mathcal{O} \left(1 \right)$ size key ring,
$k = \mathcal{O} \left(\log n \right)$ with $\epsilon = \mathcal{O} \left(1 \right)$,
$\gamma = \delta / \left[\left(1 - \lambda \right) l \log n \right]$ with δ fraction compromised nodes.

4   Concluding Remarks

In this work we have introduced a realistic model to analyze the efficiency, connectivity and security properties of any key pre-distribution mechanism for DSN. Under this model local vs. global secure connectivity properties has been analyzed using novel linear algebraic methods, and optimality trade-off has been expressed in terms of the expansion properties of the underlying graph. This is, to the best of our knowledge first such asymptotic analysis considering joint optimality and trade-off between storage, connectivity, and resiliency at the same time. Our results are existential, and suggests that the product graph $\mathcal{G} \cdot \mathcal{H}$ shall have good expansion properties to achieve optimal parameters. While a graph can be connected with a bottleneck set S which is small and $G \setminus S$ has one large connected component and many small components. This will not be good for constructing a secure sensor networks. As compromising S will be sufficient to ensure a non-functioning network. It is desired that the product graph $\mathcal{G} \cdot \mathcal{H}$ shall be a expander graph(c.f. [1], A graph $G = (V, E)$ is ϵ-edge-expanding if for every partition of the vertex set V into X and $\bar{X} = V \setminus X$, where X contains at most a half of the vertices, the number of cross edges $e \left(X, \bar{X} \right)$ are greater than $\epsilon \left| X \right|$) . Challenge for DSN is following. One need to design a **KPS** such that when $\mathcal{H}$ is a randomly generated network, embedding $\mathcal{G}$ on $\mathcal{H}$ shall ensure a ϵ-edge-expanding graph $\mathcal{G} \cdot \mathcal{H}$ for some $\epsilon > 0$, and ϵ is bounded away from zero as m, the order of graph grows. Finally, we note that a complementary thought was explored in [20], where authors have shown that some topologies arising naturally in the context of (secure) wireless networking are low-degree, expander graphs. Another interesting recent result strengthens our thought is [8]. In [8], authors have presented a deterministic key distribution scheme based on Expander Graphs. Their paper shows how to map the parameters (e.g., degree, expansion, and diameter) of a Ramanujan Expander Graph to the desired properties of a key distribution scheme for a physical network topology. In other words their work is complementary to this work in exhibiting an explicit example of designing *deterministic-***KPS** using Expander graphs.

We conclude this section with comparison of parameters derived in this work with some of the existing works. It must be noted that there are significant trade-offs between the parameters we have discussed. Also it must be noted that each of these works improve on one or more parameters while loosing on the other. What we derive in this work is the optimal value that is jointly achievable for parameters. We refer reader to an excellent survey on key distribution mechanisms by Çamtepe and Yener [7]. Following table (Table-2) lists design parameters derived in this work along with (a) exhaustive pair-wise key distribution scheme, (b) basic probabilistic scheme of [13], (c) random pair-wise scheme of [10], and (d) symmetric BIBD based deterministic scheme of [6]. In the table $\mathcal{O}(1)$ in probability implies constant probability, field with '-' implies not directly derivable, G indicates dependent on network graph.

Table 2. Comparison of Design Parameters

Solution	Ref.	n	m	l	k	ϵ	γ	δ
Exhaustive Pair-wise	Folklore	-		n	$2(n-1)$	G	$\mathcal{O}(1)$	$\mathcal{O}(1)$	any
Probabilistic	[13]	n	-	$2l$	G	$\frac{((n-l)!)^2}{((n-2l)!n!)}$	l/n	-
Random Pair-wise	[10]	n	-	$2np$	G	p	$\mathcal{O}(1)$	any
symmetric BIBD	[6]	n^2+n+1	n^2	$2n+2$	G	$\mathcal{O}(1)$	$1/n$	-
Expansion	this work	n	n^l	$\mathcal{O}(1)$	$\log n$	$\mathcal{O}(1)$	$\frac{\delta}{l\log n}$	δ

Acknowledgments. Author would like to thank Debapriyay Mukhopadhyay, Ranjeet K. Patro and Satyajit Banerjee for several discussions on these problems. Author would also like to thank the anonymous reviewers of ESAS 2006, for their valuable comments.

References

1. N. Alon. Eigenvalues and expanders. *Combinatorica*, 6(2):83–96, 1986.
2. N. Alon. The shannon capacity of a union. *Combinatorica*, 18(3):301–310, 1998.
3. N. Alon, L. Babai, and H. Suzuki. Multilinear polynomials and Frankl-Ray-Chaudhuri-Wilson type intersection theorems. *J. Comb. Theory Ser. A*, 58(2):165–180, 1991.
4. R. Blom. An optimal class of symmetric key generation systems. In *Proc. of the EUROCRYPT 84 workshop on Advances in cryptology: theory and application of cryptographic techniques*, pages 335–338, New York, NY, USA, 1985. Springer-Verlag New York, Inc.
5. C. Blundo, A. D. Santis, A. Herzberg, S. Kutten, U. Vaccaro, and M. Yung. Perfectly-secure key distribution for dynamic conferences. In *CRYPTO '92: Proceedings of the 12th Annual International Cryptology Conference on Advances in Cryptology*, pages 471–486, London, UK, 1993. Springer-Verlag.
6. S. A. Çamtepe and B. Yener. Combinatorial design of key distribution mechanisms for wireless sensor networks. In *ESORICS*, pages 293–308, 2004.

7. S. A. Çamtepe and B. Yener. Key distribution mechanisms for wireless sensor networks: a survey. RPI Technical Report TR-05-07, RPI, 2005.
8. S. A. Çamtepe, B. Yener, and M. Yung. Expander graph based key distribution mechanisms in wireless sensor networks. In *to appear in IEEE International Conference on Communications (ICC) 2006*, 2006.
9. D. Chakrabarti, S. Maitra, and B. K. Roy. A key pre-distribution scheme for wireless sensor networks: Merging blocks in combinatorial design. In *ISC*, pages 89–103, 2005.
10. H. Chan, A. Perrig, and D. Song. Random key predistribution schemes for sensor networks. In *SP '03: Proceedings of the 2003 IEEE Symposium on Security and Privacy*, page 197, Washington, DC, USA, 2003. IEEE Computer Society.
11. W. Du, J. Deng, Y. S. Han, and P. K. Varshney. A pairwise key pre-distribution scheme for wireless sensor networks. In *CCS '03: Proceedings of the 10th ACM conference on Computer and communications security*, pages 42–51, New York, NY, USA, 2003. ACM Press.
12. P. Erdös and A. Rényi. On the evolution of random graphs. *Institute of Mathematics Hungarian Academy of Sciences*, 5:17–61, 1960.
13. L. Eschenauer and V. D. Gligor. A key-management scheme for distributed sensor networks. In *CCS '02: Proceedings of the 9th ACM conference on Computer and communications security*, pages 41–47, New York, NY, USA, 2002. ACM Press.
14. J. Hwang and Y. Kim. Revisiting random key pre-distribution schemes for wireless sensor networks. In *SASN '04: Proceedings of the 2nd ACM workshop on Security of ad hoc and sensor networks*, pages 43–52, New York, NY, USA, 2004. ACM Press.
15. J. Lee and D. R. Stinson. Deterministic key predistribution schemes for distributed sensor networks. In *Selected Areas in Cryptography*, pages 294–307, 2004.
16. J. Lee and D. R. Stinson. A combinatorial approach to key predistribution for distributed sensor networks. In *IEEE Wireless Communications and Networking Conference*, volume 2, pages 1200–1205, 2005.
17. D. Liu and P. Ning. Establishing pairwise keys in distributed sensor networks. In *CCS '03: Proceedings of the 10th ACM conference on Computer and communications security*, pages 52–61, New York, NY, USA, 2003. ACM Press.
18. D. Liu and P. Ning. Location-based pairwise key establishments for static sensor networks. In *SASN '03: Proceedings of the 1st ACM workshop on Security of ad hoc and sensor networks*, pages 72–82, New York, NY, USA, 2003. ACM Press.
19. D. Liu, P. Ning, and R. Li. Establishing pairwise keys in distributed sensor networks. *ACM Trans. Inf. Syst. Secur.*, 8(1):41–77, 2005.
20. A. Panconesi and J. Radhakrishnan. Expansion properties of (secure) wireless networks. In *SPAA '04: Proceedings of the sixteenth annual ACM symposium on Parallelism in algorithms and architectures*, pages 281–285, New York, NY, USA, 2004. ACM Press.
21. R. D. Pietro, L. V. Mancini, A. Mei, A. Panconesi, and J. Radhakrishnan. Connectivity properties of secure wireless sensor networks. In *SASN '04: Proceedings of the 2nd ACM workshop on Security of ad hoc and sensor networks*, pages 53–58, New York, NY, USA, 2004. ACM Press.
22. F. Xue and P. R. Kumar. The number of neighbors needed for connectivity of wireless networks. *Wirel. Netw.*, 10(2):169–181, 2004.

Cryptographic Protocol to Establish Trusted History of Interactions

Samuel Galice[1], Marine Minier[1], John Mullins[2], and Stéphane Ubéda[1]

[1] CITI INSA-Lyon - ARES INRIA Project
CITI, INSA de Lyon, Bâtiment Léonard de Vinci
21 Avenue Jean Capelle, 69621 Villeurbanne Cedex
FirstName.Name@insa-lyon.fr
[2] Département de génie informatique, École Polytechnique de Montréal,
P.O. Box 6079, Station Centre-ville, Montréal (Québec), Canada, H3C 3A7
john.mullins@polymtl.ca

Abstract. In the context of ambient networks, this article describes a cryptographic protocol called Common History Extraction (CHE) protocol implementing a trust management framework. All the nodes are supposed to share the same cryptographic algorithms and protocols. An entity called imprinting station provides them with two pairs of public/private keys derived from their identities. Also, two strange nodes wanting to initiate an interaction have to build a seed of trust. The trust between two nodes is based on a mutual proof of previous common met nodes.

Keywords: cryptographic protocol, trust management framework, Identity based encryption.

Introduction

Nowadays, wireless communications are a critical aspect of computing devices, and offer open solutions for providing mobility and autonomous actions: a smart device as the center of a Personal Area Network is only one major device in an environment where every object will soon be able to communicate. Devices in radio range can potentially establish self-organized networks of two or more objects. In such a context, the peer-to-peer communication capabilities of smart objects will not be restricted simply to access fixed networks and mobility during the use of more complex services, addressed by means of ad hoc communication capabilities, will necessarily receive more attention.

However without centralized trusted agents, we are facing a risk management problem requiring a specific security model and associated cryptographic techniques. Also, we propose a trust decision based on the use of informations cryptographically proved, to reduce this risk. Roughly, smart devices record past interactions between autonomous nodes in a *history* (after a bootstrap phase); to interact, nodes first search previous common met nodes in their histories; then, they mutually authenticate; and finally, they prove, using a security protocol

L. Buttyan, V. Gligor, and D. Westhoff (Eds.): ESAS 2006, LNCS 4357, pp. 136–149, 2006.
© Springer-Verlag Berlin Heidelberg 2006

presented here, that these common interactions really took place. If the number of such common interactions is sufficient that is, upper a certain threshold, then the interaction may occur [17].

The security protocol proposed here is based on the notion of cryptographic ID first introduced by A. Shamir [25], adapted to elliptic curves by D. Boneh and M. Franklin [5] for the cipher and used by Chen, Zhang and Kim [8] for a signature without a trusted PKG (Private Key Generator). The main advantages to use elliptic curve identity based cryptography is the gain in size and in computational time in adequacy with small devices used in ambient networks such as PDAs or smart phones. Moreover, user's public key being or being derived from his identity, there is no requirement of public key directories. Also, key distribution being far simplified, this make ID-based cryptosystems advantageous over the traditional Public Key Cryptosystems (PKCs).

This paper is organized as follows: section 1 presents relevant approaches concerning trust and trust management framework and specifies the proposed history based trust approach. Section 2 provides a detailed description of our protocol while section 3 performs the security analysis of our protocol against classical attacks. Section 4 precises some parameters required for the protocol.

1 Trust Management Framework and the Common History Extraction (CHE) Protocol

Reliability trust, as the name suggest, can be interpreted as the reliability of something or somebody according to the Gambetta's definition [12]. This can be formulated as follows (Reliability Trust): "Trust is the subjective probability by which an individual, Alice, expects that another individual, Bob, performs a given action on which its welfare depends". This definition includes the concept of dependence on the trusted party, and the reliability (probability) of the trusted party, as seen by the trusting party. However, trust can be more complex than Gambetta's definition indicates. For example, Falcone and Castelfranchi [10] recognise that having high (reliability) trust in a person in general is not necessarily enough to decide to enter into a situation of dependence on that person. Therefore, we can also adopt the following definition (decision trust) by McKnight and Chervany [9]: "Trust is the extent to which one party is willing to depend on something or somebody in a given situation with a feeling of relative security, even though negative consequences are possible".

1.1 Related Works

According to [27], trust management systems are classified into three categories: credential and policy-based trust management, reputation-based trust management, and social network-based trust management. This approach depends on the way we establish and evaluate trust relationships between nodes. In credential and policy-based trust management system [2, 3, 4], a node uses credential verification to establish a trust relationship with other nodes. Their concept of trust management is limited to verifying credentials and restricting access to resources according to application-defined policies: they aim to enable access control [13]. A resource-owner provides a requesting node access to a restricted resource only if it can verify the credentials of the requesting node either directly or through a web of trust [15]. This is useful by itself only for those applications that assume implicit trust in the resource owner. Since these policy-based access control trust mechanisms do not incorporate the need of the requesting peer to establish trust in the resource-owner, they by themselves do not provide a complete generic trust management solution for all decentralized applications. Reputation-based trust management systems on the other hand provide a mechanism by which a node requesting a resource may evaluate its trust in the reliability of the resource and the node providing the resource. Trust value assigned to a trust relationship is a function of the combination of the nodes global reputation and the evaluating nodes perception of that node. The third kind of trust management systems, in addition, utilize social relationships between nodes when computing trust and reputation values. In particular, they analyze a social network which represents the relationships existing within a community and form conclusions about nodes reputations based on different aspects of the social network. Examples of such trust management systems include Regret [23, 24] that identifies groups using the social network, and NodeRanking [22] that identifies experts using the social network.

Ambient networks are environments where only a distributed reputation system, i.e. without any centralized functions, is allowed [20]. In a distributed system there is no central location for submitting ratings or obtaining reputation scores of others: each node must protect itself from potential malicious nodes using only self-contained informations and a local control. The trust data can be distributed stores where ratings can be submitted, or each participant simply records the opinion about each experience with other parties, and provides this information on request from relying parties. A relying party, who considers transacting with a given target party, must find the distributed stores, or try to obtain ratings from as many community members as possible who have had direct experience with that target party. The relying party computes the reputation score based on the received ratings. In case the relying party has had direct experience with the target party, the experience from that encounter can be taken into account as private information, possibly carrying a higher weight than the received ratings. The two fundamental aspects of distributed reputation systems are: a distributed communication protocol that allows participants to obtain ratings from other members in the community and a reputation computation method used by each individual agent to derive reputation scores of target parties based on received ratings, and possibly on other information.

In our model that uses a history based approach as the one proposed in [7], the acting peer tries to forge a direct experience with the target party using the content of their own histories. The trust level is then computed only after successful transactions corresponding with a positive reputation mechanism as described in [27].

1.2   Overview of Our Protocol

Let us first briefly describe the general architecture where trusted histories take place. All smart devices participating to this trust management architecture have to carry common specific cryptographic algorithms and protocols. This is obtained through an *imprinting phase* previous to any other interactions. Special fixed secure functional units called *imprinting stations* are supposed [26]. A device belongs to a domain associated to a specific station and receives from this station an *initial seed of trust* constructed from a secret master key s unique for each station.

Just after each node has received its initial trust germ, history is obviously empty of any interaction. The number of common nodes is of course insufficient to permit an autonomous running and thus, it is necessary a bootstrap phase. So, two persons that want to exchange some services or some informations initiate an interaction by forcing by the hand this particular meeting - as in a Bluetooth like model [14], this gives the desired history element. After this bootstrap period, the nodes use the content of their histories to accept or reject a new interaction, the human intervention is then obvious and no more forcing are needed.

Then, it starts recording a history based upon the knowledge of its interactions with encountered nodes. When two strange nodes interact for the first time, they exchange the concatenation of the public keys of their respective histories and search their common elements. The interaction takes place if the number of common nodes is upper a given threshold. Of course, they need to prove one to each other the common history that could be trusted. The cryptographic protocol described in this paper ensures that any recorded element of history cannot be used by any other node. This issue will be discussed in section 3. This mutually proved history is used to create and enforce the trust relation needed to establish service interactions. At the end of any interaction, a provable value created and signed by the other party constitutes an element of history to parties. This common value also proves the identities of the nodes in presence. The core of the cryptographic method used to extract elements of history common to interacting nodes is called *Common History Extraction* protocol. In our model, there are no trust notation or reputation principles as proposed for example in [18].

This model could be compared to a non transitive version of the one used in the "Web of trust" defined by GnuPG [11]: in our model, we (weakly) authenticate nodes and previous interactions based on successful previous meetings but only at distance one between nodes. We does not consider here a conditionally transitive trust (i.e. a contextual trust). The identity itself is proved also by the use of identity-based cryptography and moreover we use elliptic curves cryptography as basic blocks to design our protocol.

Our proposal is an alternative to pairing model requiring intervention of users and not relevant in the case of short term association between devices. Moreover, in the pairing model, authentication and encryption are made using a symmetric key derived from a PIN information physically entered on each device, making the model prone to simple off-line attack due to this shared key [14]. Although a distributed n to n pairing model with removal or banishment of devices procedures and rules to solve potential conflicts is proposed in [21] but this model only takes into account a long term virtual private network with a secure long term community. In [6] a history based trust model is also presented but dedicated to group signature and using trusty environment to generate elements of history.

2   A Detailed Description of the CHE Protocol

2.1   The Initial Seed of Trust

Each device receives a *trust germ* from its *imprinting station*. It is composed by the following initial informations: ID an identity (eMail adress or IP address or just a simple name) supposed to be unique in the domain of the imprinting station chosen by the node, $(S_{\mathrm{ID}}, Q_{\mathrm{ID}})$ a first pair of private/public key for cipher operations, a second pair of keys $(S_{\mathrm{ID}}^S, Q_{\mathrm{ID}}^S)$ for the signature and a set representing all the public parameters of the elliptic curves required along computations:

$$\text{Params: } \Omega := \langle \mathbb{F}_p, a, b, P, h, G_1, G_2, e, H_1, H_2, H_1', H_2'; P_{pub,\Omega} \rangle$$

where: a and b are the parameters of a particular elliptic curve $y^2 = x^3 + ax + b$ on $\mathbb{F}_p$; P, a particular point of this curve of prime order q; h, the cofactor defined as $h = \#E(\mathbb{F}_p)/q$; G_1, is a first additive cyclic group of prime order q built using the P point; G_2, a multiplicative cyclic group of the same order; e, a bilinear pairing from $G_1 \times G_1$ to G_2; $H_1 : \{0,1\}^* \to G_1^*$ and $H_2 : G_2 \to \{0,1\}^n$, two map-to-point hash functions required for the Boneh-Franklin's Identity Based Encryption (BF-IBE) (see [5] for more details); and $H_1' : \{0,1\}^* \times G_1 \to G_1$ and $H_2' : \{0,1\}^* \times G_1 \to \mathbb{Z}_q$, two hash functions required for the Chen-Zhang-Kim IBS signature scheme (CZK-IBS) (see [8] and annex A for more details).

Ω-values are the domain identifier values provided to each node imprinted by the same imprinting station. Every imprinting station possesses the same Ω-values except $P_{pub,\Omega} = sP$ varying along the parameter s, the master key of the station. This value depends on each station and must be absolutely kept secret by it.

None of those stations is supposed to be certified by any authority. Moreover, an independent mobile, imprinting itself, may be its own standalone security domain. Another important point is that each smart device shares the same cryptographic algorithms and protocols downloaded from the imprinting station: a fingerprint algorithm, a signature algorithm, a zero-knowledge protocol, a protocol to construct secure channel and the public parameters. The only values that each smart device has to keep secret is S_{ID} and S_{ID}^S as usually in cryptosystems.

In the context of mobile objects with low capacity, cryptography based on elliptic curves (ECC) leads to many advantages. In particular, its use makes possible to develop algorithms and protocols whose the robustness and the computational and space cost are more advantageous than usual cryptography (as RSA).

2.2 The Common History Extraction (CHE) Protocol: How the Mechanism Enhances the Reciprocal Trust

Once the initialization phase done, a node may then interact with other nodes without connexion with its imprinting station. This is the second phase of our protocol.

The "Common History Extraction" protocol extracts the common acquaintances contained in the nodes' history. We have followed the Boneh and Franklin proposition [5] to construct the secret/public key pair of each node, to cipher some messages and also to build a secure channel with a weak authentication. We also have made use of the Chen-Zhang-Kim's Identity Based signature scheme as defined in [8] to sign the required elements. Thus, each node has received two pairs of public/secret keys during the imprinting phase, one pair (S_{ID}, Q_{ID}) for the cipher operation and one pair (S_{ID}^S, Q_{ID}^S) for a signature purpose.

The first step of our protocol takes place once Alice and Bob have interacted yet. In this case, they already have built a trust bond using one of the three following possible methods: they could have already met and just have to rebuild a trust nonce; they could also have built a trust bond constructed on the previous common interactions; or during a bootstrap phase and then, the corresponding users have forced by the hand the beginning of the interaction.

At the end of their interaction, Alice and Bob build, in a secure channel using the IBE scheme a message m of reciprocal trust. They sign it. Alice stores in her history $(m, Q_B, Q_B^S, sign_{S_B^S}(m))$ while Bob stores $(m, Q_A, Q_A^S, sign_{S_A^S}(m))$ in his history.

$$
\begin{array}{lcr}
 & \text{creation of a secure channel (IBE Scheme)} & \\
A & \longleftrightarrow & B \\
 & \text{create a message } m=\text{"ID}_A \text{ and ID}_B \text{ trust each other"} & \\
A & \longleftrightarrow & B \\
 & \text{A signs } m \text{ with IBS} & \\
A & \longrightarrow & B \\
 & \text{B signs } m \text{ with IBS} & \\
A & \longleftarrow & B \\
\end{array}
$$

Suppose now that in the same way Bob and Charlie have built a secure channel to exchange a common message m'.

$$
\begin{array}{lcr}
 & \text{creation of a secure channel (IBE Scheme)} & \\
B & \longleftrightarrow & C \\
 & \text{create a message } m'=\text{"ID}_B \text{ and ID}_C \text{ trust each other"} & \\
B & \longleftrightarrow & C \\
 & \text{B signs } m' \text{ with IBS} & \\
B & \longrightarrow & C \\
 & \text{C signs } m' \text{ with IBS} & \\
B & \longleftarrow & C \\
\end{array}
$$

Following that, if Alice meets Charlie, to mutually prove that they have respectively met Bob previously, they will exchange a public part of their histories and Charlie, first, will prove to Alice that Bob trust him using m'.

$$A \xrightarrow{\text{did you meet Bob before ?}} C$$

$$A \xleftarrow{\quad (m', sign_{S_B^S}(m')) \quad} C$$

verifies m'

The reciprocal process will be repeated by Alice.

Notice also that due to the particular structure of the built message, we could easily add some semantic notions in this message and prove the associated keywords used.

3   Security Analysis

3.1   Classical Attacks

We sketch in this section the security analysis of our protocol against classical attacks. The security of each cryptographic primitives of [5] and [8] has been clearly established in the initial articles describing those primitives.

This protocol permits to guarantee the following traditional cryptographic properties: weak authenticity (as Charlie knows the Bob's public key, he could authenticate his signature), integrity is guaranteed by the hash function used in the IBS scheme as in the classical case of a certificate, confidentiality is guaranteed by the use of the cryptographic IDs. Those IDs also permit to guarantee that the first phase of our protocol was correctly done. The secure channel built at the beginning of the exchange in the first phase also prevents a man-in-the-middle attack.

The Key Escrow drawback. The use of the IBE scheme introduces the well known key escrow drawback: the PKG (here the imprinting station) could read all the messages exchanged between the nodes imprinted by itself and also cipher some due to its knowledge of each created key pair. That's why we decide to use the IBE scheme only for the creation of the secure channel, the main step of our protocol is protected by the CZK-IBS scheme where the key pair generated is unknown from the imprinting station.

Man in the middle attack. Due to the use of an IBE scheme for creating the secure channel, each node could verify the validity of an ID by testing if a message could be decipher by this ID. So, a man in the middle attack could be easily discarded between the nodes. However, due to the key escrow drawback of the IBE protocol, a man in the middle attack could be performed by the imprinting station at the creation of the secure channel but this imprinting station could not sign the corresponding message. It could forge false messages but could not prove them. So, in all cases, a man in the middle attack can not be performed.

Denial of service attack. To discard the denial of service attack from a particular node, we suppose here that the first node performing the verification of the common elements of history is the one asking for a service. Our protocol does not prevent a distributed denial of service attack originating from a coalition of nodes against a single one.

3.2 Other Attacks

A cross-domain protocol. One of the main advantage of our protocol is that it is a cross-domain protocol: two nodes, not belonging to the same security domain (or to the same imprinting station) could nevertheless interact by comparing the contents of their respective histories once they exchange the public key of their security domains (we suppose here that all the other parameters are the same). The main problem in this case is the usurpation of security domains: suppose that an attacker forges an imprinting station with a name that already exists and that it generates exactly the same IDs than the ones of another security domain. At this point two ways are possible: or the attacker also steals the public key of this domain and gives it as its own public key or the attacker gives another public key. In the first case, a node of the attacker could not decipher any message send to it due to the lack of the corresponding secret key. In the second case, the two domains differ from the values of their public keys and are not exactly the same even if they have the same name and the same nodes IDs. So, the computations performed in our protocol will be different and two nodes with exactly the same complete ID do not decipher and sign in the same way.

However, our protocol could not completely discard this problem: two nodes will possess exactly the same ID and the same public key not the same signature key (upon which we perform the last challenge). So, we could differentiate `Alice1` from `Alice2` using their signature private keys.

Non-transferability of History. Suppose now that an attacker steals Alice's identity and all her history and that an attacker could not steal the secret key (in this case the attacker would become an Alice's clone!). So, this attacker, knowing all the Alice' history, could never prove the previous interactions because he does not know the secret S_{ID_A}. However, Alice could always clone herself with some other terminals but the benefit of such an attack is very low: two nodes *Alice* in an ambient network could hardly construct exactly the same history. However, those nodes with exactly the same keys could build a very strong history and have lots of recorded elements and could interact more easily than the others. Therefore, Alice's cloned devices could be carried by different persons visiting different places in order to have different histories. This is not considered by us as a major risk since it is a social engineering attack which is difficult to conduct as well as difficult to surround by cryptographic methods.

Anonymity. Our protocol does not guarantee the anonymity of the nodes IDs and of the nodes previous meetings as done in [3]. As reported in [27], there is an inherent trade-off between trust and anonymity and our aim is to propose a trust management framework . Thus, we consider here the trust weather of the network: a minimal trust level could only be reached if the nodes reveal some informations about them. We could improve this aspect by changing the transmission of the list of the encounter nodes public keys according the weather of the network (by ciphering the list using the public key of the node with a nonce for example). We also could imagine a mechanism where the nodes broadcast the list of the public keys of the nodes they have met to increase the general trust level of the network: "who meets who ?" will become in this case a trust indicator.

4   Some Implementation Results

The main parameters in our model are the size of the common history a node requires to accept an interaction and the size of the history itself. Note that, there exists an asymmetry in interactions and the size of the common knowledge required to be receiver or to be provider do not need to be the same. Also the fact that the corresponding node belongs or does not belong to the same security domain may also influence. For inner domain relationship, the size of the common history required is clearly related to the size of the community.

4.1   Probabilistic Approach

We consider here that the size of the history is k (using a least-recently-used (LRU) eviction policy) and depends on the total number n of nodes for a given imprinting station. We then want to estimate the required number p of common nodes in the history to permit access to some services. We suppose in this subsection that the nodes meetings are random and does not depend on some laws of proximity.

We then deduce the probability that A and B belonging to the n nodes group have at most p common knowledges (excluding p): $\frac{1}{(\binom{n}{k})^2} \cdot \sum_{i=0}^{p-1} \binom{n}{i} \cdot \binom{n-i}{k-i} \cdot \binom{n-k}{k-i}$.

And then, the probability P they have at least p common knowledges is given by:

$$P = Pr(A \cap B \geq p) = 1 - \frac{1}{(\binom{n}{k})^2} \cdot \sum_{i=0}^{p-1} \binom{n}{i} \cdot \binom{n-i}{k-i} \cdot \binom{n-k}{k-i} \qquad (1)$$

We have computed the corresponding probability of success in a such case and, inspired from the birthday paradox, have observed that for a given group of size n, if the size k of the history is $n/\ln(n)$ and the threshold number p of common knowledges is about $\sqrt{n/\ln(n)}$ then the probability of success (here to create a trust link) is greater than 50%. So, as an example, if $n = 100$, $k = 22$ and $p = 5$, the success probability is about $56,6\%$ (for the same parameters and $p = 3$, this probability reachs 92%). In this case, we see that the size k of the history is reasonable and could be easily carried by each node and that the number of verifications to perform, given by the p value is also not excessive.

We have summed up in the following table some results concerning the parameters n, k and p and the P probability:

n	$k = n/\ln(n)$	$p = \sqrt{n/(\ln(n)}$	P
100	22	5	56,6 %
200	38	7	61,9 %
500	81	9	94,1 %
1000	145	13	98,9 %
2000	264	17	99,99 %
5000	588	25	100 %
10000	1086	33	100 %

4.2   Simulation Results

Our model is dedicated to smart devices, therefore such devices are belonging to a person and so resulting interaction graph is a social graph. Social graphs have been studied for a long time, first by sociologists and more recently by mathematicians [19].

The first property of social graph is the *small world* effect. This property means that even in social graph strongly geographical (so with insular part or social barriers) there exists short connecting path. More recently, some works emphasize recurrent clustering organization which can also affect the way social graph should be studied. The last property, which is very important for simulation, is the skewed degree distribution.

In order to study the p parameter of the trust model we use random graph with skewed distribution [16]. The sequence of degree is obtained through an exponential and continuous power-law distribution generator.

The aim of our simulation is to provide basic idea to verify the correct choice of the p parameter for a given community. The goal is to choose the right p parameter that give large probability of spontaneous interaction between nodes of the community and low probability of interaction between a node not belonging to the same community. This empirical approach need the knowledge of the community, in term of degree distribution. Most of community specification are arbitrary. This is a first step to automatic - or semi automatic configuration for our model and a specific community.

Let us suppose a community denoted C of 30 nodes interacting inside a social group G of 100 nodes, including the C community. We suppose that interactions are more frequent between nodes of C than between a node of C and a node of $G \backslash C$. Therefore, G also constitutes a social group and has same general properties. In our simulations, we define a community with 4 parameters: s the size of the community, d_{min} and d_{max} corresponding to the range of possible degrees of nodes, and α the exponent of the power-law distribution function. Here the parameters both of C and G:

	Nodes	d_{min}	d_{min}	α
C	30	6	12	2.4
G	100	5	10	2.4

We then study, according the p parameter the number of nodes of $G \backslash C$ that will be directly included in the C community considering a history with an infinite size. The p parameter must be chosen very carefully to prevent the community C from being drowned into the group G. We obtain the following results according the p parameter:

p	3	4	5	6
number of nodes included in the community	15-20	3-5	0-1	0
Inside C probability of spontaneous interaction	99.9%	99.98%	98.66%	92.84%

In the previous table one can see the number of nodes from $G \backslash C$ spontaneously included in the community C with respect to the value of p. Depending of parameters, the community can be relatively open - choosing a small value for p means that outsider nodes are easily included in C, or closed - choosing a high value for p makes the spontaneous inclusion of outsiders nodes difficult. The second line of the table shows that whatever the value of p, the community itself works fine with a probability of spontaneous interaction greater than 90% (computed with a history of size 15).

4.3   Implementation Aspects

Moreover, to initiate an interaction, the node that provides a service to an other sends it the concatenation of all the public keys Q_{ID} that it has in its history. Each public key is 160 bits length, so in the most popular case with a history containing 30 elements, it must send a chain of 600 bytes, that is very reasonable.

In addition, with a threshold equal to 3, the number of verifications that must be done is very low. We have tested our protocol on a PC powered by a 3 Ghz Pentium IV and have found that the duration for ciphering and signing using our protocol is about 0.78 and 0.9 ms. This is also the duration for the verification of an element.

5   Conclusion

This paper introduces a new cryptographic scheme to be included in a trust management framework dedicated to *ambient networks*. In such a context, mobile devices need to carry self-contained informations and methods to be able to make fully autonomous security decisions. Some verifications have to be done off line to replace a trusted third party. According the chosen trust policy, the validity of any trust bond can be moderate either by a timeout or by the renewal with fixed intervals of its period of validity contrary to the Bluetooth model where trust is acquired only once.

Our protocol makes use of the notion of cryptographic ID on elliptic curves combined with a history based approach to enforce the trust bond created between the nodes. We think that this approach, even if the size of the history could be a limiting factor when the community of nodes is huge, permits to prevent our framework from all the usual drawbacks as the ones that could appear in reputation models: coalition of nodes for destroying the reputation of a single node, transitivity of the trust,... Our framework takes only into account the past interactions that really happened and nothing else. So, the notion of trust is local and limited to a single node judgment.

In a near future, we want to extend the described protocol for group associations in ad-hoc networks. We also want to provide an anonymous mechanism to protect the privacy of nodes and we want to study other particular network attacks.

References

1. *The First International Joint Conference on Autonomous Agents & Multiagent Systems, AAMAS 2002, July 15-19, 2002, Bologna, Italy, Proceedings.* ACM, 2002.
2. Matt Blaze, Joan Feigenbaum, John Ioannidis, and Angelos D. Keromytis. The KeyNote Trust-Management System Version 2 - RFC 2704. RFC 2704, Available from http://www.faqs.org/rfcs/rfc2704.html, September 1999.
3. Matt Blaze, Joan Feigenbaum, and Angelos D. Keromytis. The role of trust management in distributed systems security. In Jan Vitek and Christian Damsgaard Jensen, editors, *Secure Internet Programming*, volume 1603 of *Lecture Notes in Computer Science*, pages 185–210. Springer, 1999.
4. Matt Blaze, Joan Feigenbaum, and Jack Lacy. Decentralized trust management. In *IEEE Symposium on Security and Privacy*, pages 164–173. IEEE Computer Society, 1996.
5. Dan Boneh and Matthew K. Franklin. Identity-based encryption from the weil pairing. In *Advances in Cryptology - Crypto'2001*, volume 2139 of *Lecture Notes in Computer Science*, pages 213–229. Springer, 2001.
6. Laurent Bussard, Refik Molva, and Yves Roudier. History-based signature or how to trust anonymous documents. In Oxford T. Dimitrakos, editor, *Second International Conference on Trust Management*, pages 78–92, April 2004.
7. Licia Capra. Engineering human trust in mobile system collaborations. In Richard N. Taylor and Matthew B. Dwyer, editors, *SIGSOFT FSE*, pages 107–116. ACM, 2004.
8. Xiofeng Chen, Fangguo Zhang, and Kwandjo Kim. A new ID-based group signature scheme from bilinear pairings. In *Information Security Applications, 4th International Workshop - WISA'03*, volume 2908 of *Lecture Notes in Computer Science*, pages 585–592. Springer-Verlag, 2003.
9. Norman L. Chervany and D. Harrison Mac Knight. What trust means in e-commerce customer relationships: an interdisciplinary conceptual typology. International Journal of Electronic Commerce, 6, 2, pp. 35-59, 2002.
10. Rino Falcone and Cristiano Castelfranchi. The socio-cognitive dynamics of trust: Does trust create trust? In Rino Falcone, Munindar P. Singh, and Yao-Hua Tan, editors, *Trust in Cyber-societies*, volume 2246 of *Lecture Notes in Computer Science*, pages 55–72. Springer, 2000.
11. The Free Software Foundation. The gnu privacy handbook. http://www.gnupg.org/gph/en/manual.html, 1999.
12. Diego Gambetta. Can we trust trust? In Diego Gambetta, editor, *Trust: Making and Breaking Cooperative Relatioins*, chapter 13, pages 213–237. Published Online, 2000.
13. Tyrone Grandison and Morris Sloman. A survey of trust in internet applications. *IEEE Communications Surveys and Tutorials*, 3(4), 2000.
14. Markus Jakobsson and Susanne Wetzel. Security weaknesses in bluetooth. In David Naccache, editor, *CT-RSA*, volume 2020 of *Lecture Notes in Computer Science*, pages 176–191. Springer, 2001.
15. Rohit Khare and Adam Rifkin. Weaving a Web of trust. issue of the World Wide Web Journal (Volume 2, Number 3, Pages 77-112), Summer 1997.
16. Matthieu Latapy and Pascal Pons. Computing communities in large networks using random walks. *LNCS*, 3733:284, 2005.
17. Véronique Legrand, Dana Hooshmand, and Stéphane Ubéda. Trusted ambient community for self-securing hybrid networks. Research Report 5027, INRIA, 2003.

18. Jinshan Liu and Valérie Issarny. Enhanced reputation mechanism for mobile ad hoc networks. In Christian D. Jensen, Stefan Poslad, and Theodosis Dimitrakos, editors, *iTrust*, volume 2995 of *Lecture Notes in Computer Science*, pages 48–62. Springer, 2004.
19. S. Milgram. The small world problem. *Psychology Today*, 1:61–67, 1967.
20. Filip Perich, Jeffrey Undercoffer, Lalana Kagal, Anupam Joshi, Timothy Finin, and Yelena Yesha. In reputation we believe: Query processing in mobile ad-hoc networks. *mobiquitous*, 00:326–334, 2004.
21. Nicolas Prigent, Christophe Bidan, Jean-Pierre Andreaux, and Olivier Heen. Secure long term communities in ad hoc networks. In Sanjeev Setia and Vipin Swarup, editors, *SASN*, pages 115–124. ACM, 2003.
22. Josep M. Pujol, Ramon Sangüesa, and Jordi Delgado. Extracting reputation in multi agent systems by means of social network topology. In *AAMAS* [1], pages 467–474.
23. Jordi Sabater and Carles Sierra. Regret: reputation in gregarious societies. In *Agents*, pages 194–195, 2001.
24. Jordi Sabater and Carles Sierra. Reputation and social network analysis in multi-agent systems. In *AAMAS* [1], pages 475–482.
25. Adi Shamir. Identity-based cryptosystems and signature schemes. In *CRYPTO*, pages 47–53, 1984.
26. Frank Stajano and Ross J. Anderson. The resurrecting duckling: Security issues for ad-hoc wireless networks. In *Security Protocols Workshop*, volume 1796 of *Lecture Notes in Computer Science*, pages 172–194. Springer, 1999.
27. Girish Suryanarayana and Richard N. Taylor. A survey of trust management and resource discovery technologies in peer-to-peer applications.
28. Xiaoyun Wang and Hongbo Yu. How to break md5 and other hash functions. In *Advances in Cryptology - Eurocrypt'2001*, volume 3494 of *Lecture Notes in Computer Science*, pages 19–35. Springer, 2005.

A   Chen-Zhang-Kim's Identity Based Signature Without Trusted PKG Signature Scheme (CZK-IBS)

We review here Chen-Zhang-Kim's IBS without Trusted PKG signature scheme along with their security and computational efficiency in signing and verification phases. Note that whenever we say point, it represents a point on the underlying elliptic curve on which the bilinear pairings are realized [8].

Suppose that there exists an admissible cryptographic bilinear pairing e from $G_1 \times G_1$ to G_2 where G_1 is an additive cyclic group of prime order q, G_2 is a multiplicative cyclic group of the same order and P is an arbitrary generator of G_1. Suppose also that there exists two hash functions H'_1 and H'_2 defined as follows $H'_1 : \{0,1\}^* \times G_1 \to G_1$ and $H'_2 : \{0,1\}^* \times G_1 \to \mathbb{Z}_q$. Due to the recent results concerning collisions in hash functions as MD4, MD5 and also SHA-0 published in [28], we recommend to use at least SHA-1 and its derivatives as the used hash functions in the proposed protocols.

A.1   Description

The CZK-IBS scheme is composed of four phases: the first one Extract provides a pair of signature keys built upon an identity ID, the second one Sign describes the signature process, the third one Verify checks the validity of a signature and the last one detects impersonation attacks done by the PKG.

- Extract: Each node receives from its own single identity ID a pair of secret/public keys $(S_{\text{ID}}^S, Q_{\text{ID}}^S)$ for the signature purpose:
  1. The node selects a random $r \in \mathbb{Z}_q^*$ as his long term secret key and sends rP to the imprinting station.
  2. The imprinting station computes $S_{\text{ID}}^S = sQ_{\text{ID}}^S = sH_1'(\text{ID}\|T, rP)$ and sends it to the user via a secure channel, where T is the life span of the secret key s and where $Q_{\text{ID}}^S = H_1'(\text{ID}\|T, rP)$ is the public key linked with ID.
  3. The secret key of the user is the pair (S_{ID}^S, r) and the public key is directly derived from the identity ID.
- Sign: To sign a message m using the secret key (S_{ID}^S, r) corresponding to the identity (public key) ID the following steps are performed by the signer:
  1. Choose randomly $a \in \mathbb{Z}_q^*$ and compute $U = aQ_{\text{ID}}^S$
  2. Compute $V = rH_1'(m, U)$
  3. Compute $h = H_2'(m, U + V)$
  4. Compute $W = (a + h)S_{\text{ID}}^S$.

- Signature : $\sigma = \langle U, V, W, T, rP \rangle \in G_1 \times G_1 \times G_1 \times \{0, 1\}^* \times G_1$.

- Verify : To verify a signature $\sigma = \langle U, V, W, T, rP \rangle$ of an identity ID on the message m the verifier does the following:
  1. Compute $Q_{\text{ID}}^S = H_1'(\text{ID}\|T, rP)$
  2. Compute $H_1'(m, U)$ and $h = H_2'(m, U + V)$
  3. Accept the signature if and only if the following equations hold:

$$e(W, P) = e(U + hQ_{\text{ID}}^S, P_{pub}) \tag{2}$$

$$e(V, P) = e(H_1'(m, U), rP) \tag{3}$$

- Tracing: This phase is executed to detect impersonation attacks done by the PKG. The PKG can impersonate a signature for an identity ID as follows:
  1. The PKG chooses a random $r' \in \mathbb{Z}_q^*$ and let $Q_{\text{ID}'}^S = H_2'(\text{ID}\|T, r'P)$.
  2. He then performs the above described signing on a message m to produce $\langle U', V', W', r', P' \rangle$.

The signature passes the verification test. However, he dishonesty of the PKG can be proved by the user by providing a "knowledge proof" of his secret key to an arbiter.

This scheme is secure against existential forgery under adaptively chosen message and ID attacks in the random oracle model assuming the hardness of CDHP. The scheme eliminates the inherent Key Escrow problem.

Moreover, the signing phase requires 2 map-to-point hash, 3 scalar multiplications and 1 point addition in G_1, 1 cryptographic hash (H_2') operation and 1 addition in $\mathbb{Z}_q$. The verification requires 4 pairing operations, 2 map-to-point hash, 1 scalar multiplication and 2 point additions in G_1 and 1 cryptographic hash operations.

Ad Hoc Security Associations for Groups

Jukka Valkonen[1], N. Asokan[1,2], and Kaisa Nyberg[1,2]

[1] Helsinki University of Technology
[2] Nokia Research Center
jukka.valkonen@tkk.fi, n.asokan@tkk.fi, kaisa.nyberg@tkk.fi

Abstract. A security association specifies the cryptographic keys and algorithms to be used for secure communication among the participants in the association. Key agreement in ad hoc scenarios, that is, without key management infrastructure is a challenging task, in particular, if the security association should involve a group of entities. In this paper, existing pairwise ad hoc key agreement protocols are extended for groups of arbitrary number of entities. New protocols based on both passkeys and numeric comparison (short authenticated strings) are presented. Also security properties and group management for these protocols are discussed.

Keywords: ad hoc group, security association, key agreement, passkey, numeric comparison.

1 Introduction

A *security association* specifies the cryptographic keys and algorithms to be used for secure communication among the participants in the association. If the security association involves a pair of devices, the procedure of forming a security association is called "pairing". Pairing procedures have been specified for many short range radio communication technologies like Bluetooth. In such contexts ease of use is very important since pairing will be carried out by ordinary, non-expert users. Several different techniques for improving usability have been considered. One approach is to use auxiliary communication channels. They can be Near Field Communication (NFC), infrared, audio or video channels. When such out-of-band technologies are not available, some form of user action, such as entering a passkey or verifying a checksum, is needed. In the interest of usability, user actions have to be kept as simple as possible. This has led to the development of protocols where the user action is limited to entering a short passkey [BM92, GMN04] or checking a short string [ČČH06, Vau05, LAN05].

A natural question is whether the pairing protocols can be extended to the multiparty case. In this paper, we investigate this problem and propose new group association protocols that enable easy set up and management of security for groups. We focus on practical issues of the protocols and give only informal arguments to support security claims. The rest of the paper is organized as follows. In Section 2, we discuss usage scenarios where the need for group security associations arise, and formulate requirements. In Section 3, we present the

L. Buttyan, V. Gligor, and D. Westhoff (Eds.): ESAS 2006, LNCS 4357, pp. 150–164, 2006.

problem of ad hoc authentication and an overview of related work. In Section 4, we describe how to extend the pairing protocols to the group case. In Section 5 we describe group association procedures built around the group association protocols. In Section 6, we conclude.

2   Ad Hoc Group Security

2.1   Ad Hoc Scenarios

Consider the following scenario. Many researchers from different companies and universities participate in a security research conference. While listening to a presentation, Alice gets a spark of an idea that might lead to a protocol to solve an open problem. After the session she reserves a separate meeting room and invites Bob and Carol to discuss it. They quickly implement a prototype and decide to test the implementation by running it among their laptops. Their laptops are part of the conference wireless network. But Alice does not want anyone else to know what they are doing until they are sure that the idea actually works. So they set up a shared symmetric key, among their laptops so that the messages exchanged by the protocol are encrypted.

Now consider a related, but different scenario. A group of friends get together and decide to play a game. They divide themselves into two groups which will compete against each other. Members of each team want to set up an instant messaging group so that they can privately discuss strategy among themselves without the other group overhearing them. Each group sets up its own ad hoc group security association consisting of a shared symmetric key, which will be used to protect all messages exchanged within that group. Once they start playing a couple of new friends show up late. Each joins a different group and quickly become part of the existing group communication session.

Both of these scenarios require setting up group security associations. Both scenarios involve *ad hoc* associations, in that there is no a priori key management infrastructure (such as a company public key infrastructure) that can be used to set up the group security association. In both cases, the groups are short-lived, and the initial group consists of several participants. Sometimes it might be necessary to easily and quickly add new members to existing groups without having to create a new group from scratch. Revoking the rights of a member is much rarer because the groups are short-lived anyway.

In the former case, a shared short secret, such as a passkey written on a white board in Alice's meeting room, could serve as the means of authentication for setting up the security association. In the latter case, since members of both groups are present, secretly sharing a passkey among each group only, is difficult.

2.2   Group Security Structure

Security of a group can be either centrally managed or the management can be distributed. An example of a centrally managed group is Bluetooth piconet, where one device is acting as a master and all other devices are slaves. Each slave runs the Bluetooth pairing procedure to establish a shared secret link key with the master. The master generates a temporary "master key", which it transfers to each slave separately protected using the pairwise shared secret key. The broadcasting over the piconet can then be secured using the master key. In this manner, group security association (i.e., shared group key) is established by iterating a pairwise association.

Pairwise security associations can be used also to establish security under decentralized group management. It allows any member of the group accept new members by setting up a pairwise security association with the joining device, and then transferring the group key secured using the pairwise key.

The maximum number of devices in Bluetooth piconet is limited to seven. Iterating a pairwise structure may become cumbersome and lead to degradation of security as the number of group members grows. It suffices to the attacker to break one pairwise association to get hold of the group key. In this paper we consider solutions for establishing a group security association directly without pairwise associations and without degradation of security.

2.3   Management Functions

For a group of two, basically two operations exist: either a new group is formed or an existing group is disbanded. For a group of more than two members more management functions must be supported to run the group. In this section we list the basic management functions for groups which any security association structure must support.

- **Forming a new group security association:** A shared secret key is established between a predetermined set of devices.
- **Joining latecomers:** The shared secret group key of an already existing group is given securely to a new member, who did not participate in the forming of the group.
- **Handling of "phone break":** This situation occurs when a participant receives an urgent phone call, exits the meeting room and is out of coverage for a while. Yet a smooth return to the meeting must be possible, even if a new participant had, in the meanwhile, joined the meeting.
- **Revocation of a device:** In a permanent or long lasting group security association, it should be possible to expell members from the group. With the centralized management, the master device simply generates a new shared secret key and distributes it to the remaining members using the pairwise security associations. The problem is harder to solve in a decentralized group.
- **Disbanding the group:** It should be possible to terminate a group security association.

2.4   Requirements

Devices participating in the group negotiations are typically equal peers. This means that if group management requires some designated tasks, any device should be able to perform such tasks.

Management of pairwise security associations require devices to maintain a list of devices and store the shared secret keys securely. The device has at most one security association with another device. In group association the situation changes as now a device may have more than one security association with another device. Even in such cases the user must be able to manage its security associations in such a way that no confusion about the right security association occurs. For example, at a conference, it is essential for Alice to know if she shares a file with Bob as a collaboration partner, or Bob among other conference participants.

The security threat for group association is caused by an outsider who wants to listen to the group communication or insert its own messages to the group. Therefore the management functions for the group must be designed in such a way that an unauthorized device cannot join the group without being detected. We call such an active attacker as Man-in-the-Middle (MitM). In addition to listening and inserting its own messages, we assume that the MitM can delay or block the delivery of other messages, and can take the identity of some other device that is authorized to join the group.

We set certain bounds to the capabilities of MitM. First we assume that there are groups where MitM cannot break the Diffie-Hellman key agreement using passive attacks. Secondly, and more importantly for the scope of this paper, we set an upperbound to the probability that MitM succeeds in modifying the protocol messages and inserting its own messages in one protocol instance. Depending on the application this upperbound for pairwise association is quite large and varies between 10^{-2} [WUS06] and 10^{-6} [Blu06].

If a group association is built using pairwise associations it suffices for the attacker to break into one pairwise association to get the group key. The probability of success grows fast as the size of the group grows. This can be seen as follows. Suppose that the probability for a successful attack is 2^{-7} for each of the pairwise associations and suppose that the group has 11 devices. Then the attacker doesn't succeed with probability $(1 - 2^{-7})^{10}$ and succeeds at least once with probability $1 - (1 - 2^{-7})^{10} = 0.075$. If the group has 33 devices, the probability is 0.22. Such degradation of security is undesirable and should be avoided.

3   Ad Hoc Security Association

3.1   Ad Hoc Authenticated Key Agreement and Related Work

With public key based key agreement methods such as the Diffie-Hellman key agreement [DH76], a passive listener is unable to retrieve the shared secret key the devices are negotiating. However, active MitM can establish a shared secret key with each device separately without being detected. Čagalj, et al., describe one method in [ČČH06] how an adversary can achieve this by Address Resolution Protocol (ARP) spoofing.

MitM can be detected by adding authentication to the procedure. In case the MitM attack has taken place the devices will have different results from the Diffie-Hellman negotiation. Hence the key exchange can be authenticated by verifying that the two copies of the Diffie-Hellman key are equal. Stajano and Anderson [SA99] propose that a hash of the Diffie-Hellman key is displayed on the devices and the user compares the values. As it is said in [SA99], the comparison is tedious and error-prone. To make this method secure, the output of the hash should be about 160 bits, that is, 40 hexadecimal digits.

Balfanz, et al., present a method which uses infrared as the location limited channel to facilitate comparison, and observe that it is not limited to Diffie-Hellman key exchange [BSSW02]. With their method the devices can use any public-key based key exchange protocol including, for example, SSL/TLS or IKE. In [BDG+04] a solution based on the protocol is implemented and described.

Solutions using shorter authenticated strings, more practical for human users to handle, have been previously presented in [GMN04, ČČH06, Vau05]. Very recently, short authenticated strings received new applications in practical communication systems to authenticate Diffie-Hellman keys, such as Zfone [Zim06], which is a software released by Phil Zimmermann to offer security to Voice over IP. A similar protocol was recently developed by USB-IF for Wireless USB devices [WUS06]. The protocol uses three messages and new fresh Diffie-Hellman keys must be generated for each instance of the protocol.

The three-round protocol was recently generalized by Laur, et al., in [LAN05] and Pasini and Vaudenay in [PV06] for authentication of arbitrary (not necessarily unpredictable) data. Laur, et al., gave also a security proof for the protocol in the standard model, that is, not using hash functions as random oracles [LN06]. This protocol is described in the next section. It is the starting point of the group association protocol to be presented in Section 4.2.

Passkey-based key agreement has a longer history. The seminal method is Encrypted Key Exchange (EKE) presented in [BM92]. Also generalizations to groups have been developed [AG00, DB06, ABCP06, LHL04]. The common denominator among these group protcols is the usage of EKE as the basis of the authentication, that is, the authentication is performed simultaneously while the key is negotiated by encrypting some portions of transmitted data using the shared passkey as the encryption key. The protocols also aim to solutions where the same passkey can be used multiple times, which is unnecessary for ad hoc scenarios. With one-time passkeys a security association can be established using significantly simpler protocol and less computation using, for example, MANA III [GMN04]. This protocol has also a variant where the verification is iterated more times to replace the manual check MANA III uses at the end. An extension of MANA III for group association is presented in Section 4.3.

3.2   Mutual Authentication Using Numeric Comparison

The three-round protocol from [LAN05] makes use of a cryptographic commitment scheme with certain properties to achieve a security proof. In practise, such commitment scheme is realized using a cryptographic hash function. In [LAN05] it was proposed to strengthen a collision resistant hash function with OAEP-padding. For simplicity, we give the description of the protocol using a simple commitment scheme based on a collision resistant hash function given in [Vau05].

First, let us introduce the notation to be used throughout this paper. The data to be authenticted is denoted by M. The participants (devices) of the protocol are denoted by D_i, $i = 1, 2, \ldots, n$, where n denotes the number of devices in the group. A random nonce generated by D_i is denoted by R_i. We distinguish between the sent and received copies of some data. Let D be data sent by a one party. Then a copy of D that another party receives is denoted by $\hat{D}$. We also distinguish between long and short parameters. Long is typically 128 to 256 bits and short is typically 12 to 20 bits. Let h be a collision resistant hash function with long output. We denote by f a hash function with short output constructed, for example [WUS06], as follows. The input data is hashed using SHA256. Next, the string of 32 most significant bits from the hash is extracted and interpreted as an integer, for which the residue modulo 10^k is computed, where k is the number of digits to be used in the verification. The input to the hash functions may be a concatenation of different data strings, which are simply listed separated by commas.

In Figure 1 we describe the protocol from [LAN05] using which users can authenticate data in two devices without an a priori shared secret. All communication in the protocol takes place over an insecure channel.

1. D_1 generates random data string R_1 and computes commitment $h = h(R_1)$ and sends it to D_2
   $$D_1 \rightarrow D_2\text{: } h$$
2. D_2 generates a random string R_2 and sends it to D_1
   $$D_1 \leftarrow D_2\text{: } R_2$$
3. D_1 responds by opening its commitment and sending R_1 to D_2
   $$D_1 \rightarrow D_2\text{: } R_1$$
4. D_1 computes $v_1 = f(M, R_1, \hat{R}_2)$ and D_2 computes $v_2 = f(M, \hat{R}_1, R_2)$.

Fig. 1. Cross-authentication of data using numeric comparison

After the fourth step of the protocol a secure auxiliary channel is used to compare the values v_1 and v_2. If $v_1 = v_2$, the users acknowledge the match to the devices, which then accept the data M.

The secure auxiliary channel can be realized in different ways. For example, the devices can show the values v_1 and v_2 on displays for the users so that they can compare them. Or the user can enter the string displayed by one device to another device, which then compares the entered value with its own value. Goodrich, et al. [GSS+06], propose a method which uses audio for the verification. In this method, one of the devices speaks out a phrase formed from the short string to be authenticated. The task for the user is to verify, that the heard phrase equals the phrase displayed on the other device. Other possibility is for both of the devices to speak the phrase, and the user to verify that the phrases are equal.

The commitment to a random nonce R_1 by device D_1 is necessary for the security. If the commitment is skipped then the MitM can act as follows to insert its own data $\tilde{M}$ to D_2. In the authentication, MitM listens to the protocol to learn the check value $v_1 = f(M, R_1, R_2)$ and then, in step 3, it blocks R_1 reaching D_2. Then it selects a value $\tilde{R}_1$ to replace R_1 and get the equality $f(M, R_1, R_2) = f(\tilde{M}, \tilde{R}_1, R_2)$. This is easy, as the output of f is a short value.

With the commitment, as described in Figure 1, the MitM can only guess the check value and then determine R_2 to get a match. The success probability is $2^{-\ell}$ where ℓ is the length of the output of f in bits. The security proofs given for this protocol in [LN06, PV06] show that there is no attack strategy the MitM could use to succeed with an essentially higher probability.

3.3   Mutual Authentication Using Secret Passkey

Encrypted Key Exchange (EKE) was presented by Bellovin and Merrit in [BM92]. The protocol is based on a shared secret (a passkey) between two devices. The protocol uses both symmetric and asymmetric cryptosystems, and it is designed to afford a reasonable level of security even if short passkeys are used. The security depends on the entropy of the passkey. The MitM can guess the passkey with success probability at least $2^{-\ell}$ where ℓ is the entropy of the passkey in bits. The protocol can be implemented with different public key cryptosystems, for example RSA or ElGamal, or with Diffie-Hellman key exchange. These implementations are presented in [BM92].

1. D_1 generates random data string R_1 and computes commitment $h_1 = h(1, M, P, R_1)$ and sends it to D_2
   $$D_1 \rightarrow D_2\colon h_1$$
2. D_2 generates a random string R_2, computes commitment $h_2 = h(2, M, P, R_2)$ and sends it to D_1
   $$D_1 \leftarrow D_2\colon h_2$$
3. D_1 responds by opening its commitment and sending R_1 to D_2
   $$D_1 \rightarrow D_2\colon R_1$$
   D_2 now verifies equality $\hat{h}_1 = h(1, M, P, \hat{R}_1)$ and aborts if it does not hold.
4. D_2 responds by opening its commitment and sending R_2 to D_1
   $$D_1 \leftarrow D_2\colon R_2$$
   D_1 now verifies equality $\hat{h}_2 = h(2, M, P, \hat{R}_2)$ and aborts if it does not hold.

Fig. 2. MANA III protocol using a short secret passkey

Another protocol using entry of secret passkey is MANA III [GMN04]. A description of it is given in Figure 2. To start the protocol the devices share the data M to be authenticated, and a short secret passkey P. All messages of the protocol are sent over an insecure channel.

If the devices do not abort, they acknowledge the verification to each other. Acknowledgement can take place in two ways: using a secure auxiliary channel or an insecure channel secured based on a second short shared secret passkey. In the first case, an example of secure channel is direct communication between the users. Then the devices display OK to the users, who exchange this information, and subsequently, acknowledge the result to their devices. Else, the users abort the protocol.

If a second secret passkey, say Q, is available, then the acknowledgement can be performed by repeating the protocol described in Figure 2 with an additional data string "yes", passkey Q and fresh random nonces. It is clear that a MitM can always get either P or Q by interacting with D_1 until it gets the random nonce R_1. Then it can find the passkey, after which it continues successfully with D_2. Hence, independently of which acknowledgement procedure is used, the MitM must guess one short passkey, and has success probability $2^{-\ell}$ where ℓ is the length of the shorter passkey. The passkeys for MANA III cannot be reused, since even a passive listener can derive the passkey as soon as it has the data M and both h_1 and R_1 have been revealed at the run of the protocol, whereas the passkeys for EKE can be reused.

4   Group Association Protocols

In this section, two new group association protocols are presented: one using numeric comparison and one using passkey entry. First, we recall how the Diffie-Hellman key exchange procedure can be extended for groups.

4.1   Group Diffie-Hellman Key Exchange

The Diffie-Hellman key agreement method, originally designed to negotiate keys between two devices, can be extended to establish a shared secret key among a group of devices. First, the devices must be enumerated. Let n be the number of devices. Then each device must contribute to the shared secret key. This can happen in many different ways, see [STW96]. Below we present the method called GDH.3 in [STW96].

1. $D_i \rightarrow D_{i+1}$: $g^{R_1 R_2 \cdots R_i} \mod p$, $i = 1, \ldots, n-2$
2. $D_{n-1} \rightarrow$ ALL: $\pi = g^{R_1 R_2 \cdots R_{n-1}} \mod p$
3. $D_i \rightarrow D_n$: c_i, $i = 1, \ldots, n-1$, where $c_i = \pi^{\frac{1}{R_i}}$
4. $D_n \rightarrow D_i$: $c_i^{R_n}$, $i = 1, \ldots, n-1$

Fig. 3. Group Diffie-Hellman Key Exchange

Let the n devices joining the group be numbered as D_i, $i = 1, \ldots, n$. First, the devices must negotiate Diffie-Hellman parameters. These include a large prime p and a generator for a group g. These values can also be programmed to devices or they could even be standardized. Alternatively, some other Diffie-Hellman group can be used including standard elliptic curves [Dig00]. In this paper we use the notation of multiplicative groups modulo p.

To generate a shared secret, the devices perform the steps depicted in Figure 3.

After the steps of Figure 3, the shared secret M between the devices is $M = g^{R_1 \cdot R_2 \cdots \cdot R_n} \mod p$, for each $i = 1, \ldots, n$.

4.2   Group Authentication Using Numeric Comparison

Let M be a data negotiated between a group of devices D_i, $i = 1, \ldots, n$. For example, M is the shared secret Diffie-Hellman key. Then authentication is performed to ensure that all devices share the same data M. To start, one device, say D_1 is selected to lead the key agreement protocol, which we describe next in Figure 4.

1. D_i generates a fresh long random number R_i, computes $h_i = h(i, R_i)$ using a hash function h and broadcasts h_i,
   $$D_i \rightarrow D_j: h_i, i = 2, \ldots, n, j = 1, \ldots, n, j \neq i$$
2. D_1 waits until it has received $n - 1$ hashes, picks a fresh long random number and broadcasts it
   $$D_i \leftarrow D_1: R_1, i = 2, \ldots, n$$
3. D_i waits until it receives $\hat{R}_1$ and $\hat{h}_j$ from other devices D_j, $j = 2, \ldots, n$, $j \neq i$. It then broadcasts R_i,
   $$D_i \rightarrow D_j: R_i, i = 2, \ldots, n, j = 1, \ldots, n, j \neq i$$
4. D_i, $i = 1, \ldots, n$, waits until it receives $\hat{R}_j$ from other devices D_j, $j = 2, \ldots, n$, $j \neq i$. Then D_i computes $h_j = (j, \hat{R}_j)$, $j = 2, \ldots, n$, $j \neq i$ and checks if h_j is equal to the $\hat{h}_j$ received in round 3. If the check fails, D_i aborts the key agreement procedure. Otherwise, D_i computes $f(M, \hat{R}_1, \ldots, R_i, \ldots, \hat{R}_n)$, $i = 1, \ldots, n$.

Fig. 4. Group numeric comparison protocol

After the protocol from Figure 4 has been performed, the users are asked to verify whether all the devices display the same string. If any device displays a different string, or had aborted the procedure, users should indicate failure of verification. The verification succeeds only if all the devices share same secret value M and same random values. Practical procedures for verification are discussed in Section 5.1.

The security of the group numeric comparison protocol is inherited from the pairwise protocol. In particular, it is essential that all but possibly one device send their hash commitments first before the last device sends its nonce. Assume now that two devices, say D_j and D_k reveal their nonces without commitments. Then MitM can block D_k out of the group, and form its own group with D_k by impersonating all other members of the group to D_k. It first runs the protocol with the group by impersonating D_k. Let R_i, $i = 1, \ldots, n$, be the nonces. Then MitM runs the authentication protocol in the second group it established with D_k. Let S_i, $i = 1, \ldots, n$, be the nonces for the second group. Note that MitM controls all of them, except S_k. But after seeing S_k, MitM can select S_j to achieve a match $f(M, R_1, \ldots, R_n) = f(\tilde{M}, S_1, \ldots, S_n)$, for two different data M and $\tilde{M}$. This is easy, as the output of f is a short value.

With the commitment, the success probability is $2^{-\ell}$ where ℓ is the length of the output of f in bits. The security proofs given for the pairwise protocol in [LN06, PV06] show that there is no attack strategy the MitM could use to succeed with an essentially higher probability.

4.3   Group Authentication Using Secret Passkey

In this section we show how the passkey-based MANA III protocol can be generalized for groups. First one device, say D_1, is selected to lead the protocol. Then D_1 runs the pairwise MANA III protocol in parallel with each other device. The protocol is depicted in Figure 5, where we denote by M the data to be authenticated, and by P a short shared secret passkey. All messages of the protocol are sent over insecure channels.

1. D_1 generates random data string R_1 and computes commitment $h_1 = h(1, M, P, R_1)$ and broadcasts it,
$$D_1 \rightarrow D_i: h_1, i = 2, \ldots, n$$
2. D_i generates a random string R_i, computes commitment $h_i = h(i, M, P, R_i)$ and sends it to D_1
$$D_1 \leftarrow D_i: h_i, i = 2, \ldots, n$$
3. D_1 waits until it received all commitments $\hat{h}_i$, from other devices. Then it responds by opening its commitment and sending R_1 to D_i
$$D_1 \rightarrow D_i: R_1, i = 2, \ldots, n$$
   D_i now verifies equality $\hat{h}_1 = h(1, M, P, \hat{R}_1)$ and aborts if it does not hold, $i = 2, \ldots, n$.
4. D_i responds by opening its commitment and sending R_i to D_1
$$D_1 \leftarrow D_i: R_i, i = 2, \ldots, n$$
   D_1 now verifies equality $\hat{h}_i = h(i, M, P, \hat{R}_i)$, for all $i = 2, \ldots, n$ and aborts if there is i, for which the equality does not hold.

Fig. 5. MANA III for group

After a successful execution of Group MANA III protocol the devices perform an acknowledgement protocol. Similarly, as in the case of two devices, two alternatives exist: either the users communicate the successful verification to each others, or a second instance of Group MANA III protocol is executed with an additional data string "yes", fresh passkey and fresh random nonces. The practical procedures are discussed in more detail in Section 5.2.

5   Group Association Procedures

The group association protocols discussed above require different actions by the user. The numeric comparison protocol requires the users to verify that they share the same check value with other users. The passkey based protocol assume that the users share the same passkey which is only known to the devices that are authorized to join the group. In this section we investigate in more detail how the protocols should be run in practise to achieve the expected security. In particular, we discuss how the different management functions listed in Section 2.3 can be realized in practise.

5.1   Numeric Comparison

Forming a New Group. To start the key exchange and group association protocol, the devices must be set by the users to start the protocol. The users must also negotiate one of the devices to act as a leader for the procedure. The user of the leader device counts the number, say n, of devices that are supposed to join and inputs n to the leader device.

Next, each device wishing to join the group sends a registration message, to which the leader responds with a message including the following fields: group identity, number of group members and the unique identity of the receiving device. After the given number n of devices have registered to the leading device, key negotiation as described in Section 4.1 can start.

If the number of registered devices is different from the number of devices given by the user, the procedure is aborted by the users or after a pre-defined timeout period.

After the group Diffie-Hellman protocol has come to the end the leading device starts the authentication phase using the numeric comparison.

The string displayed in the authentication phase can be verified by various means. One straightforward method is that the users compare the string displayed on their devices. This can be achieved as follows. One of the users distributes the value displayed by his device. In the numeric comparison method the value to be distributed need not be kept confidential. In a meeting scenario, for example, the value can be written on the white board even if the room has windows. Each user compares the value on his device to the distributed value.

A second way to verify the values is to let the device do the comparison. In this method, the task for the user is to input the value to the device. Now, one of the users again distributes the value derived on his device and other users type in the value to their devices. If the values match, the device signals ok to the user and an error otherwise.

In both verification methods, the user of the leader device asks the other users to notify him in case of a failure. The verification is succesfully passed only if no failure is reported. Only then the users acknowledge the displayed value and the Diffie-Hellman key can be taken into use. If some of the users report a failure, the user of the leader device tell all users to abort the procedure on their devices.

The second way clearly needs more effort from the user, as the user must type in to the device the value displayed which is quite a cumbersome procedure and thus error prone. Naturally, if the values are typed in correctly, there should be no errors in the comparison procedure, as the comparison is left to the devices. In the first method, the user has to compare two displayed short strings. The comparison should not be too difficult to perform as the strings are only about 4 digits long. Thus the first way seems to be more appropriate way to deal the verification. In both cases, however, a user may neglect to report failure.

Of course, there is no need to separate these two methods. It might be the case, that some of the devices joining the group have limited output capabilities and some limited input capabilities. It is possible to use both of the methods to verify the strings. Only for the leader it is necessary to display the value.

Joining Latecomers. In addition to the role of a leader, a group can nominate one or more members to act as a gatekeeper, whose task it is to help new members to join the group. When a device, or a group of devices wishes to join the group, it contacts the gatekeeper device. The devices wishing to join the group create a group association with the gatekeeper. For this, the same method as explained in Section 4 can be used. After the group has negotiated and a secret key established, the gatekeeper provides all necessary information including the group key of the group secured with the new key. After all necessary information has been transmitted, the association between gatekeeper and the joining devices is removed.

With this method, a situation where only one device is joining the group reduces to pairing of two devices, but also the case when multiple devices are joining simultaneously can be handled.

It is also possible for the joining group to select a representative who establishes a pairwise security association with the gatekeeper. The gatekeeper then passes the groupkey to the joining device through the representative.

Handling of "Phone Break". As described above, latecomers can join an existing group in such a manner that no changes are needed for the existing group members. Then the members of the group can temporarily move away from the group coverage, and return to the group using the existing group association parameters. Only if the group has terminated while a user of a member device being away, the return is clearly not possible. In this case the user must be informed in an authenticated manner about the termination of the group.

Leaving a Group Permanently. Leaving the group permanently means that the group association is being removed permanently from the device.

Disbanding the group. If the entire group is terminated, all of the devices must delete the group association from their association database permanently.

Revocation of a device. When a device or a group of devices needs to be expelled from an existing group, the group must be disbanded, and a new group association must be established among the remaining and possibly new members.

There are different ways in which the decision about membership revocation is taken in the group. In any case all users of the group must be informed that a new group must be formed. In case a new group is formed, the requirement for allowing phone breaks cannot be satisfied, as if a user of a member device is not present when a device is expelled, the user must be informed so that the existing group association is deleted and the device can rejoin the group through the gatekeeper.

5.2 Passkey Based Protocol

Passkeys. In EKE based group security association the passkey is not revealed in the protocol to an outsider. Hence it is possible to use the existing passkey multiple times. This fact can be exploited to make some of the management functions run smoothly. On the other hand, the longer the same passkey is used, the more likely the passkey is revealed, after which it cannot be used. Problems might also arise if the same passkey is used too many times so that an attacker has enough time and possibilities to find out the passkey.

The passkeys for MANA III cannot be reused and thus there is no need to memorize the passkeys. The general problem with passkey based ad hoc authentication in practise is how to guarantee the secrecy of the passkey, particularly if the group is large, or the group members are scattered in a shared space among non-members.

Forming a new group. The initialization procedures in case of passkey based key exchange are almost the same as with numeric comparison. In addition to selecting the leader and determing and typing in the number of devices joining the group, the users must type in to the device the passkey used in key negotiation. After this the protocol is run, and when it terminates successfully the devices should share the same secret Diffie-Hellman key. No further action is required from the users. This holds for both Group EKE and Group MANA III provided that the passkey based acknowledgement procedure is used for MANA III.

If only one passkey is used for Group MANA III then the users of the devices must acknowledge that the verification of the commitments was successful. First the leader checks its own device, and informs about the result to other devices. If the leader's verification was successful the user of the leader device asks all other users to acknowledge. If any of the devices reports failure, then the group association must be aborted.

Joining latecomers. Joining a group can be performed as explained in Section 5.1 with the difference that key negotiation is done using passkey based authentication. Now, the group formed between the joining devices and the gatekeeper can be authenticated using a shared secret passkey. For EKE this can be the same passkey as used to set up the original security association or a different one. For MANA III the passkey must always be fresh.

The rest of the functions. The other functions are very similar as in the case of numeric comparison. Phone breaks can be handled equally smoothly, and if a membership is revoked, a new group association must be set up among the remaining members.

6   Conclusions

We have examined the possibility to extend the existing pairwise ad hoc association protocols to groups of more than two members. Two new group association protocols were presented: one based on numeric comparison and one based on shared secret passkey. The main difference, which may be significant in some scenarios and for large groups in particular, is that the passkey must be kept secret.

The properties and the practical execution are very similar for both protocols, and the different management functions listed in Section 2.3, with the exception of member revocation, can be realized in practise. To achieve the same attack probability, the length of the secret passkey for MANA III should be the same as the length of the short authenticated string for numeric comparison. For both protocols, it is required that one user collects feedback from all other users of the result of their verification, which may be a cumbersome and error-prone procedure for a large group. For MANA III, the feedback could be collected protected with an additional shared secret passkey of the same length as the first one, which may be acceptable in some scenarios. For Numeric Comparison the feedback from the group devices can also be collected protected with a shared secret passkey of the same length as the string used for comparison. However, using such method with numeric comparison protocol would mean that the advantage of non-secrecy is lost.

Acknowledgements

We would like to thank Harri Haanpää for pointing out the attack described in the end of Section 4.2.

References

[ABCP06] Michael Abdalla, Emmanuel Bresson, Olivier Chevassut, and David Pointcheval. Password-based Group Key Exchange in a Constant Number of Rounds. In *Public Key Cryptography - PKC 2006*, 2006. LNCS 3958.

[AG00] N. Asokan and Philip Ginzboorg. Key Agreement in Ad-hoc Networks. *Computer Communications Review*, 23(17):1627–1637, November 2000.

[BDG+04] Dirk Balfanz, Glenn Durfee, R. E. Grinter, D. K. Smetters, and Paul Stewart. Network-in-a-Box: How to Set Up a Secure Wireless Network in Under a Minute. In *13th Usenix Security Symposium*, San Diego, CA, August 2004.

[Blu06] Bluetooth SIG. Bluetooth Simple Pairing Whitepaper. Technical report, Bluetooth SIG, 2006. http://www.bluetooth.com/Bluetooth/ Apply/Technology/Research/Simple_Pairing.htm.

[BM92] Steven M. Bellovin and Michael Merritt. Encrypted Key Exchange: Password-Based Protocols Secure Against Dictionary Attacks. In *1992 IEEE Computer Society Symposium*, pages 72–84, 1992.

[BSSW02] Dirk Balfanz, D. K. Smetters, Paul Stewart, and H. Chi Wong. Talking to strangers: Authentication in ad-hoc wireless networks. In *Proceedings of Network and Distributed System Security Symposium 2002 (NDSS'02)*, San Diego, CA, February 2002.

[ČČH06] Mario Čagalj, Srdjan Čapkun, and Jean-Pierre Hubaux. Key Agreement in Peer-to-Peer Wireless Networks. *Proceedings of the IEEE (Special Issue on Security and Cryptography)*, 92(2):467–478, February 2006.

[DB06]   Ratna Dutta and Rana Barua. Password-Based Encrypted Group Key
           Agreement. *International Journal of Network Security*, 3(1):23–34, 2006.
[DH76]   Whitfield Diffie and Martin E. Hellman. New Directions In Cryptography.
           IEEE Transactions on Information Theory, IT-22:644–654, 1976.
[Dig00]   Digital Signature Standard (DSS) (FIPS PUB 186-2), Febru-
           ary 2000.   `http://csrc.nist.gov/publications/fips/fips186-2/`
           `fips186-2-change1.pdf`.
[GMN04]   Christian Gehrmann, Chris J. Mitchell, and Kaisa Nyberg. Manual Au-
           thentication for Wireless Devices. *RSA Cryptobytes*, 7(1), 2004.
[GSS⁺06]   Michael T. Goodrich, Michael Sirivianos, John Solis, Gene Tsudik, and
           Ersin Uzun. Loud And Clear: Human Verifiable Authentication Based
           on Audio.   `http://www.ics.uci.edu/~ccsp/lac/LoudAndClear_files/`
           `icdcs.pdf`, 2006.
[LAN05]   Sven Laur, N. Asokan, and Kaisa Nyberg. Efficient Mutual Data Authenti-
           cation Using Manually Authenticated Strings. Cryptology ePrint Archive,
           Report 2005/424, 2005. `http://eprint.iacr.org/`.
[LHL04]   Su-Mi Lee, Jung Yeon Hwang, and Dong Hoon Lee. Efficient password-
           based group key exchange. In *TrustBus*, pages 191–199, 2004.
[LN06]   Sven Laur and Kaisa Nyberg. Efficient Mutual Data Authentication Using
           Manually Authenticated Strings. In *Proceedings of CANS'06 (to appear)*,
           2006. LNCS 4301.
[PV06]   Sylvain Pasini and Serge Vaudenay. SAS-Based Authenticated Key Agree-
           ment. In *PKC 2006*, 2006.
[SA99]   Frank Stajano and Ross Anderson. The Resurrecting Duckling: Security
           Issues for Ad-hoc Wireless networks. In *Security Protocols, 7th Interna-
           tional Workshop Proceedings*, 1999.
[STW96]   Michael Steiner, Gene Tsudik, and Michael Waidner. Diffie-Hellman Key
           Distribution Extended to Group Communication. In *CCS '96: Proceedings
           of the 3rd ACM conference on Computer and communications security*,
           pages 31–37, New York, NY, USA, 1996. ACM Press.
[Vau05]   Serge Vaudenay. Secure Communications over insecure Channels Based on
           Short Authenticated Strings. In *Crypto 2005*, 2005.
[WUS06]   Association Models Supplement to the Certified Wireless Univer-
           sal Serial Bus Specification, 2006.   `http://www.usb.org/developers/`
           `wusb/wusb_2006_0302.zip`.
[Zim06]   Philip   Zimmermann.   Zfone   homepage,   2006.   `http://www.`
           `philzimmermann.com/EN/zfone/index.html`.

Verifiable Agreement: Limits of Non-repudiation in Mobile Peer-to-Peer Ad Hoc Networks

Zinaida Benenson[1], Felix C. Freiling[2], Birgit Pfitzmann[3], Christian Rohner[1], and Michael Waidner[3]

[1] Uppsala University, Department of Information Technology
{zina,chrohner}@it.uu.se
[2] University of Mannheim, Computer Science Department
freiling@informatik.uni-mannheim.de
[3] IBM Research, Zurich Research Lab
{bpf,wmi}@zurich.ibm.com

Abstract. We introduce verifiable agreement as a fundamental service for securing mobile peer-to-peer ad hoc networks, and investigate its solvability. Verifiability of a protocol result means that the participants can prove that the protocol reached a particular result to any third party (the verifier) which was not present in the network at the time of the protocol execution.

1 Introduction

1.1 Motivation

The envisioned applications of ad hoc networks often follow the scenario where a group of nodes meets for a short time, conducts some transaction, such as a collaborative document editing session, a decision to take some coordinated action, or dissemination of information to all group members, and then breaks apart, perhaps forever. We call this type of the network *mobile peer-to-peer ad hoc network*.

In this scenario, there is no centralized logging of the transaction, no transaction witnesses, apart from the participants themselves. Thus, to make the result of the transaction binding, it should be made *verifiable*. That is, after the transaction is finished, each participant should be able to prove to some third party which was not present in the network at the time of the transaction that this particular transaction (1) happened, (2) was conducted by the certain group of participants, and (3) reached a particular outcome. We call this problem *Verifiable Agreement* on the transaction result. Requiring that each participant be able to carry out the proof without the help of any other participant seems to be the most safe decision, as there is no guarantee that any other participant would be reachable at the time when the proof is conducted.

Verifiable Agreement is a crucial problem for securing mobile peer-to-peer ad hoc networks. Indeed, especially if such networks are set up in emergency situations, with participants from different organizations or different countries,

L. Buttyan, V. Gligor, and D. Westhoff (Eds.): ESAS 2006, LNCS 4357, pp. 165–178, 2006.

the participants may distrust each other. Unfortunately, as we show below, the non-repudiation of the decisions made in this situation can only be reached if the majority of participants can be trusted. This puts a strict restriction on the usage of this network type for trust-critical applications.

1.2 Agreement and Contract Signing

We denote by *Agreement* a class of problems where a set of n parties $P :=$ $\{P_1, \ldots, P_n\}$ start with initial inputs $x_1, \ldots, x_n$. Some parties might be dishonest and arbitrary deviate from their programs. All honest parties must eventually, or with some high probability, terminate and agree on a common result, y, which is "valid". *Validity* defines a particular agreement problem:

- In *Interactive Consistency* [20], the parties must agree on a vector y, where the ith element must be x_i for all honest parties P_i, otherwise it can be any value.
- In *Consensus* [9], if there is a value x such that $x_i = x$ for all honest parties P_i, then $y = x$.

Other agreement problems include Byzantine Generals Problem (also called Byzantine Agreement) [17], Weak Byzantine Agreement [16], Atomic Commitment [22], Strong Consensus [10], Validated Byzantine Agreement [15].

In contrast to Secure Multi-Party Computation [12], the inputs of the parties do not need to be secret or independent.

Contract signing [7] can be considered as an agreement problem where the parties must agree either on a contract text or on a special value failed, which means that no contract was signed. The signed contract can be an outcome of the contract signing protocol only if all honest parties want to sign the same contract text. The signed contract must be *verifiable*. Informally, verifiability can be described as follows:

- Each honest party can convince a verifier V, which knows nothing about a particular protocol run, that this protocol run yielded the result y.
- If some protocol run yielded the result y, no party can convince V that the protocol yielded some result $y' \neq y$.

The result failed is usually left non-verifiable. This reflects the real-world situation where no proof of the fact that a contract was *not* signed is required.

1.3 Related Work

Apart from contract signing, which has been an active research area for several decades, the only approach to make an agreement problem verifiable, as far as we know, is undertaken in [22]. There, a specification for verifiable atomic commitment for electronic payment protocols is presented, but no explicit definition of verifiability is given. A different notion of verifiable agreement was introduced in [15]: each honest protocol participant P_i can convince any other honest participant P_j of its result, but not necessarily any outsider. Multi-party contract signing protocols are presented, e.g., in [2,11,5]. For an overview of recent work, see also [23].

1.4   Outline and Contribution

After presenting the system model in Section 2, we give a unifying definition of agreement problems which facilitates rigorous proofs, and define verifiable agreement (Section 3).

We show that in case of dishonest majorities, verifiable agreement cannot be solved (Section 4). This puts a fundamental limit on non-repudiation of transactions in mobile peer-to-peer ad hoc networks. In contrast, some agreement problems, such as Interactive Consistency, can be solved for any number of dishonest parties. We present a verifiable agreement protocol for honest majorities in Section 5.

Finally, in Section 6, we discuss our system assumptions and the applications of verifiable agreement.

2   System Model and Preliminaries

2.1   System Model

Let $P = \{P_1, ..., P_n\}$ denote the set of participats of an agreement protocol, and V denote a verifier.

Let $|X| \geq 2$ and $|Y| \geq 2$ be two finite sets representing the inputs and the outputs of individual participants P_i. We assume (w.l.o.g.) that Y contains a distinguished element failed. For a subset of parties $H \subseteq P$ we denote by X^H the set of all $|H|$-dimensional vectors with elements from X.

The parties P_i can digitally sign messages, and all parties can verify their signatures. The signature on message m associated with party P_i is denoted by $\mathsf{sign}_i(m)$.

The *adversary* can a priori choose to corrupt a certain subset of parties. It has full control over the behavior and knowledge of dishonest parties (Byzantine failures).

We assume that the adversary, as well as all participating parties, are computationally bounded. In particular, the adversary cannot forge signatures.

We consider both synchronous and asynchronous networks with reliable communication channels.

In synchronous networks, communication proceeds in rounds. In each round, a party first receives inputs from the user and all messages sent to it in the previous round (if any), processes them, and may finally send some messages to other parties or give outputs to the user.

In asynchronous networks, the sent messages can be delivered in any order and there is no upper bound on the time of message delivery. However, as the communication channels are reliable, each sent message is guaranteed to arrive eventually. The control over the message delivery is given to the adversary. A party P_i may decide to stop waiting for a certain event E. That means the following: Before P_i starts waiting for E, it sends to itself a unique timeout message *timeout* and waits for this message, too. If *timeout* arrives first, the party stops waiting for E and proceeds.

We discuss the viability of these assumptions in the ad hoc networks in Section 6.

Every protocol instance has a unique identifier *tid*. We assume that all honest parties are willing to participate in a protocol run with a fresh protocol identifier.

2.2   Preliminary Definitions

Honesty structure formalizes for which sets of honest parties the problem should be solved[1].

Definition 1 (Honesty Structure). *An honesty structure $\mathcal{H}$ for a set of parties P is a set of subsets of P such that if $H \in \mathcal{H}$ and $H \subseteq H' \subseteq P$ then $H' \in \mathcal{H}$.*

The definition reflects the intuition that any protocol that works given a certain set H of honest parties should also work in case there are *more* honest parties.

Definition 2 (conditions Q_2 and Q_3, from [13]). *An honesty structure $\mathcal{H}$ satisfies condition Q_2 if $H_1 \cap H_2 \neq \emptyset$ for all $H_1, H_2 \in \mathcal{H}$, and it satisfies condition Q_3 if $H_1 \cap H_2 \cap H_3 \neq \emptyset$ for all $H_1, H_2, H_3 \in \mathcal{H}$.*

A *threshold honesty structure* $\mathcal{H}_t$ for a threshold $t < n$ is a set of subsets of P such that $\mathcal{H}_t = \{H \subseteq P : |H| > n - t\}$. A threshold honesty structure satisfies Q_2 or Q_3 if and only if $t \leq \frac{n}{2}$ or $t \leq \frac{n}{3}$, respectively. Thus, the condition Q_2 generalizes the notion of honest majority.

We now define validity functions which will be used in the following to describe validity conditions of agreement problems.

Definition 3 (Validity Function). *Let $\mathcal{H}$ be an honesty structure. A validity function for the sets X, Y, and $\mathcal{H}$ is a function F that maps pairs $(H, x) \in \mathcal{H} \times X^H$ to subsets of Y, the allowed outputs. It must satisfy the Non-triviality condition:*

- *$\forall y \neq$ failed $\exists x \in X^P : y \notin F(P, x)$ and*
- *$\exists x \in X^P : F(P, x) \neq \{$failed$\}$.*

Non-triviality excludes all consensus problems which can be solved by the trivial protocol which always outputs a constant result y, or always fails. We do not exclude problems that allow the output failed for all initial inputs, because the result failed is sometimes unavoidable. However, in this case the non-triviality condition guarantees that there exists at least one protocol run which does not output failed. In the following, we give examples of validity functions for some well-known problems.

---

[1] The corresponding notion from the area of secret sharing is access structure. An adversary structure [13], which consists of all sets of dishonest parties a protocol can withstand, is the complement of it.

Consensus with $Y = X$ is described by:

$$F_C(H, x) := \begin{cases} \{x\} & \text{if } x_i = x \ \forall \ P_i \in H \\ X & \text{otherwise.} \end{cases}$$

Interactive Consistency with $Y = X^P$ is described by:

$$F_{IC}(H, x) := \{y \in X^P \,|\, y^i = x_i \ \forall \ P_i \in H, \ y^i \in X \text{ otherwise.}\},$$

where y^i denotes the ith element of the vector $y \in X^P$.

3 Definition of Verifiable Agreement

We first define agreement problems. Here and further in the sequel, the *timeout* messages refer only to the asynchronous model.

Definition 4. *An* agreement problem *for a validity function F (for an honesty structure $\mathcal{H}$ and input and output sets X and Y) is to devise a protocol* consensus[] *for parties $P_1, ..., P_n$. In order to start the protocol, a party P_i receives the input* (consensus, *tid*, x_i). *Here tid is a transaction identifier unique for all executions of* consensus[], *and $x_i \in X$ is P_i's local input. Upon termination, the protocol produces an output* (*tid*, y_i) *with $y_i \in Y$ for each P_i.*

The following requirements must be satisfied for all sets $H \in \mathcal{H}$ of actually honest parties and input vectors $x \in X^H$:

- Agreement: *There is a $y \in Y$ such that $y_i = y$ for all $P_i \in H$.*
- Validity: *$y_i \in F(H, x)$ for all $P_i \in H$.*
- Correct Execution: *If all parties are honest, and no party receives any timeout messages, then for all input vectors $x \in X^P$ with $F(P, x) \neq \{$failed$\}$, the parties will never agree on $y = $ failed.*
- Termination of* consensus[]: *Eventually each $P_i \in H$ terminates and produces an output $y_i \in Y$.*

Correct Execution excludes protocols that always output failed.

We now formalize the *verifiability* of an agreement.

Definition 5. *A* verifiable agreement *problem for a validity function F is to devise, in addition to the protocol* consensus[], *the protocol* verify[] *which involves only one party P_i and a verifier V which does not have any knowledge about the execution of* consensus[] *or about possible previous runs of* verify[].

Party P_i starts verify[] *with input* (show, V, *tid*, y) *where tid is the transaction identifier of an execution of* consensus[] *and y is the result obtained from this execution. The verifier receives the input* (verify, P_i, *tid*) *and eventually obtains an output* (*tid*, d_V) *where $d_V \in \{(y, $ accepted$), $ verify_failed$\}$. The following requirements must be satisfied in addition to those from Definition 4 for an honest verifier V and all sets $H \in \mathcal{H}$ of actually honest parties:*

- Verifiability of Correct Result: *If* $P_i \in H$ *obtained the output* (tid, y) *for* $y \neq$ failed *from* consensus[] *and later receives the input* (show, V, tid, y), *and if* V *receives the input* (verify, P_i, tid), *then* V *will obtain the result* $d_V = (y, \text{accepted})$, *provided no timeout messages are received during the protocol.*
- Non-verifiability of failed: *The verifier* V *never decides* (failed, accepted) *on any input.*
- No Surprises: *If some* $P_i \in H$ *obtained* (tid, y) *from* consensus[], *then* V *never obtains the result* $d_V = (y', \text{accepted})$ *on input* (verify, P_j, tid) *for any party* P_j *and* $y' \neq y$.
- Termination of verify[]: *Each* V *and each* $P_i \in H$ *eventually terminate.*

$\Diamond$

No Surprises says, in particular, that if some honest party P_i never started or not yet finished consensus[] for some tid, then the verifier cannot accept any result y for tid from some party P_j, honest or dishonest, unless P_i is guaranteed to obtain y for tid.

We now show how to define the contract signing problem within our framework.

Definition 6. Contract signing *is a verifiable consensus problem described by the following validity function:*
$X := C \cup \{\text{reject}\}$, *where* C *is a finite set of contract texts that can be signed,* $Y := C \cup \{\text{failed}\}$, *and* $\mathcal{H}$ *is the power set of* P. *Then:*

$$F_{CS}(H, x) := \begin{cases} \{contr, \text{failed}\} & \text{if } \exists \ contr \in C \text{ such that } x_i = contr \ \forall \ P_i \in H \\ \{\text{failed}\} & \text{otherwise.} \end{cases}$$

$\Diamond$

It is possible to show that the above definition of contract signing and the "usual" definition from, e.g., [2] are equivalent. We omit this proof due to space limit.

4 Impossibility of Verifiable Agreement for Dishonest Majorities

We show that if Q_2 (which generalizes the notion of honest majority) is *not* satisfied, then the Verifiable Agreement problem cannot be solved even in synchronous networks. In contrast, some agreement problems, e.g., Interactive Consistency, can be solved deterministically in this setting for any honesty structure [20]. As the synchronous network is the most strong network model, this result implies non-solvability for all other network classes.

In section 4.1 we show that no deterministic protocol can solve verifiable agreement for dishonest majorities. In section 4.2 we show that any probabilistic verifiable agreement protocol in case Q_2 is not satisfied has the error probability at least inversely linear in the number of protocol rounds. This means that in order to make the error probability of the protocol exponentially small, an exponential number of rounds is needed, which is unacceptable due to the computationally bounded protocol participants.

4.1   No Deterministic Verifiable Agreement for Dishonest Majorities

Theorem 1. *No synchronous deterministic protocol can solve Verifiable Agreement if condition Q_2 is not satisfied.*

Proof. Let $\mathcal{H}$ be an honesty structure which does not satisfy Q_2, F be a validity function for $\mathcal{H}$ and input and output sets X and Y. Assume that there is some protocol π which solves the verifiable agreement problem specified by F deterministically in r rounds.

If $\mathcal{H}$ does not satisfy Q_2, then there are sets $H_1, H_2 \in \mathcal{H}$ such that $H_1 \cap H_2 = \emptyset$. We assume, w.l.o.g., that $H_1 \cup H_2 = P$, i.e., $H_1 = \bar{H}_2$.

In this case, it is possible to collapse all parties in H_1 into one (new) party $\tilde{P}_1$, and all parties in H_2 into a new party $\tilde{P}_2$. The new resulting protocol $\tilde{\pi}$ runs exactly as the protocol π, but all messages sent in π between the parties in the set H_1 (H_2, respectively) now belong to the internal state of party $\tilde{P}_1$ ($\tilde{P}_2$) in the corresponding protocol run of $\tilde{\pi}$. Therefore, it is sufficient to consider only the two-party case $P = \{P_1, P_2\}$ in our impossibility proof.

First note that the non-triviality of validity function F implies that there are at least two different results for π in the all-honest case. One of them must be verifiable (i.e. unequal to failed). Furthermore, if some result y is allowed in the all-honest case, then that y must be an allowed result in case only one of the parties is honest, as the dishonest party might *behave* like honest in a protocol run.

We now show that party P_1 cannot obtain any verifiable result without communication with party P_2. Assume that it can be done, i.e., P_1 can obtain some verifiable result y_1 from some protocol run. Then the non-triviality of F implies that there is some result $y \neq y_1$, verifiable or non-verifiable, which can be obtained in the all-honest case. Assume that P_1 is dishonest, P_2 is honest. If the parties run π for some *tid* and party P_1 behaves like honest, then they can obtain the result y. At the same time, party P_1 can execute π for the same *tid* without party P_2 and receive the verifiable result y_1, which contradicts No Surprises (Definition 5).

The remaining case is the one where P_1 and P_2 must be able to obtain some verifiable result from the protocol and need to communicate with each other in order to do so. We assume, w.l.o.g., that the parties send messages to each other in each round, as we can always force them to send dummy messages. Consider some protocol run run_1 where both parties P_1 and P_2 are honest and obtain a verifiable result y after r rounds, see Figure 1. Honest parties are drawn as circles, messages sent in each round from P_1 to P_2 and vice versa are shown as diagonal lines. The round where the party P_i gains the result y from the protocol run is indicated as a black point.

Now we consider the protocol run run_2 where party P_1 is dishonest. It does not send any protocol messages in the last round, but all other messages are sent as in run_1. As the honest party P_2, however, send its messages in the last round, party P_1 gets all messages it needs to obtain the verifiable result y in round r. Then, as π must satisfy No Surprises (Definition 5), party P_2 must obtain the output y as well. As P_2 does not receive any messages after Round $r - 1$, it obtains y in this round.

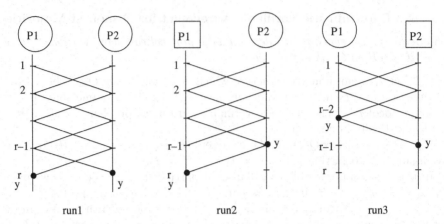

Fig. 1. No deterministic verifiable consensus for dishonest majorities. In run_1, both parties are honest. In run_2, party P_1 is dishonest. In run_3, party P_2 is dishonest.

Thus, party P_2 can obtain y after it received all messages up to round $r - 1$. Consider yet another protocol run, where P_2 is dishonest, but P_1 is honest. Until round $r - 2$ both P_1 and P_2 send their messages exactly as in run_1. In round $r - 1$, however, P_2 stops sending messages. It receives the messages from P_1 in round $r - 1$ and therefore, obtains y. However, party P_1 must obtain y, too, as explained above. Thus P_1 can obtain y after round $r - 2$.

We continue to construct the chain of protocol runs starting from run_1 where the parties need less and less messages to obtain y. In this manner, we will arrive at the the protocol run where parties P_1 and P_2 do not need to communicate at all to obtain y, which contradicts the initial assumption. Therefore, the protocol π does not exist.   □

4.2 Error Probability of Probabilistic Verifiable Agreement for Dishonest Majorities

Theorem 2. *The error probability of any probabilistic synchronous verifiable agreement protocol in case Q_2 is not satisfied is unacceptable large, i.e., at least inversely linear in the number of protocol rounds.*

Proof. We first note that any n-party verifiable agreement in case Q_2 is not satisfied can be transformed into a 2-party verifiable agreement problem, see Section 4.1. We then describe an adversary which makes the error probability of any 2-party verifiable agreement protocol which terminates in expected r number of rounds at least $\frac{1}{3r}$ only by causing the corrupted party to stop sending messages in some round i.

Let $P = \{P_1, P_2\}$ and $\mathcal{H} = \{\{P_1\}, \{P_2\}, \{P_1, P_2\}\}$, and let F be a validity function for $\mathcal{H}$. Let π be a probabilistic synchronous 2-party verifiable agreement protocol for F which terminates in an expected finite number of rounds.

We assume, w.l.o.g., that in a synchronous probabilistic protocol π between P_1 and P_2 the parties alternate in sending messages. Further, we assume that each party can get some result accepted without communication with the other party with probability at most $\frac{1}{3}$ and that there is a finite number of rounds r such that the result is accepted with probability at least $\frac{2}{3}$ after that round.

We complete the protocol such that it always runs at least r rounds. If it would terminate already in round $s < r$ we just let the parties wait till round r.

We consider only a very weak adversary: it can select the initial inputs for P_1 and P_2 and a number $i \in \{1, ..., r\}$ such that the protocol is interrupted in round i. The interruption is done by the party which should be sending in this round. The interrupting party accepts the message sent by the honest party in round $i - 1$, but sends nothing in round i and ceases to participate in the protocol run. The corresponding honest party then gets its result in round r.

The adversary is successful if No Surprises or Verifiability of Correct Result (Definition 5) are violated, i.e. if the dishonest party is able to convince the verifier V of a certain value, but the honest party is not able to do this.

Let $F(\{P_1, P_2\}, (x_1, x_2)) \neq \{\text{failed}\}$. Consider adversaries which select (x_1, x_2) as input vector. Let A_i be the adversary which interrupts the protocol run on input (x_1, x_2) in round $i \leq r$.

After the protocol is interrupted in round i, the uncorrupted party obtains some result in round r. The corrupted party obtains some result from the protocol run in round r, too, as it can pretend to be honest and to have not received any protocol messages after round i.

Let E_i denote the event that an honest verifier V accepts the output the dishonest party obtained after interrupting the protocol run in round i. The probability that it happens is denoted as $P(E_i)$. Then V accepts the output of the honest party in this protocol run with the probability $P(E_{i-1})$. E_0 denotes the probability that the output of the honest party is accepted if the interruption happens before round 1. Then $P(E_0) = P(E_1) \leq \frac{1}{3}$, $P(E_r) = \frac{2}{3}$, and the error probability of the protocol run with an adversary A_i is $P(E_i \wedge \overline{E_{i-1}})$, $i \leq r$.

Let A_{max} be the adversary A_i that maximizes the error probability. We first show the following lemma:

Lemma 1. *Let ϵ be a value such that for all rounds $i \leq r$ of a protocol $P(E_i \wedge \overline{E_{i-1}}) \leq \epsilon$. Then $\epsilon \geq (P(E_r) - P(E_0))/r$.*

Proof. (of the above lemma) For all $i \leq r$ we have $P(E_i) = P(E_i \wedge E_{i-1}) + P(E_i \wedge \overline{E_{i-1}}) \leq P(E_{i-1}) + \epsilon$, thus $P(E_i) - P(E_{i-1}) \leq \epsilon$. From that we can conclude that $P(E_r) - P(E_0) = (P(E_r) - P(E_{r-1})) + (P(E_{r-1}) - P(E_{r-2})) + ... + (P(E_2) - P(E_1)) + (P(E_1) - P(E_0)) \leq r\epsilon$ and thus, $\epsilon \geq (P(E_r) - P(E_0))/r$. □

Proof of Theorem 2 (continued):

A_{max}'s probability of success is

$$\delta_{\text{max}} := \max\{P(E_1 \wedge \overline{E_0}), ..., P(E_r \wedge \overline{E_{r-1}})\}$$

Thus we know that $P(E_i \wedge \overline{E_{i-1}}) \leq \delta_{\text{max}}$. Applying Lemma 1 with $\epsilon := \delta_{\text{max}}$ yields $\delta_{\text{max}} \geq \frac{1}{3r}$, as $P(E_r) - P(E_0) \geq \frac{2}{3} - \frac{1}{3} = \frac{1}{3}$. □

Remark 1.
A weaker version of Theorem 2 has been already proven in [6]: Their Theorem 1 shows that if a contract signing protocol terminates in r rounds, and if for some values δ, ϵ for all rounds i

$$P(E_i) > \delta \Rightarrow P(\overline{E_{i-1}}|E_i) < \epsilon \tag{1}$$

then

$$r \geq \frac{\log(\delta)}{\log(1 - \epsilon)} + 2$$

which is approximately equal to $\epsilon^{-1} \log(\delta^{-1})$.

Equation 1 implies $P(\overline{E_{i-1}} \wedge E_i) \leq \max\{\delta, \epsilon\}$, and applying Lemma 1 yields $\max\{\delta, \epsilon\} \geq 1/r$, which is basically Theorem 1 of [6].

The fact that Equation 1 implies our condition (but not vice versa) was already observed in [6]. Since we want to prove that there is *no* 2-party protocol which succeeds with high probability, the weakest possible definition of success is the most preferable one.   ◇

5   Verifiable Agreement for Honest Majorities

We first show how to extend any agreement protocol for honesty structures satisfying the condition Q_2 to a verifiable agreement protocol (Section 5.1). We present a combined protocol for synchronous and asynchronous networks.

In Section 5.2, we present a contract signing protocol for honest majorities. Note that usually contract signing should be able to withstand any number of dishonest parties as long as at least one honest party participates in the protocol. In this case, there is no chance to sign a contract in an ad hoc peer-to-peer group. However, in case the majority of parties can be trusted, our protocol is the first one which enables contract signing in this setting.

5.1   A Verifiable Agreement Protocol for Honest Majorities

Protocol 1. Let π be an agreement protocol (Definition 4) for an honesty structure $\mathcal{H}$, input and output sets X and Y and a validity function F.

- consensus[]:
    1. The parties first run the protocol π on their inputs x_i for the identifier tid. As soon as a party P_i obtains output $y_i \neq$ failed, it sends $m_i := \text{sign}_i(tid, y_i)$ to all participants.
    2. We call any set $M = \{\text{sign}_{j_1}(tid, y), \ldots, \text{sign}_{j_k}(tid, y)\}$ where $\{P_{j_1}, \ldots, P_{j_k}\} \in \mathcal{H}$ a *proof set* for (tid, y). P_i waits until it has received a proof set for (tid, y_i).
- verify[]: The verifier V accepts the result y for some tid if and only if it receives a proof set for (tid, y) where $y \neq$ failed.

                                                                              ◇

Theorem 3. *Protocol 1 solves Verifiable Agreement under the condition Q_2 in both synchronous and asynchronous networks.*

Proof. (sketch)
We only show the less obvious requirements.

Termination of consensus[] (Definition 4): Let $H \in \mathcal{H}$ be the actual set of honest parties. Then all honest parties $P_i \in H$ start π, terminate with the agreement on some result y and send the signed result (message m_i) to all parties (we assume that P_i sends m_i to itself as well). Thus, eventually each honest party P_i receives a proof set and terminates, as we assume reliable communication.

No Surprises (Definition 5): Let H be the actual set of honest parties, and assume that the verifier V receives a proof set for some $y \in Y$ with $H' \in \mathcal{H}$ as the set of all signatories of y. Since $H \cap H' \neq \emptyset$, there is at least one honest party $P_h \in H'$, and as P_h signed y, it must be the correct result. $\qquad\square$

Remark 2. If a protocol solves some agreement problem in asynchronous networks, the corresponding honesty structure must satisfy Q_3 [8]. If Q_3 is satisfied, then Q_2 is also satisfied. Therefore, in asynchronous networks, any agreement problem can be solved with verifiability, if it can be solved at all. $\qquad\diamond$

5.2 Contract Signing for Honest Majorities

Applying the construction of Protocol 1 to the binary Consensus problem with $X = Y = \{0,1\}$ (see Section 2.2), we construct contract signing for honest majorities.

Protocol 2. Let π be a protocol that solves binary Consensus, and let (sign, tid, x_i) be the input of the party P_i for the contract signing protocol. As previously, we present a combined protocol for synchronous and asynchronous networks.

(1) If $P_i \in H$ wants to sign the contract ($x_i = contr$), then it sets $c := (tid, contr)$ and sends the promise to sign $contr$ for tid to all parties: $m_{1,i} := \mathsf{sign}_i(c, \mathsf{sign})$. We call $M := \{\mathsf{sign}_1(c, \mathsf{sign}), ..., \mathsf{sign}_n(c, \mathsf{sign})\}$ a **minor proof set** for c.

P_i tries to collect such a minor proof set for c. On asynchronous networks, P_i can stop the collection process any time, on synchronous networks P_i waits until the next round. If P_i succeeded in collecting a minor proof set, then it sets $v_i := \mathsf{true}$, otherwise it sets $v_i := \mathsf{false}$.

If P_i does not want to sign the contract ($x_i = \mathsf{reject}$), then it sets $v_i := \mathsf{false}$.

(2) Protocol π is executed with input v_i. Let d_i be the result P_i obtains from this protocol run.

(3) If P_i decides $d_i = \mathsf{true}$ then it sends $\mathsf{sign}_i(c)$ to all parties.

We call any set $M_{tid} = \{\mathsf{sign}_{j_1}(c), ..., \mathsf{sign}_{j_k}(c)\}$ with $\{P_{j_1}, ..., P_{j_k}\} \in \mathcal{H}$ **major proof set** for $contr$. P_i waits until it receives such a major proof set and then stops.

The verifier V decides $(tid, contr, \mathsf{accepted})$ if and only if V receives a major proof set for $contr$.

Theorem 4. *Protocol 2 solves contract signing under condition Q_2.*

Proof. (sketch) We have to show that the protocol achieves verifiable consensus for the specific validity function F_{CS} (Def. 6). As previously, we present only the more important parts of the proof.

Validity (Def. 4): If not all honest parties wish to sign the same contract, or no contract at all, then no party will receive a minor proof set. Thus, all honest parties will start π with the input false, and π will yield the result false according to the definition of Byzantine Agreement. Therefore, all honest parties output failed, as required.

In case all honest parties wish to sign the same contract $contr$ both outputs $contr$ and failed are allowed.

No Surprises (Def. 5): Assume that the verifier V obtained the result $(tid, contr, \mathsf{accepted})$ from some party P_j. Then, P_j must have shown to V a major proof set for $contr$ with the set of signatories H'. The condition Q_2 implies that there is some honest party P_h in H'. Then P_h received the minor proof set for $contr$, which means that all honest parties received the input $contr$. Besides, P_h must have received true from π, and therefore, all honest parties received or will receive the output true from π and therefore, the result $contr$. $\square$

6 Discussion

6.1 System Assumptions

Most debatable assumption in our system model is reliable communication. In fact, many cryptographic protocols for peer-to-peer ad hoc networks, most notably, group key agreement protocols [3, 21, 4], also make this assumption. This can be justified by relying on reliable group communication services, such as [19, 18].

Another assumption is the ability of the parties to digitally sign their messages. This requires a public-key infrastructure, such as described, e.g., in [14]. For an overview of authentication mechanisms in ad hoc networks, including issues related to the public key infrastructure, see [1].

6.2 Applications

Verifiable Agreement applies to situations where the result of a transaction should be used in the future. One class of such situations arises when a distributed database is implemented in the ad hoc network and is replicated across some specified nodes, the servers. In this case, transactions conducted in the absence of the servers, should be communicated to them as soon as possible. Consider, for example, the distributed public-key infrastructure in [24]. Using verifiable agreement of the client nodes on the exclusion of "bad" nodes form the network, each agreement participant can submit the exclusion decision to the service for the purpose of certificate revocation.

Another important scenario arises when the transaction conducted by the node in the peer-to-peer group should be used in another context. Consider a meeting which is set up in ad hoc manner, perhaps in an emergency situation, where several organizations from different organizations or countries do not trust each other. They collaboratively edit an important document which they should present in their organizations after the meeting. This document may be, e.g., the minutes of the meeting. It is important to fix the current document state, such that no single party is able to change the local copy of the document undetected. Usually, this can be done using a transaction logging by a trusted site. In the absence of a trusted site, the participants may sign the commitments to the document using a contract signing protocol. To do this, however, as we showed earlier, more than the half of the participants should be trusted not to cheat. In the full version of this paper, we present a contract signing protocol for honest majorities which can be used in the above situations.

6.3 Conclusion

We introduced the notion of Verifiable Agreement, and showed its applicability in mobile peer-to-peer ad hoc networks. Limits on the solvability of Verifiable Agreement show that the non-repudiation of any action without relying on an infrastructure requires placing trust into the majority of the participants.

References

1. N. Aboudagga, M. T. Refaei, M. Eltoweissy, L. A. DaSilva, and J.-J. Quisquater. Authentication protocols for ad hoc networks: taxonomy and research issues. In *Q2SWinet '05: Proceedings of the 1st ACM international workshop on Quality of service & security in wireless and mobile networks*, pages 96–104, New York, NY, USA, 2005. ACM Press.
2. N. Asokan, B. Baum-Waidner, M. Schunter, and M. Waidner. Optimistic synchronous multi-party contract signing. Technical Report Research Report RZ 3089, IBM Zurich Research Laboratory, 1998.
3. N. Asokan and P. Ginzboorg. Key-agreement in ad-hoc networks. *Computer Communications*, 23(17):1627–1637, 2000.
4. D. Augot, R. Bhaskar, V. Issarny, and D. Sacchetti. An efficient group key agreement protocol for ad hoc networks. In *First International IEEE WoWMoM Workshop on Trust, Security and Privacy for Ubiquitous Computing*, 2005.
5. B. Baum-Waidner and M. Waidner. Round-optimal and abuse-free multi-party contract signing. In *International Colloquium on Automata, Languages and Programming*, LNCS 1853, 2000.
6. M. Ben-Or, O. Goldreich, S. Micali, and R. L. Rivest. A fair protocol for signing contracts. *IEEE Transactions on Information Theory*, 36(1), 1990.
7. M. Blum. Three applications of the oblivious transfer. Technical report, Department of EECS, University of California, Berkeley, CA, 1981.

8. G. Bracha and S. Toueg. Asynchronous consensus and broadcast protocols. *J. ACM*, 32(4), 1985.

9. M. J. Fischer. The consensus problem in unreliable distributed systems (a brief survey). In *Proceedings of the 1983 International FCT-Conference on Fundamentals of Computation Theory*, pages 127–140, London, UK, 1983. Springer-Verlag.

10. M. Fitzi and J. A. Garay. Efficient player-optimal protocols for strong and differential consensus. In *PODC '03: Proceedings of the twenty-second annual symposium on Principles of distributed computing*, pages 211–220, New York, NY, USA, 2003. ACM Press.

11. J. A. Garay and P. D. MacKenzie. Abuse-free multi-party contract signing. In *Proceedings of the 13th International Symposium on Distributed Computing*, pages 151–165, London, UK, 1999. Springer-Verlag.

12. S. Goldwasser. Multi party computations: past and present. In *PODC '97: Proceedings of the sixteenth annual ACM symposium on Principles of distributed computing*, pages 1–6, New York, NY, USA, 1997. ACM Press.

13. M. Hirt and U. Maurer. Complete characterization of adversaries tolerable in secure multi-party computation (extended abstract). In *PODC '97: Proceedings of the sixteenth annual ACM symposium on Principles of distributed computing*, pages 25–34, New York, NY, USA, 1997. ACM Press.

14. J.-P. Hubaux, L. Buttyan, and S. Capkun. The quest for security in mobile ad hoc networks. In *MobiHoc '01: Proceedings of the 2nd ACM international symposium on Mobile ad hoc networking & computing*, pages 146–155, New York, NY, USA, 2001. ACM Press.

15. K. Kursawe. *Distributed Trust*. PhD thesis, Department of Computer Science, Saarland University, 2001.

16. L. Lamport. The weak byzantine generals problem. *J. ACM*, 30(3):668–676, 1983.

17. L. Lamport, R. Shostak, and M. Pease. The byzantine generals problem. *ACM Trans. Program. Lang. Syst.*, 4(3):382–401, 1982.

18. J. Liu, D. Sacchetti, F. Sailhan, and V. Issarny. Group management for mobile ad hoc networks: design, implementation and experiment. In *MDM '05: Proceedings of the 6th international conference on Mobile data management*, pages 192–199, New York, NY, USA, 2005. ACM Press.

19. J. Luo, P. T. Eugster, and J.-P. Hubaux. Pilot: Probabilistic lightweight group communication system for ad hoc networks. *IEEE Transactions on Mobile Computing*, 3(2):164–179, 2004.

20. M. Pease, R. Shostak, and L. Lamport. Reaching agreement in presense of faults. *Journal of the ACM*, 27(2):228–234, April 1980.

21. M. Steiner, G. Tsudik, and M. Waidner. Key agreement in dynamic peer groups. *IEEE Trans. Parallel Distrib. Syst.*, 11(8):769–780, 2000.

22. L. Tang. Verifiable transaction atomicity for electronic payment protocols. In *ICDCS '96: Proceedings of the 16th International Conference on Distributed Computing Systems (ICDCS '96)*, Washington, DC, USA, 1996. IEEE Computer Society.

23. J. Zhou, J. Onieva, and J. Lopez. A synchronous multi-party contract signing protocol improving lower bound of steps. In *SEC 2006: 21st IFIP International Information Security Conference*, May 2006.

24. L. Zhou and Z. J. Haas. Securing ad hoc networks. *IEEE Network*, 13(6):24–30, 1999.

Using Radio Device Fingerprinting for the Detection of Impersonation and Sybil Attacks in Wireless Networks

Bartlomiej Sieka

[1] Computer Science Department
University of Illinois at Chicago
[2] Semihalf
tur@semihalf.com

Abstract. This paper describes an intrusion detection system to identify impersonation attacks and Sybil attacks in wireless networks. The detection system uses radio device fingerprinting and has experimental performance comparable with existing intrusion detection methods. The detection systems for Sybil attacks have not been widely investigated to date, and this contribution of the paper is novel. The paper also derives analytical formulae relating metrics of the fingerprinting classification procedure with the metrics of the intrusion detection system. The formulae can be used to guide the selection of the fingerprinting classification method, knowing the desired performance of the detection system. The use of radio device fingerprinting simplifies the task of securing a wireless ad-hoc network.

1 Introduction and Prior Art

Providing security in a wireless network is a challenging problem. The nature of radio communication makes traditional solutions developed for wire-line networks inapplicable. The challenges are further increased in ad-hoc, peer-to-peer and sensor scenarios. Node mobility, dynamic topology changes, and resource constraints at network nodes are the issues that need to be addressed when attempting to secure such networks. A natural approach is to devise protocols and algorithms that are resilient to new threats, and that will provide immunity to attacks. However, secure protocols are not a complete guarantee of solving security-related problems. Incorrect protocol design, implementation errors, and unforeseen attack vectors are some of the reasons why network security can still be compromised. A second line of defense is necessary – an Intrusion Detection System (IDS).

An IDS allows the identification of attacks on a computer system. Attacks can be detected while in progress, allowing appropriate countermeasures, or they can be detected off-line, for audit and forensics purposes. Traditionally, IDS are distinguished based on the origin of data that they record and analyze. For *host-based* detection systems, the data come from a network host, e.g., from a workstation,

L. Buttyan, V. Gligor, and D. Westhoff (Eds.): ESAS 2006, LNCS 4357, pp. 179–192, 2006.

router, firewall. The data considered in this case can be, for example, system calls, resources usage, and other operating system-level metrics. On the other hand, if the detection system focuses on the data generated by the network (e.g., packets counts, network message contents, sender/receiver patterns), it is called *network-based*. Network-based IDS are the focus of this work.

Another way to differentiate IDS is based on the type of patterns that the system is trained to identify in the audit data. If the patterns that the IDS recognizes correspond to known attacks, the system is said to employ *misuse-detection*. This kind of system is able to reliably identify hard-coded attacks, but is rather inefficient in detecting new threats. The complementary approach is called *anomaly-detection*, where the IDS identifies patterns that correspond to unusual behavior. Such behavior is treated as a possible attack. Anomaly-based systems are able to cope with previously unseen intrusions, but at the price of reporting false alarms more frequently than is the case in misuse-detection methods. Due to noise and variability present in wireless communications, anomaly-based IDS are better suited for the type of networks considered in this paper.

The research on IDS has been quite active ([1,2,3,4,5]). Apart from a multitude of specific protocols and methods, general unifying frameworks for detection systems have also been proposed ([6,7]). In particular, detection systems aimed at wireless networks have recently received a lot of attention in the scientific community ([8,9,10,11,12,13,14,15]). Most results concern themselves with attacks against routing and forwarding functions of the network. The need to secure routing stems from the fact that all nodes are assumed to take part in the routing. This is contrary to the traditional wired scenario, where routers are managed and controlled in a much more tight manner.

Wireless networks, however, have another characteristic that facilitates some hard-to-counter attacks. Due to the nature of the radio communication, the data link layer identifiers are easy to spoof. For example, in the 802.11 family of networks, MAC addresses are simply transmitted over the air, and are trusted by recipients *as is*. Hence, the main weakness of traditional detection systems proposed for wireless networks is that they use the MAC addresses to help identify attacks. Once the MAC address is spoofed, the detection system can be easily circumvented.

This paper makes the following contributions.

- It focuses on two attacks that are hard to detect using traditional approaches. They are *impersonation attack* and *Sybil attack*. *Reply attack* is also addressed. Further, this work seeks to complement existing research on wireless network IDS by employing a novel approach – radio transceiver fingerprinting. Methods to detect the impersonation attack using fingerprinting have been proposed previously ([12,14]). However, they are tied to a particular fingerprinting approach, whereas this work describes a general framework that can use any fingerprinting method.

- Detection methods for Sybil attack have not been widely investigated [16]. This work is original in proposing a fingerprinting-based detection method for this type of attack.

- Analytical formulae derived in this paper help choose parameters of the fingerprinting procedure, given the target values of performance metrics of the detection system.
- Detection metrics for the method described in this paper are presented. They are compared with metrics for other fingerprinting-based IDS, as well with metrics for traditional wireless IDS.

The rest of the paper is organized as follows. Section 2 describes radio transceiver fingerprinting methods. Section 3 presents models used. Section 4 describes the intrusion detection system, and Section 5 provides analytical formulae for its metrics. Section 6 presents the experimental data on detection performance and provides the discussion of the results. Section 7 gives concluding remarks.

2   Device Fingerprinting

Fingerprinting a wireless transceiver is a process by which one can obtain some characteristics of a given physical radio device – a fingerprint. The important property of a fingerprint is that it is not feasible for a node to forge a fingerprint of some other node. Moreover, a fingerprint is hard to repudiate, i.e., a node can not deny its own fingerprint. A fingerprinting method reliably binds the sender identity to a particular radio transmission. The consequence is that it is possible to prevent address spoofing in a wireless network.

There exists two methods of fingerprinting radio transmitters. One is called Radio Frequency Fingerprinting (RFF). It has military origins and has also been used by cell phone companies to fight cloning fraud. It is based on analyzing physical properties of the signal, and is reported to be able to fingerprint VHF FM radios, Bluetooth devices, and – more recently – 802.11 nodes ([17,18,19,20,12,21,13,22]). Another method to fingerprint a given transceiver is to precisely measure the time it takes it to perform communication functions, and infer its identity from the analysis of these timings. This approach is covered in [23] and is referred to as TAF (Timing Analysis Fingerprinting). The advantage of TAF over RFF is that it does not require costly equipment for radio signal gathering and analysis. RFF, on the other hand, gives slightly better statistical identification guarantees. However, TAF is in early stages of development, and its performance is likely to improve as it matures.

The details of acquiring the fingerprint from radio communications are left out from this work (the procedures for both TAF and RFF can be found in their respective references). Instead, this paper presents an abstract representation of the fingerprinting. Both TAF and RFF can be thought of as instantiations of this general model; the description of the model now follows.

A necessary prerequisite for fingerprinting is the transmission of radio communications by a wireless network node. Said transmission might be just one frame (RFF), or a set of frames (TAF). The fingerprinting procedure takes such radio communications as input and produces a fingerprint, which is a vector of real numbers. A fingerprint is denoted as f and the set of all fingerprints is denoted as F. Another characteristic of the communications is the identity of its sender, denoted as *id*. Finally, let *o* denote an *observation*, which is defined as a pair (f, id), where f is the fingerprint of the transmitted radio communications and *id* is the identity of its sender. An observation is a basic concept used in this work.

3   Models

3.1   Network Model

Consider a set of n wireless nodes and let this set be denoted by N. Also, let $ID = \{id_1, id_2, \ldots, id_n\}$ be the set of identities of the nodes in N. Assume that all the nodes in the network are under control of some administrative entity. The extent of the control should allow the training phase to be conducted, i.e., it should be possible for the administrator to obtain a set of authentic fingerprints for every node in N. The training phase is described in Section 4.1.

3.2   Threat Model

In general, two kinds of attacks can be distinguished with respect to the attacker's association with the network he is trying to attack. If the attacker is not associated in any way with the network, then such an attack is called *external*. If, on the other hand, the attacker is a member of the network, the attack is called *internal* (for example, an attack performed by a disgruntled employee). Internal attacks are usually harder to detect and counter, since their perpetrators are given more trust than outsiders ([24]). This paper focuses on internal impersonation attack and internal Sybil attack.

- **Impersonation attack.** In this attack, a malicious node attempts to take part in a network communication exchange pretending to be some other node. There are several reasons why an impersonation attack could be attempted. It can be done to conceal the true identity of the attacker, while performing some unauthorized or malicious action. This results in eventual consequences of those actions being attributed to, and borne by, the victim (denial of service attack). The impersonation attack can also be mounted to steal services from the node being impersonated, or use privileges belonging to it. Finally, a wireless node might impersonate some other node just out of the desire to be anonymous. In any case, a method to detect impersonation attacks is crucial for the security of the wireless network.
- **Sybil attack.** In this case, a node assumes multiple identities in the hope of achieving a malicious goal. Sybil attacks are applicable to reputation management protocols and to algorithms that require cooperated and joint computation by nodes (e.g., quorum systems, threshold cryptography, etc.). Assume that the attacker is a wireless node a belonging to N. In its simplest form, a Sybil attack by node a consists of two radio communications sent by a, such that the sender's identity in one is different than the sender's identity in the other. One of the identities is the authentic identity of node a, but not both.

- **Replay attack.** There can be two kinds of replay attacks.
  - The attacker, node a, records its radio communications and retransmits them at a later time in hope of accomplishing some unauthorized goal. For example, when certain network privileges expire with time, the node might try to gain them again by such a simple retransmission. This kind of reply attack should be dealt with by network protocols, for example, by employing sequence numbers or timestamps.
  - The attacker, node a, replays radio communications transmitted previously by some other node, say node v. But such an attack requires a to pretend to be v, and is thus reduced to an impersonation attack, described above.

Attack definitions given in this section concern themselves only with transmission originating from the attacker. However, for attacks to be of any value to the attacker, he has also to receive radio frames not intended for him. Unauthorized reception of communication messages is called eavesdropping and can be countered by cryptographic methods (encryption). Providing secrecy of communication is a widely studied topic, and is not covered here.

4 Problem Statement and Solution

The goal is to build a system capable of detecting impersonation and Sybil attacks in a wireless network. The assumption is that there exists a procedure able to compute a fingerprint for a given radio communication. The detection system works in two phases, described in the following sections.

4.1 Training Phase

The training phase is performed off-line, before the network operation begins (or before a newcomer node is allowed to join the network). During this phase, observations with authentic fingerprints are gathered in a controlled environment. A controlled environment means that there are no attack attempts on the network during the training phase. Since all the nodes are under control of one authority, this step is feasible and not difficult to perform. For example, wireless devices to be fingerprinted can be connected without the antennae, using RF cables. This provides reasonable guarantees of the authenticity of the gathered fingerprints.

The training phase results in the creation of a classification procedure. The classification procedure takes as input a fingerprint extracted from radio communication, and produces the identity of the node that sent that radio communication. Classification is not always exact, and only statistical guarantees on the prediction can be made. The classification procedure is also referred to as the *classifier*, and it can be formally characterized by function *classify*.

$$classify : F \rightarrow ID$$

Conceptually, the training phase is performed for a device at a time. For every device i, a set of authentic observations is recorded. The set of observations for all nodes is split into two sets, (1) the *train* set used for actual training, and (2) the *test* set used to quantify the performance of the classifier function. The performance of the classifier is characterized by the Estimated Classification Rate Matrix ($ECRM$), defined as follows.

$$ECRM = \begin{pmatrix} ECRM_{1,1} & ECRM_{1,2} & \dots & ECRM_{1,n} \\ ECRM_{2,1} & ECRM_{2,2} & \dots & ECRM_{2,n} \\ \vdots & \vdots & & \vdots \\ ECRM_{n,1} & ECRM_{n,2} & \dots & ECRM_{n,n} \end{pmatrix}$$

$ECRM_{i,j}$ is the probability of a fingerprint of node i being classified as a fingerprint of node j (i.e., $ECRM_{i,j} = P(classify(f_i) = id_j)$, assuming that f_i is an authentic fingerprint of node i). By definition, elements of $ECRM$ have the following property.

$$\forall i \in N : \sum_{k=1}^{n} ECRM_{i,k} = 1$$

The $ECRM$ conveys detailed information on how the classifier works with respect to all the identities. However, sometimes it is more convenient to use a single number characteristic. For this purpose let us define the Estimated Classification Rate (ECR), which corresponds to the overall "goodness" of the classifier. The higher the value of ECR, the better the classifier is at assigning identities to fingerprints. The formal definition of the ECR now follows.

$$ECR = \frac{1}{n} \sum_{k=1}^{n} ECRM_{k,k}$$

Ideally, the $ECRM$ is an identity matrix and the ECR equals 1, however this is not likely to be achieved in reality.

To summarize, the outcome of the training phase is a classification procedure able to map fingerprints to identities. This classification procedure is characterized by the $ECRM$ and ECR. The following section describes how the classifier is used to detect attacks on the wireless network.

4.2   Detection

Detection occurs during normal network operation. Assume that the radio traffic has been received and the fingerprint generated. For this work it is not relevant what/who performs these actions. It can be a base station or a specially designated node; this issue is to be decided during system deployment.

Impersonation Attack. Given an observation, the classification procedure is invoked to obtain the identity. If the identity returned by the classifier does not match the identity from the observation, the impersonation attack is reported. More formally, an impersonation attack is detected when, for a given observation (f, id), we have $classify(f) \neq id$. Otherwise it is assumed that the observation (f, id) is valid, i.e., that it is not a part of an impersonation attack. Note that $classify(f)$ is the identifier of the node attempting the attack. Since the offending node's identity is thus known, administrative actions can be taken against it. Let us define an internal impersonation attack formally. Let the attacker be a wireless node a belonging to N. An impersonation attack by a is defined as the transmission of radio communication by a with the sender's identity id, such that $id \in ID \setminus \{id_a\}$.

Sybil Attack. Detecting the Sybil attacks requires at least two observations. Assume that the sender identities are different in the two observations, but the classifier has classified the fingerprints from them as belonging to the same node. This signifies that a single node is attempting to communicate using two different identities. Here is a more formal definition of the Sybil attack. Assume that the following observations have been received: (f_i, id_i) and (f_j, id_j). If $id_i \neq id_j$ and $classify(f_i) = classify(f_j)$, then a Sybil attack is reported. It is also assumed, that the attacker mounting the attack is node a with identity id_a, such that $id_a = classify(f_i) = classify(f_j)$.

5   Analysis

There are two metrics of the impersonation and Sybil attack detection scheme that are presented here. They are Detection Rate (DR) and False Alarm Rate (FAR).

The detection rate corresponds to the ability of the system to detect an attack, and the higher the value of DR, the better the detection system is. Detection rate is an indication of how successful the scheme is at catching attacks.

The false alarm rate is a measure of how often a detected attack is in fact not an attack at all. FAR corresponds to the likelihood of the detection procedure erroneously reporting an attack. Clearly, it is important that this metric be as small as possible. One reason is that network administration personnel will stop responding to attack reports with required diligence if they are reported in error too frequently. Another reason is user annoyance. Assume that there are certain administrative actions taken against nodes detected to be launching an attack. If such a node was in fact behaving properly and despite of this is seeing an adverse action (attack countermeasures), the user controlling that node will likely complain to the network administration.

The detection rate and the false alarm rate for impersonation and Sybil attacks are analyzed in sections that follow.

5.1   Impersonation Attack

Detection Rate. Let $P(D)$ denote the probability that an attack is detected, then $DR = P(D)$. Assume an impersonation attack attempt exhibited by

observation (f_a, id_v). In this attack, the attacker (node a) tries to impersonate the victim (node v). Assuming a and v are fixed, the probability of detection
of the impersonation attack of node v by node a is given as follows.

$$P(D_{a,v}) = P(classify(f_a) \neq id_v | f_a \text{ belongs to } a)$$

$$= \sum_{k \in N \setminus \{v\}} P(classify(f_a) = id_k)$$

$$= \sum_{k \in N \setminus \{v\}} ECRM_{a,k}$$

$$= 1 - ECRM_{a,v}$$

Assuming that all attack targets are equally likely, the probability of detection
of an impersonation attack by node a is given as below.

$$P(D_a) = \frac{1}{n-1} \sum_{v \in N \setminus \{a\}} P(D_{a,v})$$

$$= \frac{1}{n-1} \sum_{v \in N \setminus \{a\}} (1 - ECRM_{a,v})$$

$$= 1 - \frac{1}{n-1} \sum_{v \in N \setminus \{a\}} ECRM_{a,v}$$

$$= 1 - \frac{1 - ECRM_{a,a}}{n-1}$$

Averaging over all possible attackers, the formula for the detection rate is as
follows.

$$P(D) = \frac{1}{n} \sum_{a \in N} P(D_a)$$

$$= \frac{1}{n} \sum_{a \in N} (1 - \frac{1 - ECRM_{a,a}}{n-1})$$

$$= 1 - \frac{\frac{1}{n} \sum_{a \in N} (1 - ECRM_{a,a})}{n-1}$$

$$= 1 - \frac{1 - \frac{1}{n} \sum_{a \in N} ECRM_{a,a}}{n-1}$$

$$= 1 - \frac{1 - ECR}{n-1}$$

False Alarm Rate. If $P(FA)$ is the probability of a false alarm, then $FAR = P(FA)$. Assume a benign observation (f_i, id_i), where the fingerprint f_i truly belongs to the node with identity id_i. Assuming i is fixed, we can express the probability of a false detection of an impersonation attack based on observation (f_i, id_i) as follows.

$$P(FA_i) = P(classify(f_i) \neq id_i | f_i \text{ belongs to } i)$$

$$= \sum_{k \in N \setminus \{i\}} P(classify(f_i) = id_k)$$

$$= \sum_{k \in N \setminus \{i\}} ECRM_{i,k}$$

$$= 1 - ECRM_{i,i}$$

Assuming that observations are equally likely for all the nodes, we can average the above to obtain $P(FA)$, as below.

$$P(FA) = \frac{1}{n} \sum_{i \in N} P(FA_i)$$

$$= \frac{1}{n} \sum_{i \in N} (1 - ECRM_{i,i})$$

$$= 1 - \frac{1}{n} \sum_{i \in N} ECRM_{i,i}$$

$$= 1 - ECR$$

Thus, the FAR depends only on the properties of the classifier, and more specifically on the estimated classification rate. The greater the ECR (i.e., the better the classifier), the lower the false error rate.

5.2   Sybil Attack

The following two sections assume that the two observations used to detect the Sybil attack are (f_i, id_i) and (f_j, id_j).

Detection Rate. Assume that the observations indeed correspond to a Sybil attack and that the attacker is some node a. Then the probability of detecting the attack by a is given as follows.

$$P(D_a) = P(classify(f_i) = classify(f_j) | f_i, f_j \text{ belong to the same node})$$

There are n distinct cases when $classify(f_i) = classify(f_j)$, and they have the following probabilities.

Case	Probability
$classify(f_i) = id_1 \wedge classify(f_j) = id_1$	$ECRM_{a,1} \cdot ECRM_{a,1}$
$classify(f_i) = id_2 \wedge classify(f_j) = id_2$	$ECRM_{a,2} \cdot ECRM_{a,2}$
...	...
$classify(f_i) = id_n \wedge classify(f_j) = id_n$	$ECRM_{a,n} \cdot ECRM_{a,n}$

Since the n cases are disjoint, we obtain the following.

$$P(D_a) = \sum_{k \in N} ECRM_{a,k}^2$$

Assuming that all potential attackers are equally likely, then the formula for the detection rate is as follows.

$$P(D) = \frac{1}{n} \sum_{a \in N} P(D_a)$$

$$= \frac{1}{n} \sum_{a \in N} \sum_{k \in N} ECRM_{a,k}^2$$

False Alarm Rate. How likely is it the detection of the Sybil attack is incorrect? Assume that f_i and f_j belong to two different nodes i and j. Then the probability of false alarm is as follows.

$$P(FA_{i,j}) = P(classify(f_i) = classify(f_j)|f_i, f_j \text{ belong to different nodes})$$

With i and j fixed, there are n disjoint cases here, similar to the impersonation attack scenario. Their probabilities are given below.

Case	Probability
$classify(f_i) = id_1 \wedge classify(f_j) = id_1$	$ECRM_{i,1} \cdot ECRM_{j,1}$
$classify(f_i) = id_2 \wedge classify(f_j) = id_2$	$ECRM_{i,2} \cdot ECRM_{j,2}$
...	...
$classify(f_i) = id_n \wedge classify(f_j) = id_n$	$ECRM_{i,n} \cdot ECRM_{j,n}$

The n cases are disjoint, so the probability of a false alarm is given as follows.

$$P(FA_{i,j}) = \sum_{k \in N} ECRM_{i,k} \cdot ECRM_{j,k}$$

$$= (ECRM \times ECRM^T)_{i,j}$$

Assuming now that any pair of legitimate senders is equally likely, then the overall probability of a false alarm is as follows.

$$P(FA) = \frac{1}{n(n-1)} \sum_{i,j \in N \wedge i \neq j} P(FA_{i,j})$$

$$= \frac{1}{n(n-1)} \sum_{i,j \in N \wedge i \neq j} (ECRM \times ECRM^T)_{i,j}$$

6 Discussion

This paper describes a detection system that uses radio device fingerprinting to identify impersonation and Sybil attacks. The performance of the scheme presented here is compared with other detection systems in Table 1.

Table 1. Performance metrics for different IDS. (Authors in [15] give only absolute values of false alarm counts, so a meaningful comparison with false alarm rates is not possible.)

IDS	Attack					
	Impersonation		Sybil		Blackhole	
	DR	FAR	DR	FAR	DR	FAR
TAF [23]	96.7%	13.4%	77.0%	5.8%	–	–
RFF [14]	89% - 100%	0%	–	–	–	–
mobility [13]	87.3%	23.9%	–	–	–	–
cooperative [9]	–	–	–	–	85%	1%
decentralized [15]	–	–	–	–	90% - 100%	?

TAF corresponds to the detection framework described in this paper. Metrics have been computed using analytical formulae given in Section 5. Classifier performance data required as input in the calculations was taken from [23], and their details are shown in Figure 1.

$$ECRM = \begin{pmatrix} 1.000000 & 0.000000 & 0.000000 & 0.0300000 & 0.000000 \\ 0.000000 & 0.763158 & 0.042105 & 0.131579 & 0.063158 \\ 0.003509 & 0.094737 & 0.870176 & 0.008772 & 0.022807 \\ 0.000000 & 0.168421 & 0.010526 & 0.801754 & 0.019298 \\ 0.000000 & 0.078947 & 0.022807 & 0.003509 & 0.894737 \end{pmatrix}$$

$$ECR = 0.866$$

Fig. 1. An example of the estimated classification rate matrix and the corresponding estimated classification rate. Figure contains experimental data reported in [23].

Both *RFF* and *mobility* focus on the detection of impersonation attacks only. As it is to be expected, *RFF* performs better than *TAF* in detecting this type of attack. However, both methods that are based on fingerprinting are advantageous over *mobility*.

A majority of wireless IDS focus on detecting forwarding and routing misbehavior, the blackhole attack being one of the examples. Performance metrics for *cooperative* and *decentralized* methods are given for comparison purposes. The detection rates for fingerprinting-based schemes are comparable to the rates for the traditional approaches. The false alarm rates, however, are higher in case of impersonation attacks. Higher false alarm rates can be attributed to the inherent difficulty in countering spoofing in the wireless scenario.

Overall, the impersonation attack detection system described in this paper has acceptable performance, similar to other examples from the literature.

Another contribution of this paper are the analytical formulae derived in Section 5. They can aid in selecting appropriate classification methods to use with the underlying fingerprinting procedure. Assume that certain values of performance metrics (i.e., DR and FAR for impersonation and Sybil attacks) are desired. One can then evaluate several classifiers and decide which ones guarantee required overall performance of the IDS.

7   Conclusions

Achieving security in wireless networks is a difficult task. Despite efforts aimed at preventing attacks, a second line of defense is necessary - an intrusion detection system. This paper addresses detection of internal attacks using radio device fingerprinting. In particular, the following contributions are made.

- A formal model for the detection of impersonation attack and Sybil attack in a wireless network is presented. Also, a general detection system based on fingerprinting is described.
- An original, fingerprinting-based approach for detecting Sybil attack is proposed.
- Performance of the detection system in terms of detection rate and false alarm rate is investigated. Relationship between DR and FAR and the properties of the fingerprint classification procedure (i.e., $ECRM$ and ECR) are derived analytically. This allows to set and verify requirements of the classification procedure to be used as a basis for the IDS.
- Experimental detection metrics for the detection scheme proposed are compared with metrics for other fingerprint-based methods, as well as with traditional detection systems.

An interesting future research topic would be to employ radio device fingerprinting to detect external attacks in a wireless network.

Acknowledgment

Ajay D. Kshemkalyani provided many useful comments, which greatly helped to improve this paper.

References

1. Lunt, T.: Detecting intruders in computer systems. In: Proceedings of the 1993 Conference on Auditing and Computer Technology. (1993)
2. Anderson, D., Frivold, T., Valdes, A.: Next-generation intrusion detection expert system (NIDES): A summary. SRI-CSL-95-07 (1995)

3. Ilgun, K., Kemmerer, R., Porras, P.: State transition analysis: A rule-based intrusion detection approach. IEEE Transactions on Software Engineering **21**(3) (1995) 181–199
4. Kumar, S., Spafford, E.H.: A software architecture to support misuse intrusion detection. In: Proceedings of the 18th National Conference on Information Security. (1995) 192–204
5. McHugh, J.: Testing intrusion detection systems: A critique of the 1998 and 1999 DARPA intrusion detection system evaluations as performed by Lincoln Laboratory. ACM Transactions on Information and System Security **3**(4) (2000) 262–294
6. Lee, W., Stolfo, S.J.: A framework for constructing features and models for intrusion detection systems. ACM Transactions in Information and Systems Security **3**(4) (November 2000) 227–261
7. Vigna, G., Valeur, F., Kemmerer, R.A.: Designing and implementing a family of intrusion detection systems. In: Proceedings of ESEC/FSE'03. (2003) 88–97
8. Zhang, Y., Lee, W.: Intrusion detection in wireless ad-hoc networks. In: Proceedings of the MOBICOM'00. (2000) 275–283
9. Huang, Y.A., Lee, W.: A cooperative intrusion detection for ad hoc networks. In: Proceedings of the 1st ACM Workshop on Security of Ad Hoc and Sensor Networks. (2003) 135–147
10. Zhang, Y., Lee, W., Huang, Y.A.: Intrusion detection for mobile wireless networks. Wireless Networks **9** (2003) 545–556
11. Otey, M., Parthasarathy, S., Gothing, A., Li, G., S. Narravula, D.P.: Towards NIC-based intrusion detection. In: Proceedings of SIGKDD'03. (2003) 723–728
12. Hall, J., Barbeau, M., Kranakis, E.: Enhancing intrusion detection in wireless networks using radio frequency fingerprinting. In: Proceeding of Communications, Internet, and Information Technology (CIIT), St. Thomas, US Virgin Islands (2004) 46–56
13. Hall, J., Barbeau, M., Kranakis, E.: Anomaly-based intrusion detection using mobility profiles of public transportation users. In: Proceedings of the IEEE International Conference on Wireless And Mobile Computing, Networking And Communications (WiMob'2005), Vol. 2. (2005) 17–24
14. Hall, J., Barbeau, M., Kranakis, E.: Detecting impersonation attacks in future wireless and mobile networks. In: Proceedings of the Mobile Ad-hoc Networks and Sensors Workshop (MADNES). (2005)
15. de Silva, A., Martins, M., Rocha, B., Loureiro, A., Ruiz, L., Wong, H.: Decentralized intrusion detection in wireless sensor networks. In: Proceedings of Q2SWinet'05. (2005) 16–23
16. Newsome, J., Shi, E., Song, D., Perrig, A.: The Sybil attack in sensor networks: Analysis and defenses. In: Third International Symposium on Information Processing in Sensor Networks, IPSN 2004. (2004) 259–268
17. Ureten, O., Serinken, N.: Bayesian detection of radio transmitter turn-on transients. In: Proceedings of NISP'99. (1999) 830–834
18. Ureten, O., Serinken, N.: Detection, characterisation and classification of radio transmitter turn-on transients. In: Proceedings of the NATO ASI on Multisensor Data Fusion. (2002) 611–616
19. Hall, J., Barbeau, M., Kranakis, E.: Detection of transient in radio frequency fingerprinting using phase characteristics of signals. In: Proceedings of the 3rd IASTED International Conference on Wireless and Optical Communications (WOC), Banff, Alberta, Canada (2003) 13–18

20. Tekbas, O., Serinken, N., Ureten, O.: An experimental performance evaluation of a novel radio-transmitter identification system under diverse environmental conditions. Canadian Journal of Electrical and Computer Engineering **29**(3) (July 2004) 203–209
21. Ureten, O., Serinken, N.: Bayesian detection of Wi-Fi transmitter RF fingerprints. Electronic Letters **41**(6) (March 2005) 373–374
22. Ureten, O., Serinken, N.: Wireless security through RF fingerprinting. Accepted for publication in Canadian Journal of Electrical and Computer Engineering (2006/2007)
23. Sieka, B.: Active fingerprinting of 802.11 devices by timing analysis. In: IEEE CCNC06, Las Vegas, NV, USA (2006) 15–19
24. Yang, H., Ye, F., Yuan, Y., Lu, S., Arbaugh, W.: Toward resilient security in wireless sensor networks. In: Proceedings of MobiHoc'05. (2005) 34–45

Author Index

Lecture Notes in Computer Science

For information about Vols. 1–4274

please contact your bookseller or Springer

Vol. 4319: L.-W. Chang, W.-N. Lie (Eds.), Advances in Image and Video Technology. XXVI, 1347 pages. 2006.

Vol. 4318: H. Lipmaa, M. Yung, D. Lin (Eds.), Information Security and Cryptology. XI, 305 pages. 2006.

Vol. 4317: S.K. Madria, K.T. Claypool, R. Kannan, P. Uppuluri, M.M. Gore (Eds.), Distributed Computing and Internet Technology. XIX, 466 pages. 2006.

Vol. 4316: M.M. Dalkilic, S. Kim, J. Yang (Eds.), Data Mining and Bioinformatics. VIII, 197 pages. 2006. (Sublibrary LNBI).

Vol. 4313: T. Margaria, B. Steffen (Eds.), Leveraging Applications of Formal Methods. IX, 197 pages. 2006.

Vol. 4312: S. Sugimoto, J. Hunter, A. Rauber, A. Morishima (Eds.), Digital Libraries: Achievements, Challenges and Opportunities. XVIII, 571 pages. 2006.

Vol. 4311: K. Cho, P. Jacquet (Eds.), Technologies for Advanced Heterogeneous Networks II. XI, 253 pages. 2006.

Vol. 4309: P. Inverardi, M. Jazayeri (Eds.), Software Engineering Education in the Modern Age. VIII, 207 pages. 2006.

Vol. 4308: S. Chaudhuri, S.R. Das, H.S. Paul, S. Tirthapura (Eds.), Distributed Computing and Networking. XIX, 608 pages. 2006.

Vol. 4307: P. Ning, S. Qing, N. Li (Eds.), Information and Communications Security. XIV, 558 pages. 2006.

Vol. 4306: Y. Avrithis, Y. Kompatsiaris, S. Staab, N.E. O'Connor (Eds.), Semantic Multimedia. XII, 241 pages. 2006.

Vol. 4305: A.A. Shvartsman (Ed.), Principles of Distributed Systems. XIII, 441 pages. 2006.

Vol. 4304: A. Sattar, B.-H. Kang (Eds.), AI 2006: Advances in Artificial Intelligence. XXVII, 1303 pages. 2006. (Sublibrary LNAI).

Vol. 4303: A. Hoffmann, B.-H. Kang, D. Richards, S. Tsumoto (Eds.), Advances in Knowledge Acquisition and Management. XI, 259 pages. 2006. (Sublibrary LNAI).

Vol. 4302: J. Domingo-Ferrer, L. Franconi (Eds.), Privacy in Statistical Databases. XI, 383 pages. 2006.

Vol. 4301: D. Pointcheval, Y. Mu, K. Chen (Eds.), Cryptology and Network Security. XIII, 381 pages. 2006.

Vol. 4300: Y.Q. Shi (Ed.), Transactions on Data Hiding and Multimedia Security I. IX, 139 pages. 2006.

Vol. 4299: S. Renals, S. Bengio, J.G. Fiscus (Eds.), Machine Learning for Multimodal Interaction. XII, 470 pages. 2006.

Vol. 4297: Y. Robert, M. Parashar, R. Badrinath, V.K. Prasanna (Eds.), High Performance Computing - HiPC 2006. XXIV, 642 pages. 2006.

Vol. 4296: M.S. Rhee, B. Lee (Eds.), Information Security and Cryptology – ICISC 2006. XIII, 358 pages. 2006.

Vol. 4295: J.D. Carswell, T. Tezuka (Eds.), Web and Wireless Geographical Information Systems. XI, 269 pages. 2006.

Vol. 4294: A. Dan, W. Lamersdorf (Eds.), Service-Oriented Computing – ICSOC 2006. XIX, 653 pages. 2006.

Vol. 4293: A. Gelbukh, C.A. Reyes-Garcia (Eds.), MICAI 2006: Advances in Artificial Intelligence. XXVIII, 1232 pages. 2006. (Sublibrary LNAI).

Vol. 4292: G. Bebis, R. Boyle, B. Parvin, D. Koracin, P. Remagnino, A. Nefian, G. Meenakshisundaram, V. Pascucci, J. Zara, J. Molineros, H. Theisel, T. Malzbender (Eds.), Advances in Visual Computing, Part II. XXXII, 906 pages. 2006.

Vol. 4291: G. Bebis, R. Boyle, B. Parvin, D. Koracin, P. Remagnino, A. Nefian, G. Meenakshisundaram, V. Pascucci, J. Zara, J. Molineros, H. Theisel, T. Malzbender (Eds.), Advances in Visual Computing, Part I. XXXI, 916 pages. 2006.

Vol. 4290: M. van Steen, M. Henning (Eds.), Middleware 2006. XIII, 425 pages. 2006.

Vol. 4289: M. Ackermann, B. Berendt, M. Grobelnik, A. Hotho, D. Mladenič, G. Semeraro, M. Spiliopoulou, G. Stumme, V. Svátek, M. van Someren (Eds.), Semantics, Web and Mining. X, 197 pages. 2006. (Sublibrary LNAI).

Vol. 4288: T. Asano (Ed.), Algorithms and Computation. XX, 766 pages. 2006.

Vol. 4287: C. Mao, T. Yokomori (Eds.), DNA Computing. XII, 440 pages. 2006.

Vol. 4286: P.G. Spirakis, M. Mavronicolas, S.C. Kontogiannis (Eds.), Internet and Network Economics. XI, 401 pages. 2006.

Vol. 4285: Y. Matsumoto, R.W. Sproat, K.-F. Wong, M. Zhang (Eds.), Computer Processing of Oriental Languages. XVII, 544 pages. 2006. (Sublibrary LNAI).

Vol. 4284: X. Lai, K. Chen (Eds.), Advances in Cryptology – ASIACRYPT 2006. XIV, 468 pages. 2006.

Vol. 4283: Y.Q. Shi, B. Jeon (Eds.), Digital Watermarking. XII, 474 pages. 2006.

Vol. 4282: Z. Pan, A. Cheok, M. Haller, R.W.H. Lau, H. Saito, R. Liang (Eds.), Advances in Artificial Reality and Tele-Existence. XXIII, 1347 pages. 2006.

Vol. 4281: K. Barkaoui, A. Cavalcanti, A. Cerone (Eds.), Theoretical Aspects of Computing - ICTAC 2006. XV, 371 pages. 2006.

Vol. 4280: A.K. Datta, M. Gradinariu (Eds.), Stabilization, Safety, and Security of Distributed Systems. XVII, 590 pages. 2006.

Vol. 4279: N. Kobayashi (Ed.), Programming Languages and Systems. XI, 423 pages. 2006.

Vol. 4278: R. Meersman, Z. Tari, P. Herrero (Eds.), On the Move to Meaningful Internet Systems 2006: OTM 2006 Workshops, Part II. XLV, 1004 pages. 2006.

Vol. 4277: R. Meersman, Z. Tari, P. Herrero (Eds.), On the Move to Meaningful Internet Systems 2006: OTM 2006 Workshops, Part I. XLV, 1009 pages. 2006.

Vol. 4276: R. Meersman, Z. Tari (Eds.), On the Move to Meaningful Internet Systems 2006: CoopIS, DOA, GADA, and ODBASE, Part II. XXXII, 752 pages. 2006.

Vol. 4275: R. Meersman, Z. Tari (Eds.), On the Move to Meaningful Internet Systems 2006: CoopIS, DOA, GADA, and ODBASE, Part I. XXXI, 1115 pages. 2006.